Tangut Xia's Buddhist Revolution

Kong Yeh

Abstract

This examines a pivotal moment concerning Buddhism in Inner Asian history, namely the rise of Tibetan Buddhism in the Tangut Xia State (1038–1227) from the early twelfth century to the early thirteenth century. The dissertation views the Tangut Xia as a prototypical Inner Asian empire from which later empires of China and Inner Asia – the Mongol Yuan (1271–1368) and Manchu Qing (1636–1911) – arose. Buddhism, and Tibetan Buddhism in particular, has been widely acknowledged as a crucial factor that contributed to the maintenance of the political, social, and cultural structures of those empires. And I propose, to fully understand the dynamics, we must trace its origin to the Tangut State. In general, the dissertation delineates some major figures and events related to the rise of Tibetan Buddhism in the Tangut Xia and discusses their implications. It demonstrates that the success of Tibetan Buddhism in the Tangut Xia was because of some preferable fortuitous conditions of time and space as well as the efforts made by both participants.

Specifically, the dissertation investigates the Tangut assimilation of the Gsang phu ne'u thog scholastic tradition, which was initiated by Rngog Lo tsā ba Blo ldan shes rab (ca. 1059–1109), a fact that has till now remained unnoticed by previous scholarship. The advent of the scholastic tradition gave rise to an audience of Tangut monks who engaged in scholastic training in monastic settings. The many Tangut translations of the Tibetan texts from the Gsang phu scholastic tradition, because their originals are not extant, shed light on the early intellectual history of the Later Diffusion (*phyi dar*) in Tibet as well. Notably, the significant interest in Dharmakīrti's (7th c.) *Nyāyabindu* of some early Gsang phu masters, as attested by the Tangut texts, was previously unknown. The philological connections between the Tangut texts and their Tibetan counterparts provide us with many possibilities to examine the Tangut language. Hence, the dissertation also serves as an attempt to broaden our knowledge of the Tangut Buddhist language, especially with regard to its scholarly language, which was previously often overlooked.

The dissertation further examines and presents a partial annotated translation of the first volume of a twelfth-century Gsang phu scholar's work only preserved in Tangut translation, namely the *Clarification of the Words and Meaning of the Nyāyabindu* ([illegible], **Rigs pa'i thigs pa'i tshig don gsal bar byed pa*). The translation establishes a substantial ground that allows us to observe the many points addressed above.

Table of Contents

Introduction

Questions and Contexts

This dissertation pursues the following three questions: 1. Why do the ethnic, political, and religious landscapes of China and Inner Asia after roughly the year 1000 look so different from what they were before? 2. What roles did Buddhism play in making these changes? 3. How did the Tangut Xia State (or Xixia 西夏/Western Xia, 1038–1227), a small state once existed at the crossroads between China and Inner Asia, structure Buddhism within its realm in a particular fashion so that it could play the roles? Of course, none of these questions could be answered with a single statement. Hence, rather than providing three independent answers, this study pins the questions on a roadmap in order to establish a route that may lead us to see the dynamics of the history of China and Inner Asia subsequent to the first millennium from one crucial perspective—that is—the rise of Tibetan Buddhism in the Tangut State.

Scholars have generally agreed that Chinese society showed many new characteristics starting from the later period of the Tang dynasty (618–907). Many of these new characteristics has been discussed within the framework of the so-called "Tang-Song Transition," which I will not repeat here.[1] Central to this study, however, is the fact that the last three dynasties – Yuan (1271–1368), Ming (1368–1644), and Qing (1636–1912) – despite the discrepancies between them, differed dramatically from the earlier empires such as the Han (202 BCE–220 CE) and the Tang. Most notably, the Mongols and Manchus, the ruling classes of the Yuan and Qing, never became fully Sinicized, even though they belonged to the ruling classes of a predominant Chinese

[1] See Naito, "Gaikatsuteki Tō Sō jidai kan."

population. Unlike the ethnic minorities from the fourth to sixth centuries, who had great affection for Chinese culture and soon became almost identical to their subjects, the Mongols and Manchus intentionally kept most of their ethnic identities and related institutions. This attribute has been argued by scholars to be a major factor that made the Yuan and Qing Inner Asian empires that were distant from their Sinicized counterparts.[2]

Another salient feature of late imperial China is the pattern of the distribution of various ethnic groups. The earlier Chinese empires never had clear borders between the Han Chinese and the many ethnic minorities, perhaps with the only exception of the oasis city-states along the Silk Roads. Ethnic minorities either had settlements in the rural areas around the Chinese cities or formed communities within the cities. However, by the end of the first millennium, most of these ethnic groups were already Sinicized. In comparison, the later empires all included large regions that consisted of only homogenous ethnic groups.[3] For example, the entire Tibetan region was incorporated into the Yuan and Qing empires, whereas the Ming Empire controlled Manchuria and a portion of Mongolia at its height. What lies behind the transformation of the pattern is the fact that these ethnic groups actively engaged in state-building processes that consolidated their ethnic identities and social organizations. This is partly why it was much harder for the Ming Empire to tackle the Manchu uprising in 1618 than for the Tang Empire to put down the An Lushan Rebellion in 755.

In the religious sphere, profound transformations also took place. Most significantly, Tibetan Buddhism had become an indispensable component in the religious lives of the royal

[2] For the concept of "Inner Asian empire," see Introduction to Millward, et al., *New Qing Imperial History*, and Ding and Elliott, "How to Write Chinese History in the Twenty-First Century."

[3] Of course, a homogenous ethnic group may be said to have various subgroups internally.

families and many of the northerners in China. Concerning the textual aspect, some Tibetan Buddhist texts such as *The Clarification of What Is Knowable* (Tib. *Shes bya rab gsal*, Ch. *Zhang suozhi lun* 彰所知論) composed by 'Phags pa Blo gros rgyal mtshan (1235–1280) were translated into Chinese. Also, the first printing blocks of that portion of the Tibetan Buddhist canon called *Bka' 'gyur* were prepared in 1410 under the order of the Yongle Emperor (r. 1402–1424) of the Ming. Several later emperors continued to sponsor printing blocks for new versions of the Tibetan canon. In addition to textual production, physical locations related to Tibetan Buddhism also formed. For example, Mt. Wutai (Ch. Wutai shan 五臺山) became a significant site for pilgrimage in late imperial China;[4] royal monasteries such as the Gro tshang rdo rje 'chang (Ch. Qutan si 瞿曇寺) were established as crucial intermediaries between the ruling house of the empire and Tibetan Buddhists;[5] and Chengde 承德, the summer retreat of the Qing emperors, had itself become a hub of Tibetan Buddhism.[6] However, the most influential changes undoubtedly occurred in institutions. Under the narrative of "patron-priest relationship" (Tib. *yon mchod*), eminent Tibetan monks were appointed as imperial preceptors (Ch. *di shi* 帝師, Tib. *ti shri* / *de'u shi*, etc.). While maintaining close personal relationships with the emperors and providing religious services to them, they oversaw the religious affairs of the empire. None of these are seen before the year 1000, not least because of the long history of rivalry between the Tibetan Empire and Tang China.

The historical trends presented above are obviously also interrelated and form an organic whole. Keeping one's ethnic identity is apparently an essential measure to prevent the

---

[4] See Chou, *Mount Wutai.*

[5] See Sperling, "Notes on the Early History of Gro-tshang Rdo-rje-'chang and Its Relations with the Ming Court."

[6] See Part III of Millward, et al., *New Qing Imperial History.*

disappearance of that very people. It then results in an increasingly homogenous region, which reinforces that identity. A common religious belief – here Tibetan Buddhism – further consolidates the diverse identities together and maintains that organism.

What I hope to achieve with this study is to trace the origin of the aforementioned dynamics that are typical of late imperial China. To do so, I will turn to a period before the rise of the Mongols. And, geographically, instead of focusing on a typical Inner Asian empire, I will direct my attention to a prototypical Inner Asian empire, namely, the Tangut State.

The Tangut State

The Tangut State (see fig. 1) is traditionally regarded as nothing but a Sinicized dynasty of the history of China despite its Tangut founders. Albeit nominally overseen by the Mongol editor Tuo Tuo, the *History of the Tangut State* (*Xiaguo zhuan* 夏國傳), the official history of the Tanguts composed by Chinese historians of the Yuan, it concludes with the following statement:

> 夏之境土，方二萬餘里，其設官之制，多與宋同。朝賀之儀，雜用唐、宋，而樂之器與曲則唐也。[7]
>
> The territory of the Xia has a circumference of more than 20,000 *li*. Its institution of setting up the offices is largely similar to the Song. For the etiquette in the court, it adopts those of both the Tang and the Song. Its musical instruments and vessels are those of the Tang.

The passage obviously leaves us with the impression that the Tanguts conceived their state on a typical Chinese Tang-Song model. However, the impression is, by and large, misleading. Chinese institutions and cultural tradition only constituted a part of the Tangut State. And the

[7] SS 40, 14028.

Tangut State never became completely Sinicized. In fact, Tangut identity played an important role in the political and social lives of the state. Let us examine in the following passages several aspects of how the Tanguts kept their identity despite Chinese political and cultural influence.

Western Xia, the Tangut Kingdom
As of 1150 when it was at the greatest extent
Mongol Tribes
Qocho
(Subject of the Western Liao)
Heishui Commandary (Khara-khoto)
Heishui River
(Black Water River)
Wulahai
Yumen Pass
Shazhou (Dunhuang)
Changle
Guazhou
Sanjiaochuan
Heqing Circuit
Jinsu Circuit
Suzhou
Right Tributary Commandary
Dingzhou
Xingqing (Zhongxing)
Shunzhou
Ganzhou (Zhenyi Prefecture)
Left Tributary Commandary
Xiazhou
Yinzhou
Xiliang (Liangzhou)
Xiping (Lingzhou)
Niuxinting
Longzhou
Hongzhou
Yellow River
Renduo Spring
Jingsai Commandary
Tibet
Sanchuankou
Yan'an
Xi'anzhou
Xining
Huangzhou
Huizhou
Qingzhou
Jishi Circuit
Lanzhou
Haoshuichuan
Jurchen Jin
Longzhou
Fengxiang

Figure 1. The Tangut State in ca. 1150.[8]

The Tangut State created their own writing system to write their language in 1036, an act considered integral to their state-building process but with lasting effects on their literary culture. The *Tiansheng Legal Code That Revises the Old and Ascertains the New* ([illegible],

[8] Map based by SY - Own work, CC BY-SA 4.0, https://commons.wikimedia.org/w/index.php?curid=63702760, with extra names added by Zhouyang Ma in blue.

henceforth the *Tiansheng Legal Code*), published around 1150 and the primary legal code of the Tangut State,[9] specifies the existence of a Great Academy of Tangut ([illegible]), responsible for Tangut education, in addition to a Great Academy of Chinese ([illegible]).[10] One significant achievement of Tangut education was that Tangut poetry was written in Tangut script. Stylistically, it was markedly different from Chinese poetry,[11] and it served as a literary epitome for Tangut identity. Tangut texts discovered at Khara-Khoto contain many Tangut poems composed by Tangut poets, while so far there is no evidence that Tangut poets composed poems in Chinese. Notably, these compositions continued until at least the last years of the reign of Emperor Renxiao 仁孝 (r. 1139-1193),[12] indicating an enduring interest in writing Tangut poems for over 150 years since the invention of the script.

The Tangut State also made significant strides in the field of music, establishing a Tangut Academy of Musicians ([illegible]) alongside the Chinese Academy of Musicians ([illegible]).[13] As a result, Tangut music most likely had its own unique aesthetics and styles.

In the realm of social life, the Tangut culture was not completely replaced by Chinese culture, either. For example, a recently discovered bronze token for Chinese chess in Inner Mongolia has engravings in both Chinese and Tangut characters for the word "horse" (see fig. 1). One side of the token has the Chinese character *ma* 馬, and on the other side we have the Tangut

---

[9] For a discussion of this source, see below.

[10] Du and Popova, *"Tiansheng Lüling" yanjiu*, 164.

[11] For a study of Tangut poetry, see Liang, *Xixiawen "Gongting shiji" zhengli yu yanjiu.*

[12] For the dating, see *Xixiawen "Gongting shiji" zhengli yu yanjiu*, 16.

[13] Du and Popova, *"Tiansheng Lüling" yanjiu*, 154.

character *rjijr* 𗹏.[14] This suggests that the Tanguts were attempting to maintain their cultural identity even in a game that was essentially Chinese.

Figure 2. Token for Chinese chess with both Chinese and Tangut words, "horse."[15]

The Tanguts also kept some of their own military traditions and institutions. A military institution of the Song, which is called *bei wei* 背嵬, puzzled scholars for some time. *Bei wei* was an elite army in the Song military. However, the term obviously is a phonetic transcription of a foreign language, thus showing it that was not originally a Chinese tradition. Recently, scholars have pointed out that *bei wei* came from the Tangut word *pej ˙wejr* 𗼃𘃛, which literary means

[14] Mi and He, "Xin jian Xia Han hebi qingtong xiangqi zi chutan," 52.

[15] Mi and He, "Xin jian Xia Han hebi qingtong xiangqi zi chutan," 52.

"back-guard."[16] Some bronze badges (see fig. 2) bearing the title attest to this conclusion. The fact that a *pej ·wejr* would be executed if the person he guards is killed in the battle indicates that it is a variety of the military tradition of comitatus, a tradition shared by Central Eurasian peoples.[17]

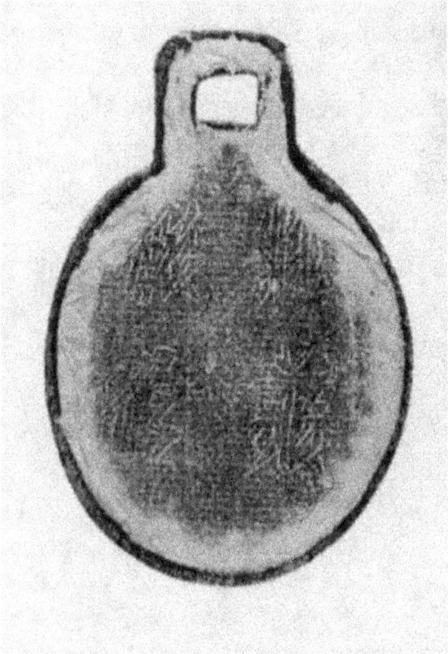

Figure 3. A Tangut bronze badge engraved with "back-guard, waiting for orders" (𗨁𗩾𗿢𗟲).[18]

In addition, women played a significant role in the political life of the Tangut State. While this phenomenon was also present in the Tang Empire, which was heavily influenced by Inner Asian traditions regarding gender, it was not as prominent in the Song dynasty. In the Tangut State, empress dowagers frequently served as regents and *de facto* rulers of the state when the emperor was young. In particular, Empress Dowager Liang 梁 (d. 1099), the mother of Qianshun 乾順 (r.

[16] See Fan and Sun, "Song Xia bei wei jun zai tan."

[17] For the tradition of comitatus, see Beckwith, *Empires of the Silk Road*, 12–23.

[18] Luo, "Xixia shouyu pai," 23.

1086–1193), was a talented military strategist who led the Tangut army herself and defeated the Song army on several occasions. This is reminiscent of Empress Dowager Xiao 蕭 (953–1009) of the Khitan Liao Empire, who also served as a military leader.

Finally, religion, particularly Buddhism, played a critical role in Tangut statecraft. While Buddhism held a significant place in the Tang Empire, it was never the dominant religion. In the Song dynasty, Confucianism became a crucial component of the Chinese identity with its revival. However, the Tanguts made Buddhism their state religion and it set the guiding principles of governance. Even though the *History of the Tangut State* mentions that Renxiao "reverentially made Confucius the emperor" (尊孔子為帝),[19] Confucianism never became the state ideology. In a Tangut reference book, *The Ocean of Meanings Established by the Nobles* ([illegible]), one of the opening verses says:

> [illegible]，[illegible]。
> [illegible]，[illegible]。[20]
>
> Wise words, when reaching the ignorant who are infused with anger, make them tremble.
> Noble compassion and the determined lord make the politics of the country just.
> Buddhist principles, the principles of deliverance, edify the ignorant.
> King's principles, as long as they are set up, settle the civil affairs.

Since one version of the *Ocean of Meaning* contains a colophon that states its woodblocks were "newly carved by the office of carving" ([illegible]) in 1182,[21] we know that the

[19] SS 40, 14030.

[20] #143, 1b8–2a1.

[21] #684, 29b7–8. The date is recorded as "the tenth day of the fifth month of the thirteenth year of the Qianyou reign, the *renyin* year" ([illegible]), thus 1182.

sentiment expressed in the reference book was approved by the state, despite the unknown compiler(s). In the verse quoted above, Buddhism is elevated to a position in which it is regarded as a means of educating the people. It is also, among other things, placed before the "king's principles," which stands for secular rule.

Furthermore, it would be incorrect to say that Buddhism only played a nominal role in the Tangut State. Buddhism was institutionalized as an integral part of the state administration, as indicated by the *Tiansheng Legal Code*. According to the code, the Tangut State had two Buddhist departments, namely, the Monastic Secretariat of Merit ([illegible]) and the Lay Secretariat of Merit ([illegible]). While all the governmental departments were divided into five ranks, the first rank contained only the Central Secretariat ([illegible] < Ch. Zhongshu 中書) and the Bureau of Military Affairs ([illegible] < Ch. Shumi 樞密); and these two Buddhist departments, together with some other offices, ranked second, showing their importance.[22] Additionally, as will be discussed in Chapter Two, the Tangut State had monk officials who shared power with other officials, further demonstrating the influence of Buddhism on governance. These Buddhist institutions were not present in the Song dynasty.

Therefore, although the Tanguts did adopt some Chinese traditions, they established and sustained their state by maintaining a strong Tangut identity. The Tangut State was a unique blend of the Chinese Tang-Song state model and Tangut political, military, cultural, and intellectual traditions.

The Tangut State was unique in its approach to organizing a multi-ethnic state. While multi-ethnic dynasties were fairly common in Chinese history, until the Tang dynasty, all regimes

---

[22] Du and Popova, *"Tiansheng Lüling" yanjiu*, 126.

can be said to have been predicated on the "Sinicization model."[23] This model assumed that there was a center of Chinese civilization whose influence gradually decreased as one moved away from the center. All non-Chinese ethnic groups within the influence of the center would eventually be Sinicized and become Han Chinese. However, the Tanguts did not follow the model. We have seen that the Tanguts did not pursue a policy of Sinicization. Instead, the Tangut rulers intentionally emphasized the boundaries between the various ethnic groups within the Tangut State and Song China. They did not attempt to establish a single ethnic identity, but rather sought to maintain the identities of the major ethnic groups within the state, including Tanguts, Chinese, Tibetans, and Uyghurs, and sustain the state on the basis of the diversity of these ethnic groups. We will discuss this in more detail in Chapter One, Section 3.

Let us consider an example from the *Tiansheng Legal Code*. In the twelfth chapter of the code, there is a section that prescribes how the subjects of the Tangut State should dress. One article states the following:

> [illegible]：[illegible]，[illegible]，[illegible]，[illegible]。[24]
>
> **Article**: When Chinese subjects violate the law requiring them to wear the Chinese-style hair-wrapper, those who hold official titles will be fined one horse, while common people will receive thirteen strokes as punishment.

The passage implies that the Tangut rulers were against Chinese people adopting the Tangut style of dress, which would have given them privileges reserved for Tanguts. However, there is more to it. The passage suggests that the ruling class did not want the Chinese people to adopt the dress

---

[23] For the Sinicization model, see Wang, *Zhongguo*, chaps. 1–2.

[24] #114, 22a8–9.

styles of any other ethnic groups, including Tibetans and Uyghurs, because of the specific mention of the Chinese-style hair-wrapper that should be worn. This indicates that the Tangut rulers wanted the Chinese people within the realm to maintain their own distinct Chinese identity.

Keeping intentional boundaries between different ethnic groups is a characteristic shared by the later Inner Asian empires of the Yuan and Qing. This policy allowed the ruling class to maintain their ethnic privileges and also made governance more effective by enabling specific policies tailored to the cultural traditions of various ethnic groups. The Tangut State was one of the earliest regimes to adopt this approach to ruling a multiethnic country.[25]

Considering the two phenomena discussed above, namely the Tangut State's approach to maintaining the identity of the ruling ethnic group without becoming fully Sinicized and intentionally keeping clear, social boundaries between different ethnic groups, the state served as a prototype for later Inner Asian empires. Therefore, in this dissertation, the Tangut State is considered a prototypical Inner Asian empire.

A Buddhist Revolution

This dissertation explores the significant impact of the rise of Tibetan Buddhism on the formation of the Tangut prototype. While Tibetan Buddhism played a crucial role in late imperial China, its origin can be traced back to the Tangut State. Although the Tanguts had mainly practiced Chinese Buddhism since the establishment of their regime, they began to assimilate Tibetan Buddhism on a massive scale around 1130, leading to a profound transformation of the religious

[25] While the Khitan Liao Empire can also be seen as a potential precursor due to its northern and southern institutions, its method of organizing different ethnic groups was more of a dual system rather than an organic single system. Although a comparison between the Khitan Empire and the Tangut State could be intriguing, it falls beyond the scope of this dissertation.

landscape in the region. Chapter Two, Three, and Four are devoted to this topic, but it is worth briefly considering some of the key issues here.

First, Tibetan monks assumed a pivotal role in the religio-political life of the Tangut State, introducing new Buddhist teachings, especially tantric teachings, that captured the interest of the Tangut people. They quickly became the most important spiritual leaders in the region, and the Tangut emperors appointed them as their personal Buddhist masters. Tangut monks began to study under Tibetan monks and adopt Tibetan names of religion, while the common people of the Tangut State regarded the Tibetan lamas as central figures of veneration.

The influence of the Tibetan monks in the Tangut State is vividly illustrated in a thangka painting discovered in Khara-Khoto (see fig. 4). The painting depicts a Tibetan lama, portrayed on a larger scale, seated in the middle as the main figure and venerated by two Tangut nobles depicted in a smaller scale. This motif of a Tibetan monk being revered by foreign patrons, which was never seen in paintings of previous centuries, attests to the overwhelming charisma of Tibetan monks in the Tangut State.

Figure 4. Tibetan lama worshipped by Tangut noble persons. Twelfth century. Khara-Khoto. The State Heritage Museum, St. Petersburg.[26]

Institutionally, Tibetan monks occupied a central position in the religious life of the Tangut State, as evidenced by the existence of institutions such as the imperial preceptor. The imperial preceptor was the most important religious figure in the Tangut State, with a position superior to all other monk officials. While it is unclear if the position of imperial preceptor was exclusively reserved for Tibetans, all the imperial preceptors in Tangut history that have been identified so far were Tibetans.

[26] Piotrovsky, *Lost Empire of the Silk Road*, 238.

Furthermore, the emergence of Tibetan Buddhism in the Tangut State brought about a significant transformation in the content of Tangut Buddhism. As explored in Chapter Three, some canonical Buddhist works were translated from Tibetan into Tangut. Chapter Four delves into the translation of philosophical and scholastic compositions from Tibetan into Tangut. However, the most crucial aspect was the translation of a vast number of Tibetan tantric texts, providing the Tanguts with a crucial new approach to spiritual attainments.[27]

The spread of Tibetan Buddhism in the Tangut State also had an impact on Tibet itself. The fact that foreign rulers started to be interested in Tibetan Buddhism made it possible for Tibetan Buddhists to find auspices outside of Tibet. This incentive gave rise to the "patron-priest" narrative. It can be said that, since the Tangut period, seeking external patronage and political alliances became a central theme in the history of Tibet.

All the above-mentioned dynamics were carried further to the Yuan, Ming, and Qing empires and were critical in structuring the religio-political lives of these empires.

Sources

While the scarcity of sources presents a significant challenge in the pursuit of this dissertation, I used as many primary sources as possible to engage in this project in Tangut, Tibetan, and Chinese.

The discovery of Tangut texts in Khara-Khoto in the early twentieth century provided scholars with abundant materials for studying Tangut culture. However, the majority of the texts are Buddhist in nature, and very few contain historical narratives, unlike the Chinese or Tibetan

[27] Tangut translations of Tibetan tantric texts have long been a subject of scholarly inquiry. Hence, I will not deal much with these translations in this dissertation. For such pieces of scholarship, see Sun, *Xixiawen "Jixiang bianzhi kouhe benxu" zhengli yanjiu*, Solonin, *Dapeng zhanchi*, and Yu, "Shenshen guangming."

historical records. This makes the writing of Tangut Buddhist history challenging, but by analyzing fragments of information in Tangut texts, we can still gain some crucial insights into the history of Tibetan Buddhism in the Tangut State.

One of the most significant sources of information about Tangut law, as mentioned above is the *Tiansheng Legal Code.*[28] This legal code was an important aspect of the Tangut State's institutional framework, and most of it has been preserved intact. Thus, it serves as a valuable resource for investigating the institutional aspect of Tangut Buddhism. Some other texts, such as the *Ocean of Meanings Established by the Nobles*, also provide valuable insight into Tangut history. Furthermore, while Tangut Buddhist texts do not directly provide historical information, the prefaces, postscripts, and colophons attached to them can offer insight into the contexts in which these texts were produced. Therefore, these attached parts of the Buddhist texts will be essential sources to examine in order to gain a better understanding of the history of Tangut Buddhism.

Tangut Buddhist texts can also be invaluable historical material if examined properly. Although the Tangut translations of Tibetan Buddhist texts do not directly provide information on historical events, contextualizing them within the intellectual history of Tibetan Buddhism can provide insights into the nature of Tibetan Buddhism received by the Tangut State. For example, by an examination of the prevalence of works on Buddhist epistemology and logic that were translated into Tangut, we can discover that the Tangut State established an academic curriculum of Tibetan Buddhist Studies. This will be the central issue discussed in Chapters Four and Five.

---

[28] For the dating of the *Tiansheng Legal Code*, see Du, *"Tiansheng Lüling" yu Xixia fazhi yanjiu*, 26–27. A major clue here is that the record from the Song dynasty indicates that the Tangut State published a *Legal Code That Ascertains the New* (Ch. *Dingxin lü* 鼎新律) in 1150. This seems to be the *Tiansheng Legal Code*.

On the Tibetan side, there are several historical sources that are critical to this dissertation. *The Red Annals* (*Deb ther dmar po*), written by Tshal pa Kun dga' rdo rje (1309–1364), is a religious history that provides important historical information. Additionally, Tibetan biographical writings are essential, particularly the biography of Ti shri Ras pa Shes rab seng ge (1164–1236), written by his disciple Ras pa dkar po (1198–1262), which is an indispensable source. Ti shri Ras pa was the last imperial preceptor of the Tangut State, and his biography documents many significant events from his arrival in the Tangut State in 1196 to the demise of the regime in 1227. Not only does his biography record events related to himself, but it also mentions the activities of other Tibetan masters in the Tangut State, making it a particularly valuable text. Many of the materials in his biography appear to come directly from Ti shri Ras pa's diary because they contain many accounts written in the first person.

Tibetan Buddhist compositions are utilized to achieve the goal of contextualizing the Tangut translations of Tibetan texts. The Tibetan texts from the *Collected Writings of the Bka' gdams School* (*Bka' gdams gsung 'bum*) are particularly relevant to the topics examined in Chapter Four and Five and are used extensively.

The availability of Chinese sources related to the current project is extremely limited. The Yuan historians never wrote an independent history of the Tangut State as they did for the Liao and Jin dynasties. The *History of the Tangut State* is only consists of one chapter of the *History of the Song*. Additionally, Chinese sources, which were generally written by Chinese literati, may be biased, as seen in the portrayal of Sinicization in the *History of the Tangut State*. Finally, the contact between the Tangut State and the Southern Song was severed by the fall of the Northern Song, resulting in a dramatic reduction of records from the 1130s onwards. Yet, that period will be the primary temporal scope of our examination.

Despite the scarcity of Chinese sources related to the current project, some proved to be useful particularly for delineating the major political events in the Tangut State. The *Xixia Chronicles* (*Xixia shushi* 西夏書事) written by the Qing scholar Wu Guangcheng 吳廣成 (fl. 1796–1850) will be a major text in this regard. Although a relatively late source, it is much more comprehensive than previous histories.

In addition to textual materials, paleographical and art materials from the Tangut period are also used in this dissertation.

Conventions

The Tangut phonetic reconstructions in this dissertation follow the system of Gong Hwang-cherng and are only given when relevant to the discussion. For Tibetan texts, Wylie transliteration is used. Throughout this dissertation, the polity of Xixia, also known as the Great State of White and High (𗴂𗹭𗂧𘜶), is consistently referred to as the Tangut State. While there are good reasons also to call it the Tangut Empire due to the diverse peoples under its rule, I hesitate to do so for two main reasons. Firstly, it did not have the expansive territorial control of other polities of its time, such as the Khitan Empire. Secondly, it was often subject to other empires, such as the Khitan Liao and Jurchen Jin empires. In this dissertation, Tangut emperors are referred to by their Chinese names and not their posthumous titles, so for example, Renxiao 仁孝 (1124–1193) is used instead of Renzong 仁宗.

The dissertation uses the following sigla:

#	Inventory number of Tangut texts from the Institute of Oriental Manuscripts, Russian Academy of Sciences. E.g., #6446.

Дх. Inventory number of Dunhuang and Khara-Khoto texts from the Institute of Oriental Manuscripts, Russian Academy of Sciences. E.g., Дх. 2822.

Or. Oriental collection of the Dunhuang Manuscripts from the British Library. E.g., Or.12380/2145.

Tang. Catalog number in Gorbacheva and Kychanov, *Tangutskiye rukopisi i ksilografy*. E.g., Tang. 231.

TK. Inventory number of Tibetan texts from the Institute of Oriental Manuscripts, Russian Academy of Sciences. E.g., TK. 327.

TX. Inventory number of Tibetan texts from the Institute of Oriental Manuscripts, Russian Academy of Sciences. E.g., TX. 67.

Chapter One: The Tangut State in an Integrative Inner Asian Imperial History

1. Writing History Within and Beyond Regions

Historians rely on a selected range of raw materials to construct a meaningful narrative. Without this selection, they risk either succumbing to an illusion of pure objectivity that generates disjointed stories or becoming overly skeptical and subjectively biased. To achieve a balance between subjectivity and objectivity, historians must investigate history within defined limits. As E.H. Carr once noted, "The historian starts with a provisional selection of facts and a provisional interpretation in the light of which that selection has been made – by others as well as by himself."[29]

However, when we look at the development of Asian Studies in the West, we find that its nineteenth century precursors had little choice in selecting their scope of inquiry. Instead, their field of inquiry was imposed upon them, as seen in designations such as Sinologists, Japanologists, Sanskritists, and Orientalists. These labels indicate that the materials under examination were limited to literature written in certain languages. As a result, western scholars of that time did not produce a true history of the East, since Orientalism failed to generate an accurate discourse about the Orient.[30] Additionally, texts written in a common language do not necessarily convey a common story. The invention of the term "Buddhist Hybrid Sanskrit" exemplifies the tension between a language-oriented perspective and an attempt to extract specific subject matter from the literature.

[29] Carr, *What is History?*, 35.

[30] Said, Introduction to *Orientalism*, App, *The Birth of Orientalism*.

In the post-World War II era, a shift occurred in Asian Studies that successfully redefined the scope of inquiry by dividing Asia into natural geographical regions, such as East Asia, South Asia, and the Near East. This approach allowed for a more nuanced and comprehensive understanding of Asian history.

The division of Asia into distinct geographical regions has been successful in addressing the internal dynamics of each region. For example, recent academic works on early modern East Asian history have revealed economic interconnections between China, Japan, and the Dutch East India Company,[31] examined religious trends of Chan Buddhism across China and Japan in the seventeenth century, [32] and argued for the rise of Korean national consciousness during the East Asian War from 1592 to 1598 and its aftermath. [33]

However, these frameworks are limited by their focus on single countries or regions, which risks superimposing the discourse of the nation-state onto historical periods where such a notion did not exist. For instance, the "Tang-Song Transition," a classical periodization of Chinese history, assumes a continuity from the Tang to Song as a single narrative of the Chinese state.[34] This oversimplification overlooks the fact that the empire we call "Tang" controlled more territories and peoples, even at its weakest point, than at any time during the Song's nearly three-hundred-year existence. By juxtaposing the Tang (618–907) and the Song (960–1279) while leaving out the connections between the Tang and the Khitan Liao, Jurchen Jin, and Tangut State, we imply that the histories of the Tang and the Song are a single, homogenous history of the Chinese nation.

---

[31] Blussé, *Visible Cities.*

[32] Wu, *Leaving for the Rising Sun.*

[33] Haboush, *The Great East Asian War and the Birth of the Korean Nation.*

[34] Naitō, "Gaikatsuteki Tō Sō jidai kan."

However, a theory of history based on a narrative of the nation-state for pre-modern periods is only provisional and requires further scrutiny. When examining critically, an approach to the history of a sub-continental region becomes also unsatisfactory in several instances. One of these is its inability to fully integrate frontier regions into the framework of a sub-continental history. Here, let us observe the Tibetan Plateau for example. Tibet was certainly much involved in East Asian political history from the advent of the Tibetan Empire (618–842), which was already in constant conflict with the Tang Empire. However, considering the remarkable religious history of Tibet, the natural geographical boundaries of the formidable Himalayan ranges could by no means stop the Buddhists who strive for obtaining true teachings from the South Asian sub-continent in both the Early Diffusion (*snga dar*) and the beginning of the Later Diffusion (*phyi dar*) periods of Buddhism. And it should be no exaggeration that much of the formation of Tibetan civilization was conditioned by this greater South Asian cultural framework.

Let us now consider the sub-continental region of Inner Asia, which may include Tibet as a part. Unlike other regions in Asia that were intentionally delineated, Inner Asia has been passively assigned to cover what is not covered by East Asia, South Asia, the Near East, etc. Nevertheless, scholars have attempted to identify the trends that weave together an Inner Asian history. For example, the evolution of nomadism, which undoubtedly includes much of the northern Tibetan cultural area, is a story that unfolded throughout Inner Asia's history. However, we must note that Tibet's resistance in the field of religion sets it apart from the rest of Inner Asia. Tibetan civilization was barely traceable in the pre-Islamic Inner Asia, and there was almost no Tibetan civilization that developed out of the Islamic Inner Asia. Consequently, it is challenging to fully incorporate the history of Tibet into any of the sub-continental regions.

Of course, there are methods that will make it possible to transcend beyond the limits of sub-continental boundaries and avoid the dangers of nation state narratives. One direction is to further reduce the scope of inquiry to local level, thus making local history a crucial genre in historical writings. Local history sheds light on historical trends on local level and attempts build linkage between political, social, economic and intellectual realities. Local histories are by all means contingent on narratives of larger scopes and reveal to one degree or another those marco patterns on micro levels. Here, we encounter works such as Robert Hymes' exemplary study on Fuzhou of the Song, which addresses the significance of the "localist turn" between the Northern and Southern Song dynasties, [35] Peter Bol's examination on Wuzhou from the Song to the Ming, which connects the social change and intellectual transformation, [36] and Paul Nietupski's research on Labrang Monastery from the eighteenth century, which not only unveils the instrumental function of a Tibetan monastery in consolidating local society but also shows the Tibetan region of A mdo as a "middle ground" that facilitated the political, economic, and cultural exchanges between the authority in Beijing and Lhasa. [37] These works demonstrate the importance of local histories in providing nuanced perspectives on the complexities of historical development, and offer a means to overcome the limitations of sub-continental boundaries and nation state narratives.

However, local histories do not always conform to these narratives and can even challenge the dominance of macro histories. For example, Sukee Lee's study on Mingzhou shows a relatively strong presence of government, thus challenging the impression of a completely local literati-

---

[35] Hymes, *Statesmen and Gentlemen.*

[36] Bol, *Localizing Learning.*

[37] Nietupski, *Labrang Monastery.*

governed society in the Southern Song.[38] Similarly, my own research on Mi nyag in Khams during the early Qing indicates that local monastic power was a significant force that sought to expand its influence eastwards, thereby resisting the dominant narrative that Tibet could only passively accept Qing rule in Sino-Tibetan relations during the later imperial period of Chinese history.[39] These local histories offer important insights into the complexities of historical realities and demonstrate the need to incorporate diverse perspectives and voices in our understanding of the past.

It is possible to further narrow the scope of historical inquiry by focusing on the history of a single family or individual. Biographical writing utilizes the life of a particular person or family as a nexus for exploring the political, social, cultural, and economic realities of a given time and place. By situating the subject within its temporal and spatial context, the writer reveals not only the properties of that context but also the relationships between the subject and its surroundings. For example, Pamela Crossley's study of three generations of a Manchu family establishes the links between these banner men and the world that shaped their lives, revealing a changing world that the Qing Empire attempted to keep static.[40] Similarly, Kurtis Schaeffer's examination of the life of O rgyan chos skyid (1675–1729), a legendary Tibetan nun, sheds light on a range of issues related to monastic institutions, social structures and mobility, autobiographical writing, and gender in early modern Tibet.[41]

So far, scholarship on historical writing predominantly features a trend of reductionism. However, it is important to consider the feasibility of increasing our scope of inquiry, without

---

[38] Lee. *Negotiated Power.*

[39] Ma, "The Rise of the Monastic Power in Minyak and the Sino-Tibetan Relations."

[40] Crossley, *Orphan Warriors.*

[41] Schaeffer, *Himalayan Hermitess.*

reaching the extreme of global history, which can be seen as one single subject of study. One way to transcend sub-continental boundaries without going to the other extreme is to focus on two sub-continental regions as a "provisional selection," as described by Carr. Trans-regional studies that look at two sub-continental regions have several merits, including breaking natural geographical boundaries and dissolving imagined communities of nation states, which allows scholars to explore historical dynamics across regions and reveal political, cultural, and economic trends in their own right. Contemporary projects based on "Intra-Asian Networks" have yielded fruitful results, for example, revealing close economic ties between much of the East Asian and Southeast Asian worlds in the early modern and modern contexts, and uncovering histories of global trade, colonialism, migration and diaspora, religious movements, and cultural transformations.[42]

Building upon the model of transregional history, "integrative history" further reveals the possibility of writing a history within and beyond regions. "Integrative history" is a term coined by Joseph F. Fletcher later in his life.[43] According to Fletcher, integrative history is a single *macrohistory* that investigates the organism of many different microhistories in different regions. Hence, unlike transregional history that addresses mainly the dynamics between different regions, integrative history emphasizes the whole that emerges from its parts. Fletcher emphasized the significance of this method, stating that "However beautiful the mosaic of specific studies that make up the 'discipline' of history may be, without a *macrohistory*, a tentative general schema of the continuities or, at the least, parallelisms in history, the full significance of the historical peculiarities of a given society cannot be seen."[44] Fletcher's premature death prevented him from

[42] For a summary of the field of Intra-Asian Networks, see Hamashita, "Introduction to Intra-Asian Networks."

[43] See Fletcher, "Integrative History." For a review of his intellectual framework, see Zhong, *Chongshi neiya shi*, 181–247.

[44] Fletcher, "Integrative History," 4.

fully developing his theory, but his basic principles, which he described as "conceptually simple," are all available to us. He succinctly puts his approach as follows: "first one searches for historical parallelisms (roughly contemporaneous similar developments in world's various societies), and then one determines whether they are causally interrelated."[45]

This dissertation adopts the theory of integrative history to explore an integrative Inner Asian imperial history. While following the general guidelines of applying Fletcher's principles to my subject, my dissertation diverges from his own use of integrative history to study Asia in the early modern period in several ways. First, in terms of space, I have chosen only a part of the East Asian world and a part of its Inner Asian counterpart instead of putting almost the entire Asiatic continent under scrutiny. This divergence is predicated on the second one, which is the temporal scope. Fletcher examines predominantly Asia in 1500–1800, pursuing the notion of "early modern," to perceive how an integrative early modern history of Asia arose from this period. In contrast, Inner Asian imperial history does not involve modernity but reveals a picture of the internal logic underlying the development of East and Inner Asian histories. The birth of Inner Asian imperial history, as I will show later, should be no later than the birth of the Mongol Empire in the early thirteenth century, which was a complete political realization of that history.

Thirdly and perhaps most importantly, Fletcher's fledgling theoretical framework of integrative history is represented as a linear theory that leaves out the interdependencies among various parallelisms. In Fletcher's exemplary article, every parallel historical phenomenon triggers another, thus creating a causal chain. For example, the parallelism of population growth caused the speed-up of the "pace of history" and ignited more economic activities, which in turn gave rise to urbanization. The rise of new urban classes facilitated the reinvigoration of religious energies

---

[45] Fletcher, "Integrative History," 3–4.

and also broke the balance between urban areas and nomadic steppes.[46] This observation, although making sense in many ways, remains imperfect. It is hard to judge, for instance, the cause for population growth, which is the fundamental driving force.[47] Besides, a few causal links are rather doubtful. Urbanization and economic growth surely contributed to the decline of nomadism, and the incursion of the Russian imperial power into the Pontic steppe starting in the seventeenth century is perhaps an ideal illustration of this. However, the decline of nomadism was not necessarily caused by those factors. The Qing Empire, the Russian counterpart in the east, successfully sidelined the Dzungars in Inner Asia in the eighteenth century obviously not by means of new urban elements.[48] To further polish this framework would not simply mean to correlate the parallelisms on the most general level and build up a casual chain. Instead, using smaller building blocks of analysis allows us to discover latent interconnections between regions and see why a history as such is integrative. This involves, for example, asking questions such as "does a parallelism in region A contribute to the same parallelism in region B?" And, further the question, "does parallelism I in region A contribute to parallelism II in region B?" The following section will show the practice of these theories.

2. The Birth of an Integrative Inner Asian Imperial History

In tracing the roots of an integrative Inner Asian imperial history, we must take into consideration the immediate pre-Mongol era. This inquiry encompasses three major regions in East and Inner Asia: the Tibetan Plateau, the Eastern Lowlands, and the Northern Areas. The

46 Fletcher, "Integrative History," 34–35.

47 Fletcher, "Integrative History," 34: "It is hard to find the cause or causes of that."

48 Peter Perdue points out this sharp contrast between the Qing case and other empires in resulting the decline of nomadism. See Perdue, *China Marches West*, 11.

Tibetan Plateau pertains to the general Tibetan cultural area, while the Eastern Lowlands refer to the agricultural regions in the East Asian subcontinent, roughly equivalent to the Northern Song's extension. The Northern Areas comprise territories located north of the previous two, including the Mongolian Plateau, Manchurian Plain, and certain parts of Central Asia where the Western Liao (Khara-Khitai) Empire (1124–1218) exerted its influence in the twelfth century (see Fig. 1). However, these labels are tentative and conceptual, aiming to avoid political associations with nation-states. Moreover, defining clear boundaries proves difficult, as the so-called "Sixteen Prefectures" of that period represent a shared area between the Eastern Lowlands and Northern Areas. The Tangut State, the primary focus of my dissertation, exemplifies an overlap of all three regions. As we will see, these transitional zones are pivotal in understanding the interconnections that secured the building blocks of Inner Asian imperial history.

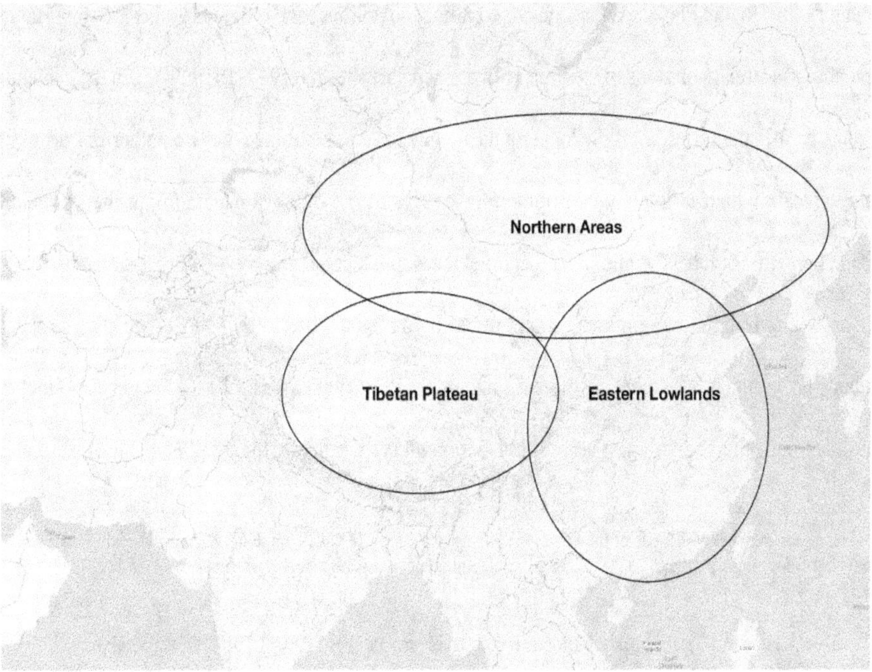
Northern Areas
Tibetan Plateau
Eastern Lowlands

Figure. 1 The three regions of Inner Asian imperial history

Now, let us turn to the parallelisms of a preliminary observation on the three regions.

Parallelism I: Advancement of Political Institutions

The political history of Early Medieval[49] East Asia and Inner Asia was, in brief, a Great Game between several great empires. Single imperial authority existed in these empires, such as the *btsan po* of the Tibetan Empire, emperors of the Tang, khans of the Türks and Uyghurs. These empires controlled expansive lands and people and attempted to gain more land by utilizing the resources they had. Therefore, military conflicts were a common scenario throughout the age. After a period of uncertainties and chaos following the collapse of the empires in the nineth and early tenth century, new forms of political institutions emerged in the three regions in the eleventh century. In Tibetan Plateau, a tendency to combine the political and religious authorities in a single person was already obvious in the time of Lha bla ma Ye shes 'od (947–1019/24).[50] In the eleventh to the twelfth centuries, multiple local monastic powers that combined the two authorities arose in the plateau, which ultimately contributed to the rise of the Sa skya hegemony in the thirteenth century. This practice would later become the sophisticated theory of *chos srid zung 'brel*, "combining religion and politics," exemplified by the later Tibetan regimes, especially the Dga' ldan pho brang government in the seventeenth century, which served as a model for Tibetan politics until the beginning of the twenty-first century. Similarly, the establishment of the Song

[49] Here I adhere Beckwith's use of this term as referring to a period in which an "Early Medieval World Order" existing from roughly the early seventh century to the nineth century. See Beckwith, *Empires of the Silk Road*, 158–162.

[50] van der Kuijp, "A Fifteenth Century Biography of Lha bla ma Ye shes 'od (947-1019/24): Part One: Its Prolegomenon and Prophecies," 341–375.

Dynasty in the Eastern Lowlands signified the start of two significant political institutions that, despite disruptions, continue even in today's China to a large extent. The first is the centralized government. Afraid of being rebelled against and overthrown again by frontier warlords and military officials who had done such things so often in the Tang and Five Dynasties, the Song rulers decided to withhold the paramount political and military power in the hand of the central government. The second institution, civil governance, then followed the first one. Literati, instead of aristocrats and military officers from great families, started to share power with the ruling imperial house.[51]

The advancement of political institutions in the Northern Areas is perhaps too obvious to be even noticed. In Barfield's theory, peoples who lived in Mongolia throughout the ages are depicted as rather parasitical. These people relied heavily on the prosperity of the southern dynasties that controlled Northern China. Therefore, once the Chinese dynasties fell, the steppe empires also broke, thus creating synchronized dynastic cycles.[52] Barfield has not taken the chance to examine the internal developments of the peoples of the Northern Area. In the tenth to the eleventh centuries, a general observation is that tribal peoples started the state-building process. Before this period, northern peoples who invaded China during the fourth to sixth centuries had to almost adopt the complete set of political institutions derived from the Han Empire.[53] The history of this period shows a strong tendency of the tribal peoples to build a state in their own in the Northern Areas. A striking phenomenon is the creation of written languages. The Khitans, Tanguts,

---

[51] For general description of these institutions and their significance, see Hartman, "Sung Government and Politics," and Deng, *Zuzong zhi fa*, 103–280.

[52] Barfield, *Perilous Frontier*, 8–16.

[53] For example, the Rites of Zhou was a paradigmatic work for many tribal peoples to conceive their institutions. See Yoshiaki, "Goko Jūrokkoku Hokuchō ki ni okeru Shurai no juyō o megutte."

and Jurchens created their own scripts in tandem with their announcements of the founding of states. Other administrative innovations were also made. Notable is the so-called "duo-administrative system" initiated by the Khitan Liao, which aimed at keeping the ruling ethnic group that was normally outnumbered and other groups separate while maintaining an integrative system.[54] It was further developed by the Yuan and Qing dynasties in late-imperial Chinese history.

Parallelism II: Emergence of New Social Classes

New social classes emerged in all three areas from the tenth to eleventh centuries. In Tibetan Plateau, elite monks became a dominant social class in later Tibetan history. Monks in the Tibetan Empire were an integral part of the monastic institutions, which were ultimately a component of the statecraft. The status of the monks was similar to that of early Japan, which adopted Buddhism as an indispensable part of state-building.[55] After the demise of the empire, the monks started to enjoy much autonomy. Their authority was reinforced by the growing consciousness of the importance of *bla ma* as a fourth category of refuge-taking in addition to the Buddha, Dharma, and Saṅgha. Elite monks could receive great reverence together with patronage from secular rulers. They could cultivate hordes of devoted disciples and followers who formed the basis for supporting their remarkable social-economic presence in society. In the Eastern Lowlands, the destruction of the great aristocratic families, the envision of a civil government, and the development of the invigorating civil examinations all fostered the new literati class, which would later permeate through the local societies from the national level in the twelfth century.[56] In

[54] Di Cosmo, "State Formation and Periodization in Inner Asian History," 32–34.

[55] Minowa, *Nihon bukkyōshi*, 28–29.

[56] For this long trend of transformation, see Chen. "The State, the Gentry, and Local Institutions: The Song Dynasty and Long-term Trends from Tang to Qing."

the Northern Areas, the rise of a new class of military aristocrats was manifest. In traditional organizations of tribes, tribes of clans tied by kinship were the basic units of society. Manufacturing a formidable war machine was nothing more than the charismatic ruler tying together and mobilizing these unites, just like what Modu did for Xiongnu in the third century BCE. In the eleventh and twelfth centuries, we see northern empires trying to dissolve the old tribal units and replace them with standardized battalions commanded by military officers who pledged personal loyalty to the ruler and appointed by the ruler.[57] We should remember that the event of Temüchin's rise itself was such an exceptional case in Inner Asian history since he almost never relied on his own clan for wars. Instead, strongmen such as those in the legendary "Baljuna covenant" who maintained a close personal relationship with him played paramount roles.[58] This new class of course formed the basis for later organizations such as the Manchu banners.

Parallelism III: Transformation of Intellectual and Religious Frameworks

One would almost naturally expect a parallelism of intellectual history, having seen the above two parallel historical phenomena. And as expected, we indeed witness significant intellectual and religious transformations in the three regions. The start of the Later Diffusion period in the eleventh century in the Tibetan Plateau signified, as Ronald Davidson terms, the "Tibetan Renaissance," in which the revival of Buddhism was instrumental in the rebirth of Tibetan culture after the collapse of the Tibetan Empire.[59] New tantric lineages were transmitted into the Tibetan plateau by prominent figures such as 'Brog mi Shākya ye she (fl. eleventh century)

---

[57] The Mongol reorganization of tribes is an example, see Morgan, *The Mongols*, 89–90.

[58] Jackson, "The Mongol Age in Eastern Inner Asia," 28–30.

[59] Davidson, Introduction to *Tibetan Renaissance*.

and Mar pa Chos kyi blo gros (fl. eleventh century). New tantric teachings became an essential part of Tibetan Buddhism later in history. But apart from the influx of tantric teachings, there also arose a distinct form of Tibetan scholasticism concurrently with the rise of the Gsang phu ne'u thog (henceforth Gsang phu) monastic tradition.[60] Therefore, although Tibetan Buddhist writings generally talk about a continuity of Buddhism in two different periods, historically speaking, we are faced with two forms of Buddhism, of which the former one should perhaps be termed as "Buddhism in Tibet," and the latter, "Tibetan Buddhism." For the intellectual transformation in the Eastern Lowlands, a rough-and-ready answer that may be mor accessible could be "from Confucianism to Neo-Confucianism," a conclusion already manifest in the early theory of the Tang-Song Transition.[61] To further elaborate it with still concise words, it is necessary to quote from Peter Bol, "Put most simply, early T'ang scholars supposed that the normative models for writing, government, and behavior were contained in the cumulative cultural tradition. Debates over values were arguments over the proper cultural forms. But by the late Sung, thinkers had shifted their faith to the mind's ability to arrive at true ideas about moral qualities inherent in the self and things, and the received cultural tradition had lost authority."[62] Beginning with the Guwen 古文 (ancient style) Movement in the early ninth century, literati under the Tang and Song dynasties were trying to find their *dao* 道, the "way," which was woven by *wen*, the "culture."[63] The *dao*, having been presented by great thinkers such as Wang Anshi 王安石 (1021–1086), Su Shi 蘇軾 (1037–1101), and Cheng Yi 程頤 (1033–1107) in the eleventh century, gained its

[60] As it forms a central object of investigation in Chapter Four, this issue is only addressed briefly here.

[61] Miyakawa, "An Outline of the Naito Hypothesis and Its Effects on Japanese Studies of China," 545.

[62] Bol, *This Culture of Ours*, 2–3.

[63] Bol, *This Culture of Ours*, 123–147.

ultimate discourse orchestrated by Zhu Xi 朱熹 (1130–1200), Lü Zuqian 呂祖謙 (1137–1181) and their followers in the twelfth century. *Daoxue* (almost interchangeable with *Lixue*, Neo-Confucianism), or the learning of *dao* became then an important subject of historical writing and civil examination in the late Yuan Period.[64] The affluence of the Chan schools of Chinese Buddhism to prominence no doubt marked another important intellectual trend in the eleventh century in the Eastern Lowlands.[65]

The transformation took place in the Northern Areas is one that is easy to observe – the reception of foreign ideas and religions. Although the exact influence of Buddhism in the Türk empires remains doubtful, the Uyghur Khaganate (744–840) was introduced with Manichaeism in the eighth century.[66] Its most important successor, the Qocho Kingdom (843–1209) whose political center was in the Turfan Basin, gradually became crucial nodes of Buddhism.[67] In the east, the Khitan Liao shows a strong presence of the Huayan School of Buddhism, which originated in the Tang.[68] The Jurchen Jin partly inherited the intellectual culture of the Northern Song.[69] And, pending the end of the state, *Daoxue* also started to spread.[70] The Quanzhen School of Daoism, which was also in close interaction with the early Mongols, arose first in Jin's realm and almost

---

[64] Xiao, *Yuandai de zuqun wenhua yu keju*, 49.

[65] Albert Welter, *Monks, Rulers, and Literati*, 1–25.

[66] Using the Karabalgasun inscription, Émmanuel-Édouard Chavannes and Paul Pelliot dated the introduction of Manichaeism to the Uyghur Khaganate in 763. See Chavannes and Pelliot, *Un traité manichéen retrouvé en Chine*, 223.

[67] Wilkens, "Buddhism in the West Uyghur Kingdom and Beyond."

[68] For the Huayan School in Liao, see Chikusa, "Ryō dai Kegonshū no ichikōsatsu: Omo ni, shinshutsu Kegonshū tenseki no bunkengaku teki kenkyū."

[69] Peter Bol, "Seeking Common Ground: Han Literati Under Jurchen Rule."

[70] Tillman, "Confucianism under the Chin and the Impact of Sung Confucian Tao-hsüeh."

immediately had an unneglectable influence in the state.[71] Buddhism had already been in the area for centuries before the establishment of the Tangut State, which then utilized Buddhism, as Ruth Dunnell argues, as an indispensable part of state-building.[72] Having received Buddhist input first from the Liao and Northern Song, the Tangut State turned to the Tibetans for teachings in the twelfth century. These trends of course culminated in the mid-thirteenth century when the Mongols were officially converted by Tibetan Buddhists and formed the so-called *yon mchod* or "patron-priest" relationship with Tibetan monks.

More parallelisms can be found, but for now, these three are enough for us to analyze their interconnections. Not unexpectedly, connections between parallelisms on the most general level are not difficult to articulate. To support political reform, a new social class is necessary, which is further fostered by that reform. The new class also generates new needs for intellectual and religious culture, whose discourse solidifies the status of the new class. This is also true when we examine either of the three regions. For example, the growing prominence of literati created the social background for intellectual transformations in the Song.[73]

However, as posted before, our questions should be far more than the mere inquiry on the surface level. Considering the nature of an integrative history of the three regions, it is imperative that we consider the interconnections between other smaller units. There can be little doubt that region B's parallelism can be partly conditioned by Region A's same parallelism. The decisive evidence is provided by parallelism III in the Tibetan Plateau and Northern Areas. Without the revival of Tibetan Buddhism, the Mongols could have gained no basis for their conversion in

---

[71] For the Quanzhen School under the Jin with its continuity in the Yuan, see Yao, "Buddhism and Taoism under the Chin," in *China Under Jurchen Rule*, eds. Tillman and West, 153–158; Wang, *In the Wake of the Mongols*, 65–85.

[72] Dunnell, *The Great State of White and High*, 34–49.

[73] Bol, *This Culture of Ours*, 32–75.

history. Further, we embark on making sense of the connections between two parallelisms in two different regions. This task is not insignificant since, if such connections existed and did so to a remarkable extent, then we have more reasons to assume a single history that derived from these regions.

We might first examine the relations between the state-building (parallelism I) in the Northern Areas and the rise of the literati class (parallelism II) in the Eastern Lowlands. The building of a state and its institutions needs talents who are skilled in such designs. A portion of literati who were cultivated by the Great Song yet were disappointed by their dim future chose their overlords elsewhere. And the tribal rulers who were anxious about state-building had little reason to reject these newcomers. Two defectors, for example, were well commented upon in the writings of Song literati and historiographers, although the details of their lives remain opaque. We do not know their actual names. The names, Zhang Yuan 張元 (or 張源) and Wu Hao 吳昊, were no doubt fake, but they were to show their loyalty to Yuanhao 元昊 (1003–1048), the first emperor of the Tangut State. It is at least clear that Zhang Yuan was an extraordinarily talented literatus who only failed his examination on the final stage, the court exam. The failure to obtain the degree outraged him and made him a defector to the Tangut State. Both of them participated actively in the projects of Yuanhao and helped the emperor defeat the Song troops in the first three campaigns that the Song launched to eliminate the Tangut State after their claim of independence.[74] It is hard to imagine that the northern states could have been as successful as they were in history had the Song literati class not been so strong.

[74] For the story of Zhang Yuan and Wu Hao, see Wu, *Xixia shi gao*, 32.

Further investigation confirms the link between the state-building (parallelism I) in the Northern Areas and the intellectual transformation (parallelism III) in the Eastern Lowlands. It is an often-overlooked fact that the new intellectual culture formed in the Tang-Song Transition was not only an internal development but also a response to the external world. By building statecraft, the northern peoples had become more formidable rivals than ever. The tribal coalitions were replaced by states and dynasties, which were much stronger and more enduring. Literati in the south were forced to rethink their relationship with these "barbarians" in the north. Han Yu, in his famous essay "Yuan dao," 原道 or "On the Way," already wrote the following passage, "Confucius composed the *Spring and Autumn Annals*. When the Chinese states used barbarian rituals, he regarded them as barbarian; when the barbarians advanced to the Central Country[75], he regarded them as peoples of the Central Country."[76] The dichotomy of Yi/Xia 夷/夏 or Diyi/Zhongguo 狄夷/中國 once became a major issue in the Song.[77] It should also be noted that Wang Anshi's New Policies, which he formulated in response to the financial pressure brought by the military threat posed by the states in the Northern Areas, was a political agenda as well as Wang's own vision for the *Shengren zhi dao* 聖人之道, the "Way of the Sages."[78]

---

[75] Central Country here translates *Zhongguo* 中國. A normal translation "China" is often misleading in this context. I here follow Bol's rendering. See Bol, "Geography and Culture."

[76] Han Yu, "Yuan dao," in QTW, juan 558, 12: 孔子之作《春秋》也，諸侯用夷禮，則夷之。進於中國，則中國之。

[77] This is evident in the writings of Song literati. See Ge, *Zhai zi Zhongguo*, and Tackett, *The Origins of the Chinese Nation*. However, I think we need to be careful when this phenomenon is branded as the rise of "nationalism." Nationalism is a term specifically conditioned by eighteenth century Europe and does not necessarily apply to the situations of the Song. While Ge and Tackett provided some persuasive reasons for why the phenomenon should be "nationalism," I suggest putting this phenomenon in the context of Song intellectual culture in which literati's articulations of inter-state relations frame a part of their intellectual scheme.

[78] Bol, *This Culture of Ours*, 212–53.

Besides, another essential connection arose between the religious transformation (parallelism III) in the Northern Areas and the rise of a new social class (parallelism II) in the Tibetan Plateau. The patron-priest relationship formed between the rulers from the north and the Tibetan monks solidified the social status of elite monks to be a leading class in Tibetan society. This development saw its first climax in Inner Asian imperial history when Kubilai Khan (1215–1294) appointed Sa skya patriarch 'Phags pa as both his Imperial preceptor and the governor of the three provinces of Tibet (*bod chol kha gsum*). A well-known passage from the *Blue Annals* (*Deb ther sngon po*) by 'Gos lo tsā ba Gzhon nu dpal (1392–1481) might be quoted here, "Having relied on the fact that the Se chen Emperor (=Kubilai) offered the three provinces of Tibet to 'Phags pa rin po che as the offering for initiation, the master engaged in the activities of a master."[79] Earlier development of this connection of course existed in the Tangut State, which will be further examined in the following chapters.

A conspicuous feature emerges when we analyze the interconnections on the level of these small parallel units. We do not recognize many interconnections between the parallel developments of the Tibetan Plateau and the Eastern Lowlands. But the Northern Areas was intensive connected to both. Therefore here, we come to an important observation of this dissertation, that is, the initial rise of the Mongol Empire, which has always been an intriguing historical phenomenon to explain, was attributed measurably to the interconnections of these parallelisms. The sudden explosion of the Mongol world thus was not accidental, far from it. It was, instead, a response to the call of the birth of Inner Asian imperial history, which was

[79] *Deb sngon*, 268:

> *'phags pa rin po che la gong ma se chen gyis / bod chol kha gsum po thams cad dbang yon du phul ba la brten nas bla mas bla ma'i bya ba mdzad cing /.*

conceived through the long ages starting from the nineth century. As a people in the Northern Areas, the Mongols inherited and continued most of the driving forces of history that their predecessors had. After decades of conquests, the Mongols realized a single Inner Asian imperial history in forming a single political entity—the Yuan Empire. This also explains why the extension of the Yuan, bordering the Golden Horde and the Chagatai Khanate, was one as such. It covers almost exactly the three regions discussed above and manifests the sophisticated internal connections with a single empire.

While the rise of the Mongols is viewed as the start of Inner Asian imperial history, this dissertation focuses on the period immediately preceding the formation of the Mongol Empire, which can be referred to as the formative period of the integrative Inner Asian imperial history. This period begins around 1130 and ends around 1230, and it is important in understanding the interconnections between the three regions of Inner Asian imperial history. In 1127, the Jin army conquered Kaifeng from the Northern Song, marking the beginning of a process that would eventually put the Eastern Lowlands and Northern Areas under a single rule. In 1124, on the brink of the Liao's collapse, Yelü Dashi (1094–1143) led his people to the west and founded the Western Liao. The Western Liao defeated the Seljuqs in the Battle of Qatwan in 1141 and took control of a part of Central Asia. And, when the Western Liao became a subject of the Mongol Empire in 1218, it provided the Mongols with valuable resources for their campaigns. In 1139, Renxiao 仁孝 (1124–1193) was enthroned as the ruler of the Tangut State, ushering in a long period of stability and prosperity. Under his reign, Tibetan Buddhism was introduced to the Tangut State. About one century later, the Mongols first took Zhongdu (present day Beijing) from the Jin in 1215 and fully conquered the state in 1234. Chinggis Khan destroyed the Khwarazmian Empire in 1220 and finally subdued the Tangut State in 1227, the same year he died. In 1244, in response to a call from Köden (1206–1251), the Mongol prince who ruled the old Tangut land, Sa skya Paṇḍita Kun dga' rgyal mtshan (1182–1251) and his nephew 'Phags pa left Gtsang in 1244 to meet the Mongols in Liangzhou (present day Wu Wei, in Gansu Province). This period marked the end of the old world and the creation of a new order.

Having discussed the temporal scope – what I have called the formative period of the integrative Inner Asian imperial history – of the dissertation, let us now turn to the geographical scope of it – the Tangut State. As we have seen in fig. 1, there is an area where the three regions overlap, and that would be roughly the geographical center of the Tangut State. Indeed, the Tangut State in the formative period of the integrative Inner Asian imperial history fostered many of the key factors that would later shape an Inner Asian empire. And we might term the Tangut State as a "prototypical Inner Asian empire."

3. The Tangut State: A Prototypical Inner Asian Empire

In 1176, the Tangut government erected a stele at the bank of the Black Water River (Heishui he 黑水河) near Zhenyi Prefecture (Zhenyi jun 鎮夷郡, also known as Ganzhou 甘州)[80]. This bilingual stele consists of a Chinese inscription on one side and a Tibetan inscription on the other.[81] While much of the Tibetan inscription is now hardly legible, an examination of the parts that are still readable shows that the contents of both inscriptions are similar. According to the

[80] Ganzhou (present-day Zhangye 张掖) is what the prefecture is normally called throughout Chinese history. The Tangut government renamed it Zhenyi, "suppressing the barbarians." In Chinese administrative divisions during the Sui-Tang period, *jun* and *zhou* are both on the prefectural level, but *jun* may denote that the prefecture is more military than civil in nature, normally established on the borderland areas.

[81] For previous scholarship on the stele, see Wang, "Xixia Heishui qiao bei kaobu," and Sato, et al., "Kan Zō gappeki Seika 'Kuromizu hashi hi' saikō."

Chinese inscription, the stele was erected as an imperial edict. And the addressees of the edict were gods in the valley of the Black River.

The emperor – who was Renxiao in this case – first praises the contribution of a certain Bodhisattva Excellent-Awakened-Noble-Light (Xianjue Sheng Guang pusa 賢覺聖光菩薩), a figure whose identity is a mystery,[82] for building a bridge on the Black Water River, which allowed the people to cross the Black Water River without danger. Then, he says that he visited the bridge before and made offerings to the gods, which enabled the gods to remove the danger of the flood of the river. And, finally, he says he has made offerings again this time and hopes the gods could help him forever pacify the floods of the river, benefit the people under his rule, and protects the state. Six persons who participated in the project of erecting the stele are recorded at the end of the inscription.

An issue that has been discussed by previous scholars is why the emperor chose to make offerings again in 1176 and erect the stele. For this, I suggest we turn to the *Xixia Chronicles*. Under the year 1176, the author Wu Guangcheng wrote the following entry:

> In the seventh month of the autumn, there was drought. Locusts appeared extensively. The crops of the prefectures of Hexi[83] were almost eaten up.[84]

---

[82] This could be a real historical figure, an imperial preceptor called Xianjue 賢覺 in the Tangut State. Or it could be a legendary figure of the Han dynasty called Xianjue Sheng Guang pusa, whose story was popular in the Ganzhou region. See Sato, et al., "Kan Zō gappeki Seika 'Kuromizu hashi hi' saikō," 11.

[83] 河西, which literally means the "west of the [Yellow] River." It is roughly equal to present day Gansu Province.

[84] Wu, *Xixia shushi jiaozhu*, 474: 秋七月，旱。蝗大起，河西諸州食稼殆盡。

Since the stele was erected in the ninth month, it seems it is related to the drought of the seventh month. What is curious is the emperor asked to local gods to help stop the floods instead of a drought. Perhaps there were floods after the drought? This is something that cannot be solved at this moment.

Let us now turn to the inscriptions. Both inscriptions read as follows:[85]

勅：	om swa [*sti] /
鎮[夷][86]郡境内黑水河上下所有隱顯一切水土之主——山神、水神、龍神、樹神、[土]地諸神等——咸聽朕命！	[---su?] / / gy[a][-] 'j[i] na [-]u'I stod [---] gnas pa'i / [---]'i lha dang / [k]lu['i] lha dang / shing [sa] lha la sogs pa [---b?---] / [*bdag] gi bka' nyon cig /
昔賢覺聖光菩薩哀愍此河年年暴漲，漂蕩人畜，[故]以大慈悲興建此橋，普令一切往返有情，咸免徒	sngon 'phags pa byang chub sems [*dpa'---] 'od zer[87] gyis / [---] yi [---]u chu brug chen po [---] / myi [---] mang po la gnod [---] [']bangs byabs [---/?] s[-]o[---k?]y[---]y[---y]es b[---] g[---] / rgyal khan[-][88]gyi [---g?---] dang / bde brgya cha [---] /

---

[85] I use the transcriptions of both texts from Sato, et al., "Kan Zō gappeki Seika 'Kuromizu hashi hi' saikō," 8, 15–17. The same article also contains the photographs of both sides of the stele. For the Chinese text, characters in the brackets, which are not entirely legible are supplied by Sato, et al based on the legible strokes of them as well as the context. Since they do not have a punctuation for the Chinese text, the punctuation of the Chinese text is mine. For the Tibetan text, the following convention is used by Sato, et al.:

> [abc] Letters are reconstructed with certainty based on the legible strokes.
> ab[c?] Despite the legible strokes, the letter cannot be determined.
> [*abc] Letters, which are missing due to their obliteration, are reconstructed without certainty.
> [abc(/def)] The letters can be identified in multiple ways.
> [---] Due to obliteration, the number of missing letters is unknown.
> ab[-] One letter is missing.

[86] The character *yi* 夷, "barbarians," seems to have been purposefully damaged. Did the Mongols efface it or is it a result of Tanguts' self-censorship after the Mongol conquest? We do not know.

[87] Based on the Chinese equivalent, it seems we can reconstruct the full name as 'Phags pa Byang chub sems dpa' Sangs rgyas bzang po 'od zer.

[88] Probably *khams*  instead of *khan*[-], thus making the term *rgyal khams*, corresponding the Chinese *guo* 國. The lower right corner of the ma  in the stele is always lengthened, which makes it look like *na* if the stroke on the right is obliterated.

涉之患，皆霑安濟之福。斯誠利國便民之大端也。	/ [bdag] sngon 'phags pa bya[ng] chub sems d[pa' b?---'od] zer [---]u[---] zam [pa] de mthong bas / dad ba dang [---]y[---] nas / de la [g]nas pa'I lha klu khyed rnams [---] gyi [---]m rgya chen p[o] [---] / de [---] khyed rnams kyis chu'I gnod pa mtha' dag zhI bar byas [*---/ / bda]g gi bsam pa dang mthun par byung bas [---] yang shin du [-]i[---]gs so /
朕昔已曾親臨此橋，嘉美賢覺興造之功。仍罄虔懇躬，祭汝諸神等。自是之後，水患頓息。固知諸神冥歆，朕意陰加，擁祐之所致也。	
今朕載啓精虔，幸冀汝等諸多靈神，廓慈悲之心，恢濟度之德，重加神力，密運威靈 。庶幾水患永息，橋道久長，令此諸方有情，俱蒙利益，佑我邦家，則豈惟上契，十方諸聖之心，抑亦可副。朕之弘願也，諸神鑒之，毋替朕命！	/ da dung [*sngar b]zhin [*du---] gang gnas pa'I lha klu khyed rnams [---y---s-] dang [---] chu [---skya]bs kyis / 'gro ba mang pos [---o---] dag b[r]tan nas zh[i] ba[r] mdzod cig / [z]am pa lam [---/?---] ba mang po la phan par bsgrub pa dang / / bdag gi [---lha?---] yul [du?-] [bzh]ugs pa'I 'phags pa rnams kyi thugs dg[---] [']d[un?] [---r]gya chen po bsgrub pa'I stong grogs byas pa yin no / [---] la gang gnas [pa']I lha klu khyed rnams / / bdag gi bka' bzhin du sgrubs shi[g] /
大夏乾祐七年歲次丙申九月二十五日立石	/ / me pho spre'u lo zla wa rgu pa ni shu lnga nyi ma la rdo yig bslangs /
主案郭那正成 司吏駱永安 筆手張世恭書 瀉作使安善惠刊	/ / spyi'I zhal snga ba cin yi bkyin tse g.yo ti cho / / si'u kyam g.yo yan [--- /]
小監王延慶	/ / yi ge brko myi zhi' dgan zhan hyi / / yi ge 'bri myi klog sphy[i---o---] /
都大勾當鎮夷郡正兼郡學教授 王德昌	/ / a lu gu do[89] [tshe(/je)] she / yig mkhan lca'u si dkan /

Translations of both texts are as follows:

Imperial decree:	Goodness!
All the lords of water and earth who are either visible or invisible in the upper and lower valleys of the Black Water River within the circumference of Zhenyi Prefecture – the god	…the god of…and the god of the Dragons, and the gods of the trees and the earth, etc.

[89] This *do* , whose lower part is obliterated, seems to be more likely a *no*, which would correspond better the *na* 那 in the Chinese text.

of mountains, the god of water, the god of dragons, the god of trees, the god of the earth, etc. – all listen to my command!

Previously, Bodhisattva Excellent-Awakened-Noble-Light was distressed by the fact that the river flooded ferociously every year, sweeping people and animals away. Therefore, by means of great compassion, he built this bridge, thus allowing all the sentient beings who travel back and forth all to be free from the fear of trudging through the water and all to be blessed by the fortune of comfort. This is indeed a great enterprise that benefits the state and eases the people.

I have previously visited the bridge in person and praised the contribution made by the Excellent-Awakened. I likewise showed my faith without reservation, sincerely bowed, and made offerings to you gods. Even since then, the peril of flood has been stopped. Hence, I know it is because of the divine protection that resulted from you gods who have enjoyed the offerings in the divine space and have silently enforced my will.

Now, I have again unleashed my absolute faith, and wish you, the many numinous gods, could enlarge your compassionate mind and amplify your salvific virtue, multiply your magical power, and intensify the exertion of your numinous might. Then, perhaps the peril of the flood could be permanently stopped, and the path of the bridge could be long-lasting. Thus, the sentient beings from many directions could all be benefited, and our country could be protected. If that were to be the case, then it is not only a pledge, but the minds of the noble ones from the ten directions would perhaps also be satisfied. This is my great prayer, and, gods, please examine it and do not disobey my command!

who dwell in the upper…Black Water[92]…listen to my command!

Previously, the Noble Boddhisattva…Light…great flood…harming many…people…cleanse the subjects…of the kingdom, and one hundred kinds of happiness…

I have previously…the Noble Bodhisattva…Light…Having seen that bridge, on the basis of the faith and…you, the gods and dragons who dwell there…extensive…that…you have made all the harm of the water pacified… it appeared according to my intention…also very…

Now, just like before, you gods and dragons who dwell in any … and … water … protect … Thus, many beings … make it everlastingly pacified! The path of the bridge … establish benefits for many, and my … the minds of the noble ones who dwell in the regions…making the support for establishing extensive… you gods and dragons who dwell in any … accomplish it according to my command!

[92] The Tibetan *'j[i] na* is a phonetic transcription of the Tangut *zji̠r nja̠* [illegible], which means "black water."

Stele erected on the twenty-fifth day of the ninth month of the *bingshen*[90] year, the seventh year of the Qianyou reign of the Great Xia.	Inscription established on the twenty-fifth day[93] of the ninth month of the fire-male-monkey year.
The supervisor Guona Zhengcheng[91],	The supervisor-in-chief, prefect of Zhenyi Prefecture, Wang Dechang
The clerk Luo Yong'an	The overseer Wang Yan[qing]
Written by the calligrapher Zhang Shigong	The carver An Shanhui
Carved by the carver An Shanhui	The scribe Klog Sphyi…[94]
The overseer Wang Yanqing	The supervisor[95] Guona Zhengcheng
The supervisor-in-chief, prefect of Zhenyi Prefecture, and professor at the prefectural school, Wang Dechang	The calligrapher Zhang Shigong

The Black Water Stele resembles the famous Liangzhou Stele erected in 1094 by Empress Dowager Liang 梁[96] and Emperor Qianshun 乾順 (r. 1086–1139) of the Tangut State in many

[90] 丙申, a year in the *ganzhi* 干支 sexagenary cycle.

[91] Guona 郭那 is the phonetic transcription of the Tangut clan name Kwo nja̠ [illegible]. Zhengcheng 正成 is not entirely clear. It could be a phonetic transcription of his Tangut name. But I tend to think it is in fact a translation of the Tangut name Tśhja śjɨj [illegible], "Correct-Established," which would work well with the Tibetan phonetic transcription *tshe she* / *je she*.

[93] The "day" is rendered as *nyi ma* instead of the usual *tshes*. This seems to indicate that the translator of the Tibetan texts wants to distinguish between the Chinese calendar and the Tibetan calendar.

[94] There is a temptation to identify this person with the clerk Luo Yong'an 駱永安 in the Chinese text. However, it is extremely difficult to regard *sphyi* as a phonetic transcription of *yong*. See Sato, et al., "Kan Zō gappeki Seika 'Kuromizu hashi hi' saikō," 20. We should not forget that he is supposedly the scribe of the Tibetan text. So, he must have the necessary skill to write Tibetan letters. Therefore, I tend to think he is a different person who is a Tibetan or Tibetanized Chinese, or Luo Yong'an had the necessary skill to write the Tibetan text.

[95] The Tibetan *a lu* should be a phonetic transcription of the Tangut *·ja lju* [illegible], which means "supervisor."

[96] This is the later Empress Dowager Liang from the Liang family, who was the mother of Qianshun. She is to be distinguished from the former Empress Dowager Liang, who was the mother of Bingchang 秉常 (1061–1086).

ways.[97] Both steles were erected under imperial orders; both steles were erected as invocations for the welfare of the people and the prosperity of the state; the inscriptions of both steles were written in the Buddhist context. However, they also differ in several aspects. The most salient difference is that the Liangzhou Stele, which also has bilingual inscriptions, was in Tangut and Chinese, whereas the Black Water Stele was written in Chinese and Tibetan. This means that Tangut, the language of the ruling ethnic group of the Tangut State, was not conceived as a part of the inscriptions. The absence of a Tangut inscription is somehow understandable because Zhenyi Prefecture / Ganzhou traditionally had mainly Chinese and Tibetan populations and had not been heavily populated by Tanguts. However, the phenomenon is still striking since the Tangut government did not see the necessity of having the Tangut inscription on the stele as a way to show the principal status of the ruling ethnic group, especially given the fact that the stele served as an imperial edict. This suggests that the Tangut government was not pushing a Tangutization agenda in its realm. Instead, it tried to keep the cultural traditions of different ethnic groups as long as the message of the government could be accessed by them properly and effectively.

The stele is also unique since it is the earliest datable Sino-Tibetan bilingual stele that was erected by a single political authority. While the famous 823 treaty stele between the Tang and the Tibetan empires is an earlier example of a Sino-Tibetan bilingual stele, it serves as a treaty between two polities. The Black Water Stele, in contrast, was erected not for Chinese and Tibetan audiences from two distinct polities but for these two ethnic groups within a single state. The tradition of erecting bilingual Sino-Tibetan steles or multilingual steles that contain Chinese and Tibetan inscriptions continued in the later empires of China and Inner Asia. Renowned examples of these

[97] For scholarship on the Liangzhou Stele, see Shi, *Xixia Fojiao shilue*, 35, 247–254, and Dunnell, *The Great State of White and High*, chap. 5.

are the 1341 Sino-Tibetan bilingual stele in Lingyan 靈岩 Monastery, Shandong,[98] the 1429 Sino-Tibetan bilingual stele in Da chongjiao 大崇教 Monastery, Gansu,[99] and the 1792 quadrilingual stele of the *Discourse of Lama* (Lama shuo 喇嘛說) in Yonghe 雍和 Temple, Beijing.[100]

While the contents of the inscriptions in both languages are similar, they are not completely identical. The differences, as I see, were intentionally made to better suit the cultural backgrounds of the Chinese and Tibetan audiences. A major difference here is at the beginning of both texts. In the Chinese text, it says "imperial edict" (*chi* 勅), whereas the Tibetan text starts with a benediction, "goodness" (or, in fact, "may there be goodness"[101]). Chinese people were of course more used to the Chinese bureaucratic system in which a statement that came from the emperor would always be understood as an imperial edict. It enhanced the emperor's authority as someone commanding the gods to do their work. The benediction in the Tibetan text, on the other hand, fit well in the Tibetan cultural context as the Tibetans were much less sensitive to the bureaucratic system but were more sensitive to the religious power. Another notable difference is the way the date is recorded in both texts. The Chinese text uses the reign title of the emperor together with the *ganzhi* 干支 sexagenary cycle. The Tibetan text, on the other hand, does not use the reign title. Instead, it

---

[98] The stele bears the command given by the state preceptor Dkon mchog rgyal mtshan to the Yuan officials that they should not take any property from the monastery. For studies of the stele, see Chavannes, "Inscriptions et pièces de Chancellerie chinoises de l'époque mongole (seconde série)," 418–421, and Wang, "Shandong Changqing Lingyan si Da Yuan guoshi fazhi bei kaoshi."

[99] Da chongjiao Monastery was built in 1417 by Dpal ldan bkra shis (1377–after 1452), the Religious Lord of Great Wisdom (Da zhi fa wang 大智法王) of the Ming dynasty. In 1427, the Ming government expanded the monastery and made it a royal monastery. For the inscriptions, see Zhang, Su, and Luo, *Xitian Fozi yuanliu lu*, 365–370.

[100] For a study of the stele, see Oidtmann, *Forging the Golden Urn*, 104, 239–243.

[101] If we read the full sentence as *oṃ svasti siddham*.

uses the sexagenary cycle whose year name consists of an element and an animal, which is customary in Tibetan culture.

Buddhism is the religion that forms the context that ties together the Tangut emperor, the Chinese and Tibetan audiences, and the gods who are the addressees. Many Chinese people in the Hexi had long been Buddhists ever since the introduction of Buddhism into China. The Tibetans who lived within the Tangut State were in general also Buddhists because of the Buddhist culture of the Tibetan Empire, which ruled the Hexi Corridor four centuries ago. The Tanguts, as will be discussed more in the next chapter, were also predominantly Buddhists. The Buddhist language used in the stele is exemplified by expressions such as "great compassion" (*da cibei* 大慈悲), "sentient beings" (*youqing* 有情), "salvific virtue" (*jidu zhi de* 濟度之德), "great prayer" (*hong yuan* 弘願), and, most importantly, by the "Bodhisattva Excellent-Awakened-Noble-Light." Hence, Buddhism was the language that the three main ethnic groups in the Tangut State – Tanguts, Chinese, and Tibetans – used to communicate with each other. In the case of the Black Water Stele, the emperor also puts the local gods in such communication, suggesting that his secular authority was exerted upon the divine beings through a Buddhist device of making offerings to them. The emperor's Chinese and Tibetan subjects, who were the viewers of the stele, benefited from the communication between the emperor and the local gods with that Buddhist language. And the subjects were directly benefited by the local gods' protection as well as indirectly benefited by the emperor's act of making offerings. The power relations between the above-mentioned four groups can thus be illustrated by the following figure:

Chinese subjects
Indirectly benefited by
Viewing the communication
Directly benefited by
Making offerings
Tangut emperor
Local gods
Granting protection
Viewing the communication
Indirectly benefited by
Directly benefited by
Tibetan subjects

Figure 2. Power relations in the Black Water Stele

Finally, what we also notice from reading the Sino-Tibetan inscription of 1176 is how the Tangut government brought talented artisans from different ethnic groups to finish the project of erecting the stele. The one who gave the order for erecting such a stele was of course the Tangut emperor himself. The supervisor, Guona Zhengcheng, was undoubtedly a Tangut.[102] Most other people, including the supervisor-in-chief Wang Dechang, were Chinese. The scribe of the Tibetan text, Klog Sphyi…, is probably a Tibetan or a Tibetanized Chinese.[103]

Let us now summarize the characteristics of the Tangut rule reflected by the Black Water Stele:

---

[102] See note 91.

[103] See note 94.

1. Maintaining the state by ethnic differences without pushing an agenda of assimilation.

2. Appealing to different ethnic groups with different political languages accessible to their different cultural backgrounds.

3. Using the Buddhist idiom as a *lingua franca* for consolidating the coherence of and the support from different ethnic groups.

4. Bringing together the talents from different ethnic groups to effectively achieve a state project.

And, as made clear in the Introduction and the last section, we may also add:

5. Ruling the state as a non-Han ethnic group without pursuing an agenda of complete Sinicization.

All five characteristics are what constitutes an Inner Asian empire like the Yuan and the Qing. Therefore, I suggest we view the Tangut State as a prototypical Inner Asian empire that is already imbued with those elements that are characteristic of the later Inner Asian empires. And what facilitated the formation of such a prototypical Inner Asian empire was, as I discussed in the last section, the intensified interactions between the three regions from which an integrative Inner Asian imperial history arose. While examining every aspect of these interactions exemplified by the Tangut State is impossible in this dissertation, in the following chapters, I will investigate particularly how these interactions made Buddhism, especially Tibetan Buddhism, a key feature that characterizes an Inner Asian empire.

Chapter Two: Tangut Buddhism in the Revolution of a Buddhist Complex

1. The Revolution of a Buddhist Complex

The use of geographical adjectives to describe Buddhism detracts from one of its most important features: its ability to transcend boundaries of language, people, and society. Throughout history, Buddhism has spread to almost every corner of Asia, with opportunities to plant its branches in a variety of soils. Following the passing of Gautama Buddha in the first half of the fourth century BCE, Buddhism was proclaimed as a religion in Northern India[104] and disseminated in two major directions, north and south. Thera Moggaliputtatissa, a legendary figure in Aśoka's time, sent missionaries to various regions to convert people to Buddhism, a fact supported by several Pāli and Chinese sources.[105] Gandhāra, for example, was converted to Buddhism by Majjhantika in the third to the first century BCE, with steady Buddhist influence being exerted over the region.[106] The Kushan Empire arose in tandem with the growth of Buddhist influence in Bacteria and among the Iranian peoples in Central Asia during the turning of the Common Era.[107] At around the same time, Buddhism reached China through Central Asia,[108] where it flourished from the third to the seventh centuries, with countless Buddhist scriptures being translated.[109] After

[104] Modern scholars now have, based on the so-called "short chronology," a general agreement that the Nirvāṇa of the historical Buddha should be placed at the first half of the fourth century BCE. See Bechert, "Introductory Essay." See also Lamotte's summary of the long and short chronologies: Lamotte, *History of Indian Buddhism*, 13–14.

[105] Lamotte, *History of Indian Buddhism*, 292–310; Dutt, *Buddhist Monks and Monasteries of India*, 107–117.

[106] Dietz, "Buddhism in Gandhāra," 53–59.

[107] Tremblay, "The Spread of Buddhism in Serindia: Buddhism Among Iranians, Tocharians and Turks Before the 13th Century," 80–83.

[108] Zürcher, *The Buddhist Conquest of China*, 22–23.

[109] For a summary of the history of Buddhist translation in China, see Wang, *Fodian hanyi zhi yanjiu*, 64–120.

spreading to China, Buddhism written in Chinese found its way further eastward, finally taking root in Japan. At the end of the sixth century, the Japanese monastic community (*saṃgha*) was inaugurated, and several nuns were ordained.[110]

The sketch above of early Buddhist transmissions in the Indian subcontinent, Central and East Asia is by no means redundant in this chapter. We notice that Buddhism flourished in the above-mentioned areas in the first millennium largely because of the motion of Buddhism and the possibility of that motion. Exchanges of people, texts, ideas, and products among different regions and societies provided ample nutrients for the growth of the Buddhist tree, whereas the isolation of an area greatly prevented the water that cultivated the plant. This situation was almost typically represented in the dramatic difference between the Sogdiana proper and Sogdian settlements along the silk roads. The Sogdians were one of the first peoples that actively promoted Buddhist presence in in China and Central Asia. But strikingly enough, we never saw, at least from available evidence, a full-fledged boom of Buddhism in Sogdiana itself.[111] Sogdians were born explores, adventurers, language specialists, and gifted merchants. The travelling Sogdians facilitated the motion of Buddhism, thus spreading the religion in their own communities in foreign lands as well as the surrounding Chinese and Central Asian peoples. However, Sogdian, the homeland of Sogdians, never became a hub of Buddhism presumably because of its isolation from Central Eurasian political and economic ties. We perceive an important implication here that the vitality of Buddhism comes partly from the vigor of a system in which Buddhism could be transmitted and exchanged. Therefore, I name this system a Buddhist Complex. A Buddhist Complex is not merely one that facilitates the spread of Buddhist doctrines and scriptures. It is a world in which many

[110] Minowa, *Nihon bukkyōshi*, 25.

[111] Xavier Tremblay, "The Spread of Buddhism in Serindia," 89–97.

fields of human knowledge grow with Buddhism as their context. Here I cite Janet Gyatso's idea of taking Buddhism as a civilizational force.[112] We see, for example, the prosody of Chinese Recent Style Poetry (Ch. Jinti shi 近體詩) has a Sanskrit origin,[113] one that is offered by the Buddhist Complex.

The growth of Buddhism in Central and East Asia during the first millennium was sustained by an Indo-Chinese Buddhist Complex (See fig. 1). The term "Indo-Chinese" highlights the importance of India as a source of Buddhist transmission in this complex. But India is not the only source. At the micro level, any region, society, or individual could be a potential point of departure for the transmission of Buddhism. At the macro level, we must also recognize China as a major source, particularly after the sixth century. Buddhism that arrived in the Korean Peninsula and the Japanese Archipelago originated in China. Moreover, we should not overlook the westward movement of Buddhism from China. Although the authenticity of the records is doubtful, Chinese historiography from the seventh century noted that monks from China converted the rulers of the First Türk Empire. Nevertheless, we can assert with confidence that Chinese Buddhism had a significant influence on the Uyghurs. Despite the preference of the Uyghur ruling class for Manicheanism, Buddhism became increasingly prevalent among the Western Uyghurs after the 9th century, with Chinese Buddhism serving as a major source for Tocharian Buddhism during this period. Lost Chinese Buddhist compositions are found in Uyghur translations, and the Tanguts translated numerous Chinese Buddhist texts, as will be discussed below.

---

[112] Gyatso, *Being Human in a Buddhist World*, 406–407.

[113] Mair and Mei, "The Sanskrit Origins of Recent Style Prosody."

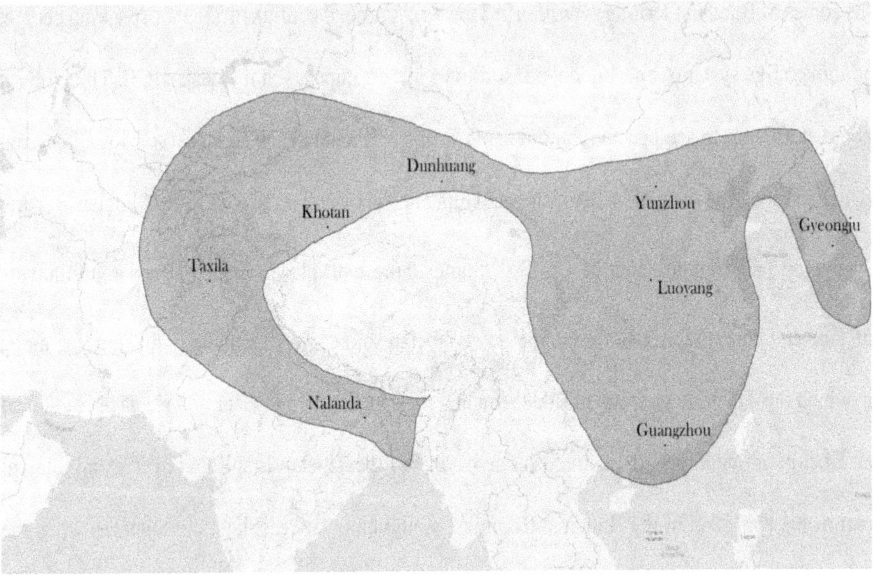
Dunhuang
Khotan
Yunzhou
Gyeongju
Taxila
Luoyang
Nalanda
Guangzhou

Figure 1. The Indo-Chinese Buddhist Complex in the beginning of the seventh century

Tibet is another member of the Indo-Chinese Buddhist Complex worth mentioning. It did not become a substantial major source in the complex during the Early Diffusion period. However, the fact that it received significant Buddhist transmissions directly from both of the major sources from the eighth century on[114] was unique. It resulted partially in the pulling of the center of gravity of the complex southward from the Tarim Basin to the Tibetan Plateau. Another factor that contributed to the shift of the center was the Tibetan military conquest of Central Asia. Buddhist resources along the Silk Road were well exploited to promote Buddhism among Tibetans. For example, the lay people and monastic communities in Dunhuang were made to copy and proofread

[114] Traditional Tibetan accounts often talk about the expulsion of Chinese Buddhist influence in the Tibetan Empire and the turn to an exclusive Indian guidance. This view, however, should be significantly reconsidered. See, for example, Kapstein, *Tibetan Assimilation of Buddhism*, 23–37; van Schaik, *Tibetan Zen*, 1–23.

the copies of Buddhist scriptures written in Tibetan.[115] Also, the influx of Tibetan-speaking people, administrative systems, and Buddhist institutions all left imprints in the oasis cities. Therefore, it is not surprising to see that the famous ninth-century Tibetan scholar-translator 'Gos Chos grub (Ch. Facheng 法成) stayed in Dunhuang and remained active after the Return-to-Allegiance Army (Guiyi jun 歸義軍) took control in 848.[116] Some Chinese officials became patrons and followers of Tibetan tantric practices after the retreat of Tibetan soldiers in Dunhuang.[117] In sum, the mode in which the Tibetans assimilated Buddhism and their incursion into Central Asia gave Buddhism in Tibet much vitality in the complex. The history of the Tibetan Empire, viewed as an integral part of the evolution of the Buddhist Complex, would have far-reaching consequences when the Indo-Chinese Buddhist Complex faced its greatest crisis.

The crisis that led to the downfall of the Buddhist Complex began brewing in the eleventh century and came to a head in the second half of the twelfth century. One major event that contributed to its decline was the Muslim expansion to the east. In the north, the Karakhanid Khanate, which had converted to Islam in the late ninth century, conquered the Kingdom of Khotan in 1006, effectively cutting off the southern route of the Tarim Basin from the complex. In the south, the Ghaznavid dynasty converted a large number of Central Asian populations and launched an invasion of the Indian subcontinent, which was continued by the Ghurids in the twelfth century. The Ghurids extended their power all the way to Bengal in 1204, marking the demise of a major

[115] Taenzer, "Changing Relations between Administration, Clergy and Lay People in Eastern Central Asia," 23–25.

[116] For a chronology of Chos grub as shown in Dunhuang manuscripts, see Wang, "Zangzu fanyijia Guan Facheng dui minzu wenhua jiaoliu de gongxian." Whether Chos grub was Tibetan or Chinese has been a point of debate. Here I follow Wang's argument to regard him as Tibetan. Pelliot chinois 4660, a proof often used to support the Chinese origin of Chos grub is analyzed in Wang's article. For Chos grub, see also Ueyama, "Dai ban koku daitoku sanzō hōshi shamon Hōsei no kenkyū (shō)," and "Dai ban koku daitoku sanzō hōshi shamon Hōsei no kenkyū (ka)."

[117] Van Schaik, "The Sweet Saint and the Four Yogas: A 'Lost' Mahāyoga Treatise from Dunhuang," 23–26.

source in the complex. Meanwhile, the Pala Empire, the last Indian regime that officially patronized Buddhism, was terminated at the end of the twelfth century.

In China, Buddhism was also facing challenges. The establishment of the Song dynasty marked an era of civil governance and the rise of literati, which was accompanied by the revival of Confucianism. This drove Buddhism to a secondary place in society. The state projects of Buddhist translation, which had been revived in the beginning of the Song, came to a complete stop after around 1000. The prosperity of Neo-Confucianism in the twelfth century further limited the space for Buddhism to thrive. As a result, the future of the Buddhist Complex appeared dim.

But the predicted dissolution of the Buddhist Complex did not occur. Instead, in the late thirteenth century, Tibet became another significant source within the complex. Tibetan Buddhism was patronized by rulers in Dadu, with 'Phags pa serving as the imperial preceptor of Khubilai in 1260, and De bzhin gshegs pa (1384–1415) going to the Ming court in 1405. Some Qing emperors such as Emperor Qianlong 乾隆 (r. 1735–1796) were even revered as the incarnations of Mañjuśrī. Additionally, Tibetan Buddhist scriptures began to be translated into Chinese, such as the famous example of the *Esoteric Collection of the Essential Way of Mahāyana*, *Dacheng yaodao miji* 大乘要道密集.[118] Observing the history of Buddhism in China and Inner Asia from the thirteenth century onwards, a new Buddhist Complex emerged, with Tibet as the most significant source. This complex is referred to as the Sino-Tibetan Buddhist Complex (See fig. 3). The translation of Buddhism into Uyghur, which broke through the boundary of the two periods, is the best evidence of the birth of the new complex. Before the eleventh century, Uyghur Buddhist texts were mainly translated from Tocharian or Chinese originals. However, starting from the thirteenth century,

[118] Some texts of this collection were composed and translated before the Yuan period. For this collection, see Shen, "*Dacheng yaodao miji* yu Xixia Yuan chao suo chuan Xizang mifa."

Tibetan texts were translated into Uyghur. An essential instance is the *Guruyoga* (*Bla ma'i rnal 'byor*) composed by Sa skya Paṇḍita.[119] Also, a block print fragment with the date 1333 is an Avalokiteśvara *sādhana* translated from Tibetan.[120] Tibetan Buddhism undoubtedly held a dominant position in the complex after the thirteenth century.

It is noteworthy that the catalogue of Uyghur Buddhist translations does not contain a single text dated to the twelfth century.[121] This absence suggests that during this period, Uyghur Buddhism did not receive significant transmissions from either China or Tibet. The reason for this "blank twelfth century" is not hard to discern: it was a time when the old Buddhist Complex was in decline, while the new complex had yet to take shape. However, the twelfth century also saw a revolution in the Buddhist Complex, with Tibetan Buddhism being assimilated into foreign lands for the first time. Tibetan Buddhists migrated into this foreign land, bringing with them their scriptures and initiating institutions to support their activities. By the beginning of the thirteenth century, a prototypical Sino-Tibetan Complex had emerged, which the Mongols later expanded into a vast region that encompassed China and Inner Asia. This foreign land that became the site of this revolution was the Tangut State.

---

[119] Elverskog, *Uygur Buddhist Literature*, 111–112.
[120] Elverskog, *Uygur Buddhist Literature*, 110–111.
[121] For descriptions of available Uyghur Buddhist texts, see Elverskog, *Uygur Buddhist Literature*.

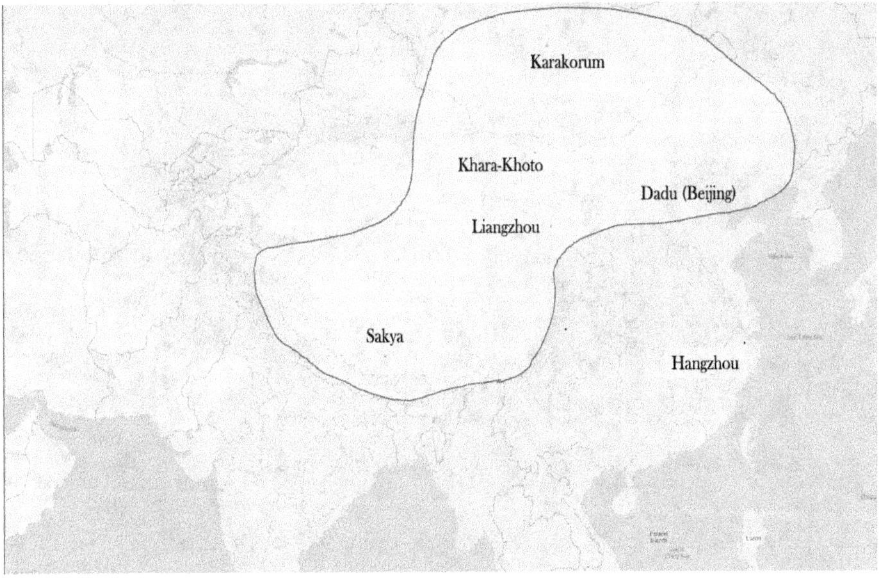
Karakorum
Khara-Khoto
Dadu (Beijing)
Liangzhou
Sakya
Hangzhou

Figure 2. Sino-Tibetan Buddhist Complex in the beginning of the fourteenth century.

That the revolution started in the Tangut realm was not accidental. If we superimpose the geographical distribution of one Buddhist Complex on that of another, we observe an overlapped area (See fig. 4). It makes up most of the territory of the Tangut State. In the Indo-Chinese Buddhist Complex, it was the most critical passage through which Buddhism was transmitted to China. In the Sino-Tibetan Buddhist Complex, it again, together with the entire Tibetan Amdo area, served as a "Middle Ground" though which Lhasa and Beijing corresponded. The geographical location thus gave the Tangut Xia the advantage to steer the flow of Buddhist transmission from one pattern to another.

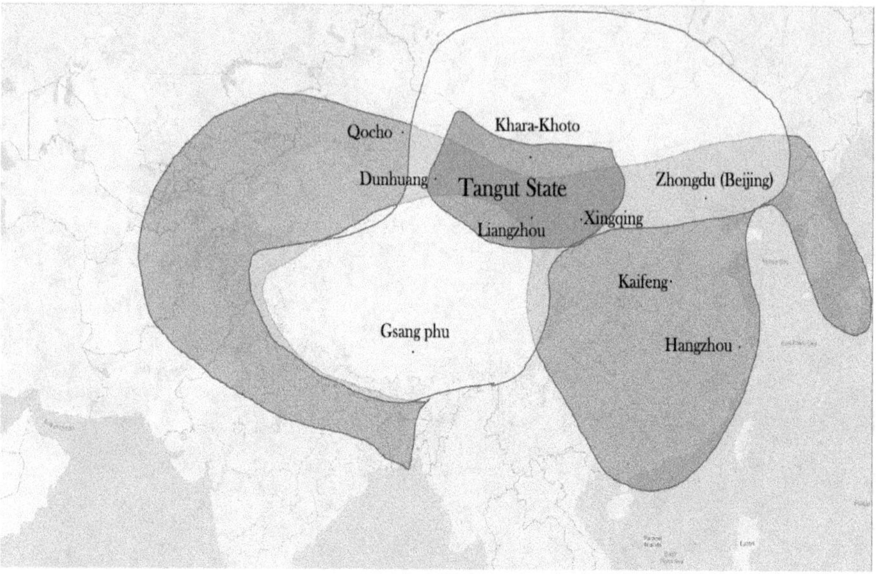
Qocho
Khara-Khoto
Dunhuang
Tangut State
Zhongdu (Beijing)
Xingqing
Liangzhou
Kaifeng
Gsang phu
Hangzhou

Figure 3. Overlapping two complexes, with major sites at the end of the twelfth century marked.

The second reason is the linguistic affinity. The Tanguts are a branch Qiangic peoples, therefore ethnically close to the Tibetans.[122] The Tangut language belongs to the Tibeto-Burman family, thus possessing linguistic features very similar to Tibetan. Straightforward examples here are the verb of existence *dju*[1] 𘃡 (Tib. *'dug*) and the verb of non-existence *mjij*[1] 𘅞 (Tib. *med*). In addition to the lexicon, the Tangut language belongs to SOV typology, which is identical with Tibetan but different from the Chinese SVO one.[123] These characteristics make Tangut translation and acquisition of Tibetan Buddhism extraordinarily efficient. As we will see in the next section, the Tangut texts almost translate the Tibetan originals morpheme by morpheme. However, instead of applying phonograms, Tangut script was created on the basis of Chinese characters. And the

[122] Wu, *Xixia shi gao*, 1–13.

[123] For an overview of the Tangut language, see Gong, "Tangut."

Tangut-Chinese character-to-character correspondence was established in works such as the *Timely Pearl in Hand*.[124] This allowed the further quick translation of the Tangut Tibetan Buddhist texts into Chinese. For example, a weird term *zhuo huo* 拙火, "clumsy fire," appear frequently in Tibetan tantric texts translated into Chinese. It turns out there is nothing clumsy about it. The Tangut original *tju¹ mə̱¹* 𗀔𗉅 is a phono-semantic translation of the Tibetan *gtum mo*, "fierce fire," an important tantric practice. Although the second Tangut character translates "fire" literally, the first one is a phonetic transcription. When translated into Chinese, both characters are taken literally. As a "bridge language," Tangut worked well for both fixing on Tibetan and Chinese. This added on the Tanguts an essential impetus for facilitating the formation of the new Buddhist Complex.

The last point is related to the political background. In the chaos of the 1120s, the Tanguts failed to take the advantage of the destruction of the Liao and Northern Song to conquer much land as planned. However, they acquired four new prefectures, namely, Xining 西寧, Le 樂, Kuo 廓, Jishi 積石, during 1136–1137 (see fig. 4). These four prefectures cover what is traditionally called the Hehuang 河湟[125] area in Chinese sources. It is also a region densely populated by Tibetans. And, in the Tibetan sources, it is referred to as Tsong kha. Although the four prefectures only amount to a relatively small portion of the total Xia territory, they are strategically critical. The Northern Song, aiming at eliminating the Tangut State, had previously allied with the Tibetan

[124] *The Timely Pearl in Hand* ([Tangut characters]). Several monographs on the work have been published. See Kwanten, *The Timely Pearl*. Huang, Nie, and Shi, *Fan Han he shi zhang zhong zhu*.

[125] Hehuang literally means "[The area between] the Huang River and the Yellow River."

chieftains in the area to attack the Tanguts.[126] In the 1100s, the Northern Song invaded the area and put it under its direct rule. This move was fatal to the survival of the Tangut State because its right flank, lacking natural barriers, was completely exposed to the strongholds of the Northern Song. However, the sudden fall of the Northern Song in 1127 left a power vacuum in the area. While the Jin nominally ruled the four prefectures afterward, its governance was unstable. Seeing the opportunity, the Tangut emperor Qianshun first launched an attack in the seventh month of 1136 and took Le and Xining.[127] Then, in the ninth month of 1137, he sent envoys to the Jin court to offer gifts in exchange of the rest of the prefectures and a formal recognition of the Tangut ownership of them. The Jin emperor, seeing the potential cost of retaking these borderland prefectures, granted Qianshun all four prefectures in exchange of their alliance.[128] The four prefectures thus remained in the Tangut realm until the final Mongol conquest in 1227.

[126] The most remarkable figure among the Tibetan local rulers is Gusiluo 唃廝囉 (Tib. Rgyal sras). For a history of Gusiluo and his relationship to the Northern Song and Tangut Xia, see Tsutomu, "The Tibetan Tribes of Ho-hsi and Buddhism during the Northern Song Period," Zhu, *Qintang sheng shuai*, and Horlemann, "The Relations of the Eleventh-Century Tsong kha Tribal Confederation to Its Neighbour States on the Silk Road."

[127] Wu, *Xixia shushi jiaozhu*, 429.

[128] Wu, *Xixia shushi jiaozhu*, 431.

Baruun Khiid
Tengger Desert
Xingqing (Capital City)
SHARA YUGUR
GANSU
Arik Gonchen
Xiliang / Liangzhou
Kangtsa
PARI
Xining
Semnyi
Pari Drigung
NINGXIA
Tulan
Tsenpo
Le
Chorten Tang
Tashi Dargye Ling
Kokonor
TSONGKHA
Martsang Drak
Tongkhor
Tangring Monastery
Jakhyung
Jishi
CHENTSA
Tseten
Jampa Bumling
Nangra
Kuo
Gori
RONGWO
Drakkar Treldzong
Gangya Drakkar Gon
Dzongkar
LABRANG
Tso Gon Ganden Choling
Amnye Machen

Figure 4. The four Tibetan prefectures acquired by the Tangut State during 1136–1137.[129]

The acquisition of the four prefectures in the 1137 not only provided security for the right flank but also bestowed strategic depth in the south. It was reasonable for the Tangut rulers to appeal to the Tibetan inhabitants in the Hehuang area to secure their rule. In fact, we do see in the latter half of the history of the Xia a slow process of shifting the national focus from the [north]east to the [south]west. The [north]eastern part of the Tangut State, consisting of prefectures such as Xia 夏, Yin 銀, Sui 綏, You 宥 and the capital city of Xingqing 興慶, was mostly populated by Tanguts and Han Chinese. In contrast, the [south]western part, including prefectures such as Gan 甘, Su 肅, Gua 瓜, Sha 沙 and the western capital Xiliang 西凉 (i.e. Liangzhou), had a significant portion of Tibetan population.

[129] Map base from Treasury of Lives: https://treasuryoflives. Names on the map base are modern place names.

Several reasons made the shift of focus imperative. During the eleventh century the eastern part had always been the frontline in the military confrontation between the Northern Song and the Tangut State. The wars in the beginning of the twelfth century had wrecked great havoc in the eastern borderland areas. The economic basis of the eastern part, as a result, was severely damaged. It was more reasonable to invest much of the administrative power in the west.[130] The acquisition of the four new Tibetan prefectures / Tsong kha area and the shift of the national focus in the twelfth century meant an increase of the necessity to consolidate the Tibetan population, especially monks who "were first of all members of local social and political communities," and were able to "mediate state control."[131]

Also, as we will see in the following chapters, the four new Tibetan prefectures / Tsong kha area became the most crucial pathway for Tibetans.

2. Tangut Buddhism in the Context of the Revolution

2.1. The Three Buddhist Traditions in the Tangut State

The Tangut State had three distinct Buddhist traditions - the Chinese tradition, the Tibetan tradition, and the local Tangut tradition - according to scholars of Tangut Buddhist studies. Among the three, the Chinese tradition was the first to be established in the Tangut State. As discussed in Chapter One, Buddhism played a critical role in the state-building process of the Tangut State. During this period, the Tanguts exclusively practiced Chinese Buddhism. Before Yuanhao

[130] This is partly seen in the shift of the trading markets (*que chang* 榷場). In the eleventh century the main market was set up in Bao'an jun 保安軍 in the northeast for trading with the Northern Song, whereas in the twelfth century the main market was established in Lanzhou 蘭州 in the south for trading with the Jin.

[131] Dunnell, *The Great State of White and High*, 160.

declared independence from the Song, he requested the Chinese Buddhist canon in 1035 by paying tributes to the Song court. The Tangut court continued to request the Chinese canon as long as the Tangut State and the Northern Song were in peace. Chinese historical sources record four additional sets of the Chinese Buddhist canon that were given to the Tangut State in 1055, 1058, 1062, and 1073.[132] It is likely that the 1035 Chinese canon formed the basis for the Tangut translation of the Chinese canon, which began in 1038 under the command of Yuanhao. The Tangut canon comprised 820 works and 3,579 volumes (*juan*).[133]

Interestingly, the principal translators who translated the Chinese canon into Tangut were neither Chinese nor Tangut but Uyghurs. Two of these translators are called Phie Tsji̱r dźiej [illegible] and Phie Sjij bji [illegible]. Both served as state preceptors of the Tangut court.[134] There was a large population in the Hexi area after the demise of the Uyghur Khaganate.[135] And, as mentioned in Chapter One and in the previous section, the Uyghurs already had a good knowledge of Chinese Buddhism by the eleventh century. These are probably the reasons that made them critical agents for introducing Chinese Buddhism to the Tanguts.

Also, it is important to point out that Chinese Buddhism was not merely transmitted from the Song to the Tangut State. The Liao Empire played a significant role in this process. Many of the commentaries translated into Tangut were composed in Chinese by Liao monks. Important figures here are the Liao monks Tongli Hengce 通理恆策 (1049–1099), Yuantong Daochen 圓通

---

[132] Shi, *Xixia Fojiao shilue*, 59–63.

[133] Shi, *Xixia Fojiao shilue*, 66.

[134] For these two figures and Uyghurs in Tangut Buddhism, see Shi, "*Xixia yi jing tu* jie," Shi, "Xixiawen *Jin guangming zuisheng wang jing* xuba kao," and Yang, "Huihu seng yu Xixiawen dazangjing de fanyi."

[135] For example, in the Return-to-Allegiance Army, despite its rulers being Chinese, consisted of many Uyghurs in its government.

道殿 (ca. 1056–1114), and Wuli Xianyan 悟理鮮演 (1048–1118), whose works on the Huayan tradition became extremely popular in the Tangut State.[136]

The Tibetan Buddhist tradition started to flourish in the 1130s. Chapter Three will detail the rise of Tibetan Buddhism in the Tangut State. But it is important to notice here that the rise of Tibetan Buddhism in the Tangut State does not amount to the conclusion that the Tanguts no longer received Chinese Buddhism from the east. Solonin has pointed out that this division is no more than an "imaginary" one since new Chinese Chan texts were still translated into Tangut in the twelfth century.[137] It is thus important here to clarify that the Buddhist revolution does not suggest the full replacement of the "old" Chinese Buddhist tradition in the Tangut State by the "new" Tibetan Buddhist tradition. Such a construction is an oversimplification of the situation. "Revolution" here emphasizes more on a transformation of the Buddhist transmissional pattern in Inner Asia and China triggered by the rise of Tibetan Buddhism in the Tangut State.

The local Tangut tradition is what arose from the influences of both Chinese and Tibetan traditions. The local tradition is also called by scholars as Sino-Tibetan [Syncretic] Buddhism.[138] I have used "local Tangut tradition" to underscore the agency of the Tanguts in facilitating the development of this tradition. I will discuss the position of the tradition in the rise of Tibetan Buddhism in Chapter Three, Section 4.

It is important to note that the traditions of "Chinese Buddhism" and "Tibetan Buddhism" are constructions from our modern perspective. While distinguishing between these traditions

---

[136] For the Liao influence on Tangut Buddhism, see Solonin, "The 'Perfect Teaching' and Liao Sources of Tangut Chan Buddhism," and Solonin, "Buddhist Connections Between the Liao and Xixia."

[137] Solonin, "Dīpaṃkara in the Tangut Context (Part 1)," 427–428. See also Solonin, *Xixia Hanchuan Fojiao wenxian yanjiu*, chap. 1.

[138] See Shen, "Lun Xixia Fojiao zhi Han Zang yu Xian Mi yuanrong," and Solonin, "Textual Evidence for Sino-Tibetan Buddhism in Xixia."

allows us to investigate the dynamics of Tangut Buddhism, the Buddhists of the Tangut State did not differentiate between them. Tangut Buddhist literature does not contain any terms for "Chinese Buddhism" or "Tibetan Buddhism," although the Tangut State was aware of the differences between Tangut, Chinese, and Tibetan monks (see section 2.3). To the people of the Tangut State, Buddhism was seen as an organism whose different traditions could inform each other and form a coherent whole. Consequently, this attitude toward Buddhism made Tangut Buddhism an open system, allowing it to continuously assimilate new Buddhist teachings from various sources.

2.2. Tangut Buddhist Language

The Tangut language used in Tangut Buddhist scriptures can be categorized into two types: the Chinese style language and the Tibetan style language. Both of these types of language were derived from the Tangut translation of the Buddhist scriptures written in either Chinese or Tibetan. Each type of language has a unique lexicon, way of expression, and syntactic structure. The Chinese style language is characterized by the following features: it translates Chinese Buddhist vocabulary on the basis of "character-to-character" correspondence, as mentioned in the previous section; it includes a large number of Buddhist terms that are phonetically transcribed from their Chinese counterparts; it uses as few particles as possible and relies on the internal connections between characters to convey meaning; and it avoids the use of long, complicated clauses. In contrast, the Tibetan style language translates Tibetan Buddhist vocabulary on the basis of "morpheme-to-morpheme"[139] correspondence. Its terms are mostly literal translations of their

[139] While characters are also considered morphemes, they are exclusively free morphemes. In the "morpheme-to-morpheme" correspondence, there are also bound morphemes.

Tibetan counterparts, and it uses particles as needed. Additionally, it does not shy away from using long, complex clauses.

As an example, let's consider the Tangut translations of the *Heart Sutra*, which are available in two versions: one translated from Chinese and the other from Tibetan.[140] Accordingly, one translation employs the Chinese style language, while the other employs the Tibetan style language. In the translation from Chinese, the word "touch" (*sprașțavya*) is translated from *chu* 觸 into *tsjụ* [illegible]. In the other translation, the same word is translated from *reg bya* into *tsjụ lew* [illegible]. While the stem *tsjụ* is the same, in the latter case, *lew* is a bound morpheme corresponding the Tibetan *bya* (further an equivalent of the Sanskrit *-tavya*). The morpheme *lew*, a gerundive particle, cannot be translated independently without putting together with its antecedent. Furthermore, the "unsurpassed full awakening" (*anuttarāṃ samyaksambodhim*) is translated from the Chinese *a nou duo luo san miao san pu ti* 阿耨多羅三藐三菩提 into *'ja*$^{?}$ *dụ*^{2} *tow*^{1} *lo*^{1} *sã*^{1} *mjiw*^{2} *sã*^{1} *po*^{1} *tjij*^{1} [illegible], thus a phonetic transcription. In the other translation, it is translated from the Tibetan *bla na med pa yang dag par rdzogs pa'i byang chub* into [illegible], "uppermost, true, full awakening," thus a literal translation. Furthermore, "the unmatched mantra" (*asamasamamantra*) is translated from the Chinese *wudeng deng zhou* 無等等咒 into [illegible], "unmatched-matching mantra," without any particle. In the other translation, it is translated from the Tibetan *mi mnyam pa dang mnyam pa'i sngags* into [illegible], "the mantra that matches with the unmatched," thus retaining both the sociative particle *dang* / [illegible] as well as the genitive particle *'i* / [illegible].

[140] For the Tangut translation based on the Chinese translation, see Sun, "Xuanzang yi *Banruo xin jing* Xixiawen yiben." For the Tangut translation based on the Tibetan translation, see Nie, "Xixiawen Zang chuan *Banruo xin jing* yanjiu."

Therefore, determining whether a Tangut translation was based on a Chinese or Tibetan original can be aided by analyzing the Tangut Buddhist language. When examining an indigenous composition, the author's use of both the Chinese style and Tibetan style languages can provide valuable clues regarding the influence of both Chinese and Tibetan traditions. By carefully analyzing the author's approach to language, we can better understand the cultural and historical context of the text.

2.3. Preceptors and Buddhist Institutions

The Tangut State had officials known as "preceptors" ([illegible]), who played a role similar to that of court chaplains in medieval Europe. Although there is no direct evidence to suggest that the Tangut government mandated that preceptors could only be Buddhist monks, all identified preceptors were indeed Buddhist monks. Their primary responsibility was to advise the royal court, and they held different ranks within the court hierarchy. The tenth chapter of the *Tiansheng Legal Code* says:

> **Article:** The preceptors of the emperor and the state[141], the crown prince, and the kings[142].
>
> The preceptors of the emperor, from whom he receives empowerment: the supreme preceptor, the state preceptor, and the virtuous preceptor.
>
> The preceptor of the crown prince: the humane preceptor.
>
> The preceptor of the kings: the loyal preceptor.

---

[141] While the phrase "emperor-state" is parsed as "the emperor and state," the two entities here are considered as a unity, namely that the emperor is nothing but the state because there is no separate entry for the preceptors of the state.

[142] Kings ([illegible]) are the members from the paternal lineage of the emperor. They receive lands and the title of king but do not form their independent kingdoms.

Article: The titles of the preceptors mentioned above are equal to the first, second, and medium ranks.[143]

> The preceptors of the emperor, from whom he receives empowerment – the supreme preceptor, the state preceptor, etc., and the virtuous preceptor, etc. – are equal to level of the first rank.
>
> The preceptor of the crown prince, the humane preceptor, is equal to the level of the second rank.
>
> The preceptor of the kings, the loyal preceptor, is equal to the level of the medium rank.[144]

Five preceptor titles are listed in these two articles: 1. the supreme preceptor ([illegible] < Ch. *shang shi* 上師), 2. the state preceptor ([illegible] < Ch. *guo shi* 國師), 3. the virtuous preceptor ([illegible] < Ch. *de shi* 德師), 4. The humane preceptor ([illegible] < Ch. *ren shi* 仁師), and 5. the loyal preceptor ([illegible] < Ch. *zhong shi* 忠師). Different preceptors would serve different members of the royal family.

However, as already mentioned in the Introduction, the preceptors of the Tangut State were not just spiritual advisors of the royal family, they were also government officials who participated

---

[143] All the secretariats of the Tangut government are divided into five ranks: first ([illegible]), second ([illegible]), medium ([illegible]), lower ([illegible]), and last ([illegible]).

[144] #170, 30a8–b7:

[illegible]

[illegible]

in the administrative affairs. The following statement shows the leadership of the Lay Secretariat of Merit and the Monastic Secretariat of Merit:

> The two Secretariats of Merit: Six state preceptors and two general controllers.[145]

This likely means that each Secretariat of Merit has three state preceptors as their chief administrators.

In addition to the five listed above, there are more preceptor titles in the Tangut State. From the Khara-Khoto texts, there is a Chinese manuscript entitled *Miscellaneous Characters*, *Za zi* 雜字 (Дх. 2822). It is a lexicon of various subjects related to the natural environment, society, government, etc. of the Tangut State. In the seventeenth section, the "section of official positions" (*guanwei bu* 官位部, see fig. 5) it lists four preceptor titles: 1. the imperial preceptor (*di shi* 帝師), 2. the state preceptor, 3. the dharma preceptor (*fa shi* 法師), and 4. the Chan preceptor (*chan shi* 禪師). We have already seen the title of the state preceptor above. The titles of the dharma preceptor and the Chan preceptor also appear in the *Tiansheng Legal Code* as [illegible] and [illegible] despite the lack of a description of their specific responsibilities.[146] However, the title of the imperial preceptor is not seen anywhere in the *Tiansheng Legal Code*.

---

[145] #170, 32a7: [illegible]： [illegible].

[146] #170, 6a9.

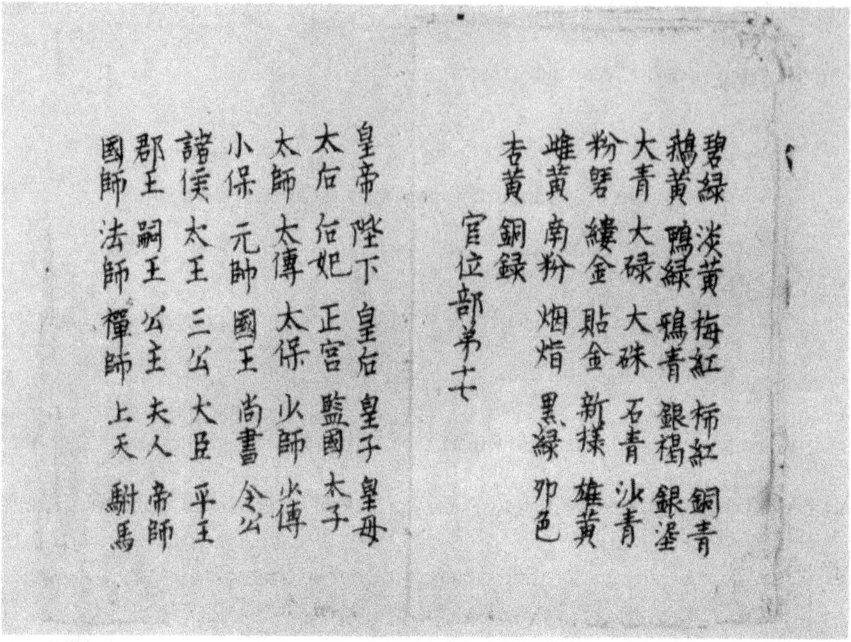
碧綠 淡黄 梅紅 柹紅 銅青
鵝黄 鴨綠 鴉青 銀褐 銀埿
大青 大碌 大硃 石青 沙青
粉碧 纏金 貼金 新樣 雄黄
雌黄 南粉 烟脂 黑綠 卯色
杏黄 銅綠
官位部第十七
皇帝 陛下 皇后 皇子 皇母
太后 后妃 正宫 監國 太子
太師 太傅 太保 少師 少傅
小保 元帥 國王 尚書 令公
諸侯 太王 三公 大臣 平王
郡王 嗣王 公主 夫人 帝師
國師 法師 禪師 上天 駙馬

Figure 5. The seventeenth section of the *Miscellaneous Characters* (*Za zi* 雜字, Дх. 2822).[147]

While some scholars pointed out that the institution of the imperial preceptor in the Tangut State served as a precedent for the same institution of the Mongol Empire,[148] some other scholars doubted whether the imperial preceptor was really important in the Tangut State as it was in the Mongol Empire mainly because the absence of the title from the *Tiansheng Legal Code.*[149] I suppose it is reasonable to regard the imperial preceptor as the paramount preceptor position in the Tangut State. And there are three reasons for this. First, the *Tiansheng Legal Code* was likely

[147] Photo from ECMS 8, 145.

[148] See Shi, *Xixia Fojiao shilue*, 137–142, and Dunnell, "The Hsia Origins of the Yüan Institution of Imperial Preceptor."

[149] See Zhang, "Di shi kao yuan," Nie, "Xixia di shi kaobian," Zhang, "'Yuan chao di shi zhidu yuanyu xixia' shuo kaobian."

published in 1150 and surely before 1169. Hence, the imperial preceptor could be a new position created after the publication of the legal code. Second, in the colophons of Tangut Buddhist scriptures where a state preceptor and an imperial preceptor are listed, the imperial preceptor is always placed above the state preceptor and enjoys a higher rank.[150] Third, Ti shri Ras pa, whose career will be discussed in detail in the next chapter, was clearly promoted from the position of the state preceptor to the imperial preceptor. Hence, I suggest that it should at least be clear that the imperial preceptor is the highest preceptor title in the Tangut State. What remains not entirely unclear is the specific responsibilities of the imperial preceptor.

All the imperial preceptors who have so far been identified are Tibetan monks. This bespeaks that the position was probably created from the very beginning exclusively for Tibetans. The only possible exception is Pu nja̱ bu̱ dźju [illegible], the earliest imperial preceptor who appears in primary sources.[151] His name does not evidently reflect a Tibetan name in religion. The former part of his name, *pu nja̱*, seems to be a phonetic transcription of the Sanskrit *puṇya*. The latter part, *bu̱ dźju*, can only be a translation, meaning "supreme-clear." It could be an equivalent for the Sanskrit *prabhāsa*. Hence, if we regard him as a person from the Indic world, then his name would be *Puṇyaprabhāsa. But we should not forget that some Tibetans tend also to use Sanskrit words in their names of religion, especially in the former part. For instance, Bcom ldan ral gri Dar ma rgyal mtshan (1227–1305), the renowned Bka' gdams monk associated with Snar thang Monastery, uses *dar ma* (Skt. *dharma*) in his name of religion, though his actual name in religion would be Chos kyi rgyal mtshan. In our case, too, the person might be a Tibetan whose name of religion is Puṇya rab gsal / Bsod nams rab gsal.

---

[150] See Chapter Three, Section 3.

[151] See Chapter Three, Section 3.

A distinct adornment that the Tangut government gives to its preceptors is the black hat, which is one of the few things that adversely influenced Tibetan Buddhist culture during the rise of Tibetan Buddhism in the Tangut State. It is well known that the patriarchs of the Karma Bka' rgyud sect wear the black hat. However, the origin of the black hat had remained debatable until the recent publications by Xie Jisheng and Cairang Zhuoma (Tsering Drölma), who convincingly concluded that the black hat originated in the Tangut State.[152] The direct evidence is the lama wearing the black hat in a *thang ka* painting of the Medicine Buddha discovered from Khara-Khoto (see fig. 6).[153] And the hat was derived from the official hat of the Tangut State (see fig. 7), an institution further adopted from the Song. Fang Zichao also pointed out that the image of a lama who wears a black hat in Cave no. 465 of Dunhuang might be Ti shri Ras pa (See fig. 8).[154]

---

[152] Xie and Cairang, "Song Liao Xia guan mao, di shi hei mao, huofo zhuanshi yu fatong zhengshuo (shang)," and Xie and Cairang, "Song Liao Xia guan mao, di shi hei mao, huofo zhuanshi yu fatong zhengshuo (xia)."

[153] The *thang ka* painting was previously regarded as a product from the Yuan period but has now been corrected to the Tangut period. See Xie and Cairang, "Song Liao Xia guan mao, di shi hei mao, huofo zhuanshi yu fatong zhengshuo (shang)," 51–54.

[154] Fang, "Duo chong shijiao xia de Di shi re ba yanjiu." A major piece of evidence Fang uses to support the idea is that the biography of Ti shri Ras pa says he taught in *stong kun*. And *stong kun* can be identified with Dunhuang. The term stong kun might also denote "the emperor of China" or simply "China." See van der Kuijp, "The Tibetan Expression 'Bod Wooden Door' (*bod shing sgo*) and Its Probable Mongol Antecedent," 125, n 104. It could also mean specifically the "Eastern Capital" (Dongjing 東京), namely, Kaifeng 開封, the capital of the Northern Song. See van Schaik, "Ruler of the East, or Eastern Capital What Lies behind the Name *Tong Kun*?" While the Northern Song was already gone during the period, Ti shri Ras pa could have still gone to Kaifeng, which remained a large city under the rule of the Jin Empire.

Figure 6. The lama wearing the black hat in the *thang ka* of the Medicine Buddha. The State Hermitage Museum, St. Petersburg.[155]

Figure 7. Official of the Tangut government. The State Hermitage Museum, St. Petersburg[156]

[155] Xie and Cairang, "Song Liao Xia guan mao, di shi hei mao, huofo zhuanshi yu fatong zhengshuo (shang)," plate 1.

[156] Xie and Cairang, "Song Liao Xia guan mao, di shi hei mao, huofo zhuanshi yu fatong zhengshuo (xia)," plate 21.

Figure 8. Lama wearing the black hat. Cave no. 465, Dunhuang. Photo by Xie Jisheng.[157]

The *Tiansheng Legal Code* also prescribes how a novice might be promoted to higher ranks. In the eleventh chapter, it says:

> Among the novices of the Buddhist monks and Daoist priests, if one knows how to chant the two scriptures of the *Lotus Sutra* and the *Humane King Sutra*, as well as know how to chant the various homages, provided that his voice is sonorous and magnetic, then monastic supervisor of the monastery to which the novice belongs and the inquisitor of the monastery, etc. could refer and report him to the Secretariat of Merit. Then, [the Secretariat of Merit] should report him to the Central Secretariat. The person himself and the related the monastic supervisor of the monastery, the deputy controller, the inquisitor of the monastery, the director of the novices who are knowledgeable and trustworthy, etc. would be interviewed. An examiner of the case should be found. [The novice] should be located in the register. If he is indeed a novice, then his skills should be assessed. If he indeed masters the above-mentioned skills, then by means of a [official] notice, he should be made a

[157] My sincere gratitude to Prof. Xie and Dr. Fang Zichao for granting me the permission to use the photo in my dissertation.

monk in-residence. Furthermore, for lay persons and other similar kinds, even if they master the above-mentioned skills, they are not allowed to be made monks.[158]

The passage shows that, at least in theory, there should be a strong presence of the state in the regulation of the monastics. The process for a novice to be promoted to a monk in-residence is a relatively complex one. It involves the monastic supervisors of the monastery, the Secretariat of Merit, and the Central Secretariat. What is important in this process is that the novice must be legally enrolled as a novice. Otherwise, even if the person has the necessary skills, it is impossible for him to become a monk. The text then continues:

> Within the state, among the lay persons and novices who belong to the Tangut, Chinese, and Tibetan Buddhist monks and Daoist priests, if one knows how to explain one scripture from among the *Prajñāpāramiā*[*sūtra*], the *Mind-Only*[159], the *Madhyamaka*[160], the *Hundred Dharmas*[161], the *Avataṃsakasūtra*, or the *Awakening of Faith*[162], understand the meaning from the beginning to the end, and knows the

---

158 #180, 32a2–b2:

> [illegible]

159 Specific reference is unclear. It could refer to the *Yogācārabhūmi*, whose Tangut translation is discovered in Khara-Khoto. Or it could refer to the *Viṃśatikā*. A Tangut text called *Commentary on the Mind-Only in Twenty* [*Verses*?] ([illegible], Tang. 200) is probably an indigenous Tangut commentary on the work.

160 It should refer to the *Mūlamadhyamakakārikā*. But it is not seen from the Khara-Khoto texts.

161 It refers to the *Treatise: A Lucid Introduction to the Hundred Dharmas of Mahāyana*, *Dacheng baifa mingmen lun* 大乘百法明門論 (T 1614, allegedly composed by Vasubandhu). A manuscript (Or.12380/226) of the Tangut translation of the text is discovered from Khara-Khoto. There are also Tangut commentaries on the work.

162 It refers to the Awakening of Faith in the Mahāyāna, *Dacheng qi xin lun* 大乘起信論 (T 1666, allegedly composed by Aśvaghoṣa).

> daily rituals, etc., provided that there is a lecturer[163] in the above-mentioned monks and Daoist priests, etc., then a state preceptor, the above-mentioned lecturer, added with a master-scholar, etc. are made to well examine his skills. If his knowledge is true, then the lay person or the novice should be included in the monks, wear red robes, and serve as a lecturer. But he does not obtain an official position. If the person is a previously mentioned Buddhist monk or Daoist priest, then a Daoist priest should become a Buddhist monk. Then, they, who wore yellow robes before, should now, in the same way, wear red robes and serve as lecturers. And they could obtain official positions. Among them, if the person is a Tangut or a Chinese monk and does not know Qieyun[164], then he is not allowed to be a lecturer.[165]

Becoming a lecturer seems to be the goal of a talented novice or a monk. However, a big difference here is that a novice or a lay person can never become an official. The official positions are only reserved for monks. Hence, when a Daoist priest wants to become an official, he must also first become a monk. This seems to implicitly support that only Buddhist monks can serve as preceptors, an assumption put forward at the beginning of this subsection. Also noticeable is the statement that Tangut and Chinese monks must know the Qieyun phonological system to become lecturers, which implies the Tibetan monks do not have to master the rhyme system. The reason for this difference is, although the Qieyun system, which originated in the Chinese language and is also applicable to the Tangut language, is not known in Tibetan literature. Therefore, here, we see again how the

---

[163] [illegible] (< *zuozhu* 座主), lit. "owner of the seat."

[164] Qieyun 切韻 is a phonological system derived from the book that bears the same title published in 601 during the Sui dynasty. See also discussion below.

[165] #180, 32b3–33a4:

> [illegible]

Tangut government tries to best accommodate the various cultural backgrounds of the Buddhists within its realm.

2.4. State Buddhism and Individual Buddhism

Tangut Buddhism can be categorized into two forms based on their distinct agencies for promotion, contents, and goals. In his 2013 pioneering work on the "systematic nature" of Tangut Buddhism, Solonin initially referred to these two forms as "official Buddhism" and "popular Buddhism."[166] In this subsection, I will further elaborate on this theory and use the terms State Buddhism and Individual Buddhism[167] to describe the nature of these two forms of Buddhism more accurately.

State Buddhism refers to the form of Buddhism promoted by the Tangut State, with the primary goal of maintaining the prosperity of the state and realizing the collective welfare of the people within the realm. This form of Buddhism is evident in the *Tiansheng Legal Code* and the postscripts authored by the ruling family, which reveal the importance of scriptures with transformative power of the state and its people. For example, as shown in the last subsection, the eleventh chapter of the *Tiansheng Legal Code* specifies that a novice must be able to chant the *Lotus Sutra* and the *Humane King Sutra* to become a monk. While the *Humane King Sutra* is associated with enhancing the political authority of the ruler and granting the state protection, the *Lotus Sutra* represents the core intention of the Tangut State to lead all people within the state to liberation. The rise of Tibetan Buddhism also provided the Tangut State with more forms of

[166] Solonin, "Xixia Fojiao zhi 'xitong xing' chu tan."

[167] The main reason for this change is that "popular Buddhism" has a very specific connotation in Buddhist studies. "Popular Buddhism," which involves combinations of Buddhism and popular cultural practices, is often considered as the opposite of the canonical and elite form of Buddhism. The persons practice this form of Buddhism in the Tangut State were obviously elite Buddhists who sought spiritual attainments with canonical methods.

protective power, as evidenced by the woodcut of a Mahākāla image from Khara-Khoto (see fig. 9). The eight Chinese characters at the top of the image read, "May the emperor live for ten thousand years! May the state be prosperous, and the people be happy!"

皇帝萬歲
國泰民

Figure 9. Woodcut of a Mahākāla image. Khara-Khoto. Thirteenth century. The State Hermitage Museum, St. Petersburg.[168]

An essential venue for the practice of State Buddhism is a religious gathering (Ch. *fa hui* 法會). In such a venue, monks perform rituals and make offerings; lives (including criminals who are sentenced to death) are released; sutras are chanted; scriptures printed by the government are distributed; and Buddhist doctrines are taught to the audience. The last activity here concerns the doctrinal subjects one must master in order to become a lecturer, as prescribed in the eleventh chapter of the *Tiansheng Legal Code* (see last subsection). While these doctrinal subjects – *prajñāpāramitā*, *madhyamaka*, the *Avataṃsakasūtra*, etc. – are not directly linked with the prosperity of the state, they are what will be taught to the audience at the religious gathering. Therefore, a lecturer has to master at least one subject in order to preach to the audience. A good example of this is the Tangut state preceptor Tśhja źjɨr [illegible] who taught the doctrines of the *Diamond Sutra* and the *Heart Sutra* to his audience at a religious gathering in 1167[169]

Another key component of State Buddhism is the Pure Land belief. It is not manifest in the *Tiansheng Legal Code* but is evidenced by the postscripts of scriptures distributed at religious gatherings.[170] Paintings such as a scroll depicting Buddha Amitābha appearing before Tangut worshippers also attest to the belief (see fig. 10).

---

[168] Piotrovsky, *Lost Empire of the Silk Road*, 169.

[169] The event is attested by the postscript of a *Heart Sutra* in Chinese, which was distributed at the religious gathering in 1167. See Nie, *Xixia Fojing xuba yizhu*, 167–168.

[170] For example, an imperial postscript is attached to the *Sūtra on the Visualization of the Bodhisattva Maitreya's Rebirth Above in Tuṣita Heaven, Guan Mile pusa shangsheng Doushuaitian jing* 佛說觀彌勒菩薩上生兜率天經 (T. 452), which was distributed at a religious gathering in 1189. See Nie, *Xixia Fojing xuba yizhu*, 173. Similar cases are many.

Figure 10. Buddha Amitābha appearing before Tangut worshippers. Khara-Khoto. Twelfth century. The State Hermitage Museum, St. Petersburg.[171]

Individual Buddhism can be described as the form of Buddhism practiced for individual benefits, particularly personal spiritual attainments. While the *Tiansheng Legal Code* does not explicitly mention the contents of Individual Buddhism, they are reflected in the actual Buddhist texts discovered from Khara-Khoto. One of the main subjects of Individual Buddhism that is

[171] Piotrovsky, *Lost Empire of the Silk Road*, 181.

derived from the Chinese Buddhist tradition is Chan Buddhism.[172] In contrast, the primary subject of Individual Buddhism that is derived from the Tibetan Buddhist tradition is Tibetan tantric Buddhism.[173] Neither tradition is mentioned in the *Tiansheng Legal Code*, nor are there any texts that belong to both traditions appended by an imperial postscript. However, a large number of Buddhist texts in the Khara-Khoto collection belong to these two subjects.

It is important to note that the two forms of Buddhism in the Tangut State, like the different Buddhist traditions, are merely provisional constructs that help us understand the systemic nature of Tangut Buddhism. In reality, there was never a clear boundary between the two forms. When a monk chanted the *Sukhāvatīvyūhasūtra*, the primary scripture of the Pure Land school, at a religious gathering, he chanted it explicitly for the benefit of all the people within the Tangut realm, but implicitly also for his own personal benefit. In fact, as we will see in the next chapter, the two forms are completely combinable. The Bka' brgyud masters in the last years of the Tangut State became the essential agents for promoting both State Buddhism and Individual Buddhism.

Returning to the integrative Inner Asian imperial history discussed in the last chapter, it is important to note that the revolution which occurred in the Tangut State during the formative period of this history led to a change in the pattern of Buddhist transmission in East Asia and Inner Asia. The previous west-east pattern was replaced by a south-north pattern, which greatly increased the interplay between the three areas of Inner Asian imperial history, particularly the Northern Areas and the Tibetan Plateau. This partly explains why later rulers who sought to

---

[172] For Chan Buddhism in the Tangut State, see Solonin, *Xixia Hanchuan Fojiao wenxian yanjiu*.

[173] For Tibetan tantric Buddhism in the Tangut State, see Solonin, *Dapeng zhanchi: Zangchuan xin jiu mizhou zai Xixia de chaunbo*.

establish themselves as legitimate emperors of an Inner Asian empire always sought to control Tibet in one way or another. The various political crises and conflicts that occurred on the Tibetan Plateau during the seventeenth to eighteenth centuries due to the campaigns of Mongols and Manchus are not as incidental as they may appear. Although isolated by natural barriers and lacking in resources during the early modern era, the plateau was a crucial locale of strategic interest. This may also partly explain why the Central Asian territories, roughly equivalent to today's Xinjiang region and significant to the Han and Tang empires, were not incorporated into the Yuan and were only conquered by the Qing after the conquest of Tibet. Thus, it can be argued that the Inner Asian Buddhist revolution had far-reaching consequences in shaping later Inner Asian history.

In the next chapter, we will examine the history of how Tibetan Buddhism arose in the Tangut State, which essentially contributed to the revolution.

Chapter Three: The Rise of Tibetan Buddhism in the Tangut State

1. Prologue: The Career of Rtsa mi Lo tsā ba Sangs rgyas grags

It is more or less agreed that the first crucial figure that tied Buddhism in Tangut and Tibet together was [R]tsa mi Lo tsā ba Sang rgyas grags [pa] (fl. early twelfth century) mainly because he was born as a Tangut and became widely known in the Tibetan cultural sphere.[174] However, the issue of how we should conceptualize his position with the rise of Tibetan Buddhism in the Tangut State is far more complicated than one may expect. And the reason is twofold. First, despite his arresting identity as a "Tangut Tibetan," he was never known for transmitting any teaching of Tibetan Buddhism directly in the Tangut State. Instead, his main achievement is remembered as passing some Indic Buddhist traditions down to the Tibetans. Second, notwithstanding his fame among the Tibetans as a Tangut, the available Tangut sources show very little information about him, thus indicating he might have never been a known quantity among the Tanguts.[175] Hence, how would we account for these facts while maintaining his significance in the Tangut-Tibetan Buddhist exchange? I will attempt to answer this question here.

---

[174] Previous scholarship on Rtsa mi Lo tsā ba is found in Sperling, "Rtsa-mi Lo-tsā-ba Sangs-rgyas grags-pa and the Tangut Background to Early Mongol-Tibetan Relations" [hereafter "Rtsa-mi Lo-tsā-ba"], 801–824 and "Further Remarks Apropos of the 'Ba'-rom-pa and the Tanguts," 4–6, 24. The exact dates of Rtsa mi Lo tsā ba are unknown. However, because when the young Rgwa Lo tsā ba Gzhon nu dpal (1105?–1198?) went to study under Rtsa mi Lo tsā ba, the latter was already an established scholar, it is likely that Rtsa mi Lo tsā ba was born in the late eleventh century and died in the early twelfth century.

[175] See Solonin, "Dīpaṃkara in the Tangut Context (Part 1)," 428, n. 6. So far as Solonin has seen, the name of Rtsa mi Lo tsā ba appears only once in Tangut script in the form of *tsar mji lu tsja wa* [illegible] in Tang. 308, #821. Interestingly, if this indeed refers to Rtsa mi Lo tsā ba, then the Tanguts appear to have used Tibetan sources as the intermediary for their indirect knowledge of Rtsa mi. This suggests that the Tanguts might have no knowledge about Rtsa mi prior to the transmission of the Tibetan Buddhist teachings. Otherwise, they could have easily used his Tangut name or title as known to the Tanguts rather than the phonetic transcription if they already had direct knowledge of him.

While a lengthy account of Rtsa mi Lo tsā ba's life is unavailable, piecemeal sources giving sketches of him can provide us with the basic contours of his life. In addition to the descriptions in such histories as the *Blue Annals*, Sperling noted some other materials that mention Rtsa mi Lo tsā ba.[176] Among them, there is a short but insightful discussion of his life in the history of Kālacakra written by the Sa skya scholar Stag tshang Lo tsā ba Shes rab rin chen (1405–1477), which says:

> As for [R]tsa mi Sangs rgyas grags, some say he was someone from the grassland near the border between the upper and lower parts of the Nyang river[177]; some say he was a grasslander of the E river valley[178]. Since [these statements] contradict what he himself wrote in the translator's colophons of the tantra and commentary that he was born in the Tangut land in the northern region,[179] he is from Tangut. When he was young, he went to India. He stayed there for a long time. He was trained as a scholar. He held the abbotship of Vajrāsana. He translated and taught the tantra and commentary of Kālacakra. His student Dring ri Chos grags as well as the students of Abhayā[karagupta][180] such as Khe Gad 'Khor [lo] grags, Ga rong Tshul khrims 'byung gnas, Rong rlings Lo tsā ba, Ra byid Lo tsā ba, and Se lo tsā ba learned from Rtsa mi. Having learned, they translated and composed treatises. However, their expositions were not received except for Se Lo tsā ba, who taught Gnyos 'Od 'bar. From him [= Gnyos 'Od 'bar], Rin chen dpal, the siddha known as U rgyan pa,[181] having requested [the expositions], guarded the expositions of

---

[176] See Elliot Sperling, "Rtsa-mi Lo-tsā-ba," 802.

[177] The Nyang river is a tributary of the Gtsang po river. It originates from the northern foothills of the Himalayan Mountains. It flows to the north, going through Rgyal rtse, and merges into the Gtsang po river in Gzhis ka rtse.

[178] E, alternatively written as G.ye or known by its later name Lha rgya ri, is a region to the southeast of Rtse thang and west of Dwags po. It locates in Chu gsum county. The name was likely derived from the name of the clan that ruled the region. See Karl E. Ryavec, *A Historical Atlas of Tibet*, 70.

[179] No colophon from his translations available to us say exactly that he was "born in the Tangut land in the northern region" (*byang phyogs mi nyag yul du skyes pa*). The information could either be a paraphrase or from a colophon not available to us.

[180] Abhyākaragupta (d. ca. 1125) was an Indian scholar with whom Rtsa mi Lo tsā ba translated many Buddhist texts. See discussion below in this section. Abhyākaragupta was a contemporary of King Rāmapāla, the Pāla king who reigned from the late eleventh century to the early twelfth century. See Bühnemann, "Some Remarks on the Date of Abhayākaragupta and the Chronology of His Works."

[181] U rgyan pa Rin chen dpal (1230–1309) was a scholar famous for his expertise in Kālacakra. For a study of his life see Li, "A Critical Study of the life of the 13th-Century Tibetan Monk U rgyan pa Rin chen dpal Based on His Biographies." His teachers included Rin chen rtse mo from B dong E monastery and the 'Brug pa Bka' brgyud

initiation and the guides [of tantric practice]. Even today, they [=the teachings] are known as the U rgyan bsnyen bsgrub.[182]

Stag tshang Lo tsā ba here correctly points out that Rtsa mi Lo tsā ba is a Tangut instead of a Tibetan. However, those who held him to be Tibetan have a reason for doing so. It goes without saying that *rtsa mi*, a confusing word, can denote not only someone of Tangut ethnicity but also, and in fact more literally, a person from grassland. Further, although he does call himself the "Tangut translator" (*mi nyag lo tsa ba*) in some colophons of his translations,[183] in some others, he clearly names himself the "Tibetan translator" (*bod kyi lo tsa ba*).[184] The dual labeling indicates both Tangut and Tibetan identities were likely accepted by him. This is, of course, quite uncommon to the Tanguts from that period. It is possible that, while Rtsa mi Lo tsā ba was born as a Tangut, he was educated in a Tibetan monastic environment or even raised in a Tibetan community within

---

master Rgod tshang pa mgon po rdo rje (1189–1258). The *Blue Annals* makes clear that he specifically studied the Kālacakra tradition of Rtsa mi Lo tsā ba for eleventh months. See Roerich, *The Blue Annals*, 699.

[182] Stag tshang Lo tsā ba Shes rab rin chen, *Dpal dus kyi 'khor lo spyi don gyi sgo nas gtan la 'bebs par byed pa'i legs bshad bstan pa'i rgya mtsho*, 68–69:

> *tsa mi sangs rgyas grags pa ni / kha cig nyang stod smad mtshams kyi 'khris rtsa kha ba yin zer / kha cig e rong gi rtsa pa yin zer ba ni / kho rang gis mdzad pa'i rgyud 'grel gyi 'gyur byang du / byang phyogs mi nyag yul du skyes par bshad pa dang 'gal bas mi nyag yin la / gzhon nu dus nas rgya gar du byon / yun ring du bzhugs / mkhas par sbyangs / rdo rje gdan gyi gdan sa mdzad / dus 'khor rgyud 'grel bsgyur cing bshad / de'i slob ma ding ri chos grags/ a bha ya'i slob ma / khe gad 'khor grags / ga rong tshul khrims 'byung gnas dang / rong rlings lo tsā ba / ra byid lo tsā ba / se lo tsā ba sogs kyi kyang / rtsa mi la mnyan nas / 'gyur bcos byas kyang gzhan rnams kyi bshad bka' ma zin / se lo tsā bas gnyos 'od 'bar la bshad / de la grub thob u rgyan par grags pa rin chen dpal gyis zhus nas dbang bshad khrid bka' rnams bskyangs / da lta'ang u rgyan bsnyen bsgrub tu grags pa rnams yin no /.*

The passage is also partially translated and discussed by Sperling. See Sperling, "Rtsa-mi Lo-tsā-ba," 802–803, 813, n. 15.

[183] See, for example, the colophons of Peking nos. 2174 and 5092 in the *Tenjur*.

[184] See, for example, the colophons of Peking nos. 4550 and 4612 in the *Tenjur*.

the Tangut State.[185] In many aspects, his life resembles more the typical career of an illustrious Tibetan translator in the early phase of the Later Diffusion rather than the experience of a Tangut engaging in the training of Tibetan Buddhism. He traveled to India, obtained teachings, translated Sanskrit texts, and taught Tibetan students. Significantly, at least from the available evidence, he chose to translate those texts into Tibetan rather than Tangut, thus showing he viewed Tibetan as the scholarly language with which he was familiar.

Clearly, Tibetans from several generations later were still amazed at Rtsa mi Lo tsā ba's achievements, especially at the fact that he, as a Tangut, became the abbot of Vajrāsana, the holy site of Indian Buddhism. When Tshal pa wrote a short biography of Zhang G.yu grags pa Brtson 'grus grags pa (1123–1193, henceforth Lama Zhang), he included a brief biographical sketch of Rgwa Lo tsā ba Gzhon nu dpal (1105?–1198?), who was one of Lama Zhang's masters and had studied under Rtsa mi Lo tsā ba. The passage says:

> Having taken full monastic vows with Rngog Lo tsā ba's student Dbang ston, he was given [the religious name] Gzhon nu dpal. He relied upon many lamas in both Mdo and Dbus. Having learned many teachings, he went to India. He touched the feet of [i.e., bowed down to] the lama and paṇḍita [R]tsa mi Sangs rgyas grags pa. Although his ethnicity was Tangut, he resided there like the crown jewel of all Indian paṇḍitas. He also touched the feet of the Second Omniscient One of the Age of Decline, Paṇḍita Abhyākaragupta. He asked [both of them] for initiations and instructions without remainder.[186]

---

[185] Sperling regards Rtsā mi Lo tsā ba as a member of the Tangut royal family. While the claim has become very influential in scholarship, it may require some reappraisal. First, if Rtsā mi Lo tsā ba were indeed a member of the royal family, then we would expect to see more traces of him in Tangut materials. Yet the reality is the opposite. Second, the conclusion is solely based on a passage from a fifteenth century family history written by Dpal ldan chos kyi bzang po. Moreover, the passage itself is not without problems as it is a bit inconsistent with the statement at the beginning of the family history. While the colophon says the family was "in the nephew lineage of Rtsa mi Lo tsā ba" (*rtsa mi lo* [supply: tsā] *ba'i dbon po'i rigs su*), the beginning of the text says it is the "nephew lineage of the Tangut Rgyal rgod" (*mi nyag rgyal rgod dbon po rigs*). See Dpal ldan chos kyi bzang po, *Sde pa g.yas ru byang pa'i rgyal rabs rin po che bstar ba*, 167, 197. As we now know Rgyal rgod refers to Emperor Zunxu 遵頊 (1163–1226). It is impossible for the family to be from both the nephew lineages of and of Rgyal rgod and Rtsa mi Lo tsā ba, whose birth predates that of the former about one century. Hence, it is necessary for us to be cautious on this point.

[186] Tshal pa, *'Gro mgon rin po che'i rnam thar bsdus pa dgos 'dod re skong ma'i 'grel pa*, 122:

Tshal pa no doubt gained the impression of Rtsa mi Lo tsā ba based on some stories passed down by Lama Zhang and his peers. In fact, when we look back to the time of Lama Zhang, we see that more people knew of Rtsa mi Lo tsā ba's career. In a brief account on the history of Mahākāla written by 'Jig rten mgon po Rin chen dpal (1143–1217), the founder of the 'Bri gung sect of the Bka' brgyud school, Rtsa mi Lo tsā ba was highly praised for his achievement as a scholar and adept in India. 'Jig rten mgon po started the text by narrating an early story of Mahākāla. In the story, for the purpose of subduing a non-Buddhist master who was preaching doctrines that were detrimental to Buddhist teachings, Mahākāla, having transformed himself into a raven, flew to Śrī Parvata (Dpal gyi ri), and informed Nāgārjuna and his spiritual son Āryadeva. Then Āryadeva, having been invited to Nālandā, subdued the non-Buddhist master. Following the story, 'Jig rten mgon po wrote:

> The great scholar born in the Tangut land, the lama who attained spiritual accomplishment, Rtsa mi, having emerged and obtained the initiation from Lama Vajrāsana[187], spoke the application of meditative activities. Then, he bestowed [the teachings] to the great lama [Gzhon nu] dpal as a way of guarding the teachings, and guarded him like a son.[188]

---

rngog lo tsā'i slob ma dbang ston la bsnyen rdzogs mdzad nas / gzhon nu dpal du btags / mdo dbus gnyis su bla ma mang po bsten / chos mang du bslabs nas rgya gar du byon / bla ma paṇḍita tsa mi sangs rgyas grags pa de / gdung rus me nyag yin yang rgya gar gyi paṇḍita thams cad kyi gtsug gi nor bu ltar bzhugs pa dang / snyigs dus kyi kun mkhyen gnyis pa paṇḍita a bhya ka ra gupta'i zhabs la gtugs/ dbang dang gdams pa ma lus pa zhus /.

[187] This could refer to either Vajrāsana the Great (Tib. Rdo rje gdan pa chen po) or Vajrāsana the Minor (Tib. Rdo rje gdan pa chung ba, alias Amoghavajra), both of whom were abbots of Vajrāsana from the tenth to eleventh centuries. The particle las that comes after *bla ma rdo rje gdan pa* in this passage is a bit difficult to understand. I have temporarily take it as going together with the phrase *dbang rab tu thob*.

[188] 'Jig rten mgon po, *Dpal ye shes kyi mgon po nag po chen po'i lo rgyus bsdus pa*, 235:

Rtsa mi Lo tsā ba was known for being a great master in the transmission of teachings related to Mahākāla.[189] Here, 'Jig rten mgon po places Rtsa mi Lo tsā ba after Nāgārjuna and Āryadeva in the lineage. Not only that, but he also treats Rtsa mi Lo tsā ba was a disciple of Vajrāsana. Only after Rtsa mi Lo tsā ba did the teachings come into the hands of a Tibetan.

The peculiar case of Rtsa mi Lo tsā ba in the transmissive lineage of Mahākāla is also reflected in the reported speeches of him documented in Tibetan sources. Here, an important text we need to refer to – as pointed out by Sperling – is the biography of Rgwa Lo tsā ba written by Lama Zhang, which contains a lengthy story of how Rgwa Lo tsā ba met Rtsa mi Lo tsā ba and studied under his guidance.[190] Interestingly, their first conversation embodies not a completely pleasant experience. The text reads:

> Having put aside ten of the forty-seven *srang* of gold he had, [Rgwa Lo tsā ba] made a maṇḍala with the [remaining] thirty-seven and he offered it to Lama [R]tsa mi. He said, "I request for myself in this very lifetime an instruction of the Buddha that others don't have." Thus, Lama Rtsa mi replied, "What are you talking about? How is an instruction that others don't have possible?" And [Rgwa Lo tsā ba] said,

---

de nas bla ma rdo rje gdan pa las mi nyag gi yul du sku 'khrungs pa'i mkhas pa chen po dngos grub brnyes pa'i bla ma rtsa mis mngon du gyur te / dbang rab tu thob nas las sbyor rnams gsungs so / de nas bla ma dpal chen po la chos skyong du gnang ste / bu bzhin tu skyong bar gyur pa yin no /.

[189] See Sperling "Rtsa-mi Lo-tsā-ba," 804–806.

[190] For a discussion and translation of the story, see Sperling "Rtsa-mi Lo-tsā-ba," 802–803, 809–813, n. 14. However, Sperling's translation is not impeccable. For example, the direct speech marker *byed* was treated by him in some places as an auxiliary verb. Also, *zlas* (prs. *zlo*), which appears several times in the story, was translated by him as "to mutter." Yet, in this context, it is better to understand it as "to report," "to inform." The version of the text Sperling used contains some flaws as well. Hence, using a different version, I have retranslated all the pieces of story presented below.

> "I request a precept that does not require the change of concentration." Thus, he bestowed him a precept, the Ṣaḍaṅgayoga, which essentially makes the essence of emptiness and compassion arise in one's continuum.[191]

Rtsa mi Lo tsā ba was clearly not very happy about the ambitious young man from Tibet as he asked too much and was unwilling to have a focus. The story then proceeds with the result Rgwa Lo tsā ba had after two and a half years of meditation:

> After two and a half years had passed, a sign that [Rgwa Lo tsā ba] had purified his mind-continuum appeared. At that time, when Lama Abhyākara asked him through the window, he reported [the sign]. Because of that, at that point, [the sign] ceased. Then, he asked Lama [R]tsa mi about it. The reply was that, even though Abhyākara was a scholar, his qualities of meditation were not great. [Rtsa mi Lo tsā ba] said, "Still, generate perseverance and meditate. And [the sign] will come; do not have doubt that the sign will not come. On the basis of those, don't report the sign that has arisen even to me!"...[192]

---

[191] Zhang, *'Gro ba'i mgon po zhang g.yu brag pa'i gsung mdzad pa rnam thar gyi skor*, 186–187:

> *gser srang bzhi bcu rtsa bdun yod pa'i bcu bzhag nas / sum cu rtsa bdun la maṇḍala byas nas / bla ma tsa mi la phul lo / bdag la tshe 'di nyid la sangs rgya ba'i man ngag gzhan la med pa zhig zhu byas pas / bla ma tsa mi'i zhal nas khyod ci zer ba yin / gzhan la med pa'i gdams ngag ga la 'ong zhes gsungs pa dang / dmigs pa spo mi dgos pa'i gdams ngag cig zhu byas pas / sbyor ba yan lag drug po zhes bya ba gnad kyi sgo nas / stong nyid snying rje'i snying po can rgyud la skye bar byed pa'i gdams ngag 'di gnang ngo /.*

[192] Zhang, *'Gro ba'i mgon po zhang g.yu brag pa'i gsung mdzad pa rnam thar gyi skor*, 187–188:

> *lo phyed dang gsum lon nas thugs rgyud 'byongs pa'i rtags byung ba la / bla ma a byā ka ras skar khung na tshur dris pa la bzlas pas der 'phro chad do / de nas bla ma tsa mi la zhus pas / bla ma a byā ka ra mkhas pa yin yang bsgoms pa'i yon tan mi che bas lan pa yin / da rung sdug sran bskyed la bsgom dang 'ong gis mi 'ong ba'i dogs med kyis / rtags byung ba de nga la yang ma zlo zhig gsungs nas /...*

Abhyākara[gupta] was the Indian paṇḍita with whom Rtsa mi Lo tsā ba completed most of his translations. However, according to the above text, Rtsa mi Lo tsā ba did not have confidence in Abhyākara to lead Rgwa Lo tsā ba to spritual attainment through meditation. And he believed that his instructions would benefit Rgwa Lo tsā ba more on the path to success. It turned out that Rtsa mi Lo tsā ba was correct since an extraordinarily auspicious sign appeared after six years of meditation. However, Rtsa mi Lo tsā ba was again displeased by the plan Rgwa Lo tsā ba made after having the good news. The text reads:

> After six years had passed, [Rgwa Lo tsā ba] saw an exalted sign and the vision of the body of an arising Tāra. The Tāra said, "Son! Go to the Grove of Coolness, the great cemetery. There, all spiritual attainments will appear." Having said that, she disappeared. Then, [Rgwa Lo tsā ba] made a request to Lama [R]tsa mi, "I will go to the Grove of Coolness to perform the *gtor ma* ritual." Thus, [Rtsa mi Lo tsā ba] said, "You Tibetans are extremely unruly. Meditate in silence!" Having said that, he did not allow him to go.[193]

Although Rtsa mi Lo tsā ba ultimately allowed Rgwa Lo tsā ba to go after about another year and a half, at this point, he was dissatisfied with Rgwa Lo tsā ba's proposal. What is quite striking here is that he reprimed Rgwa Lo tsā ba by saying, "you Tibetans" (*khyod bod*)[194]. We have seen before

[193] Zhang, *'Gro ba'i mgon po zhang g.yu brag pa'i gsung mdzad pa rnam thar gyi skor*, 188:

> *lo drug lon tsa na / rtags bzang po dang sgrol ma bzhengs sku'i zhal mthong nas / sgrol ma'i zhal nas bu khyod dur khrod chen po bsil ba'i tshal du song zhig / der dngos grub thams cad 'byung bar 'gyur ro / zhes gsungs te mi snang bar gyur to / de nas bla ma tsa mi la bdag bsil ba'i tshal du gtor ma zhig gtong du 'gro bar zhu byas pas / khyod bod lhag chad che kha rog bsgoms gsungs nas ma gnang bar /.*

[194] The phrase might also be understood as "you, Tibetan!" due to the obscurity of the number. However, I suggest a plural for the word because, in the last occurrence of this phrase, which is about 2 folios earlier, has "all you Tibetans" (*khyed bod thams cad*). There, there is no doubt about a plural ending. See Zhang, *'Gro ba'i mgon po zhang g.yu brag pa'i gsung mdzad pa rnam thar gyi skor*, 184.

that Rtsa mi Lo tsā ba indeed labeled himself in many places a Tibetan translator. But here, interestingly, he intentionally alienated himself from Tibetans and pointed out their weakness of them as students. Hence, even though Rtsa mi Lo tsā ba might have used Tibetan in the communication with Rgwa Lo tsā ba, it seems he never thought he was of the same ethnic group as Rgwa Lo tsā ba was.

A passage that has a similar overtone is found in the brief history of Mahākāla written by 'Jig rten mgon po that we mentioned earlier. The text documented an important statement of Rtsa mi Lo tsā ba when he received the offering from Rgwa Lo tsā ba:

> Lama Rtsa mi himself also bestowed the precepts without remainder to Lama [Gzhon nu] Dpal. He [=Rgwa Lo tsā ba] gave away eighteen *srang* of gold he sent from Tibet as an offering to the lama. Rtsa mi also gave the following advice: "On the one hand, the offering is too much. Since we are both yogins, it is not necessary to be like this. On the other hand, it is too little. It is an offering made to me, a great person of India, by him, a great person of Tibet." So it is stated.[195]

Here, again, Rtsa mi Lo tsā ba disassociated himself from Tibet and Tangut by calling himself "a great person of India" (*rgya gar gyi mi chen zhig*) and Rgwa Lo tsā ba "a great person of Tibet" (*bod kyi mi chen zhig*). Interestingly, the fact that he saw himself as a great person of India also echoes the previous account that he "resided there like the crown jewel of all Indian paṇḍitas"

---

[195] 'Jig rten mgon po, *Dpal ye shes kyi mgon po nag po chen po'i lo rgyus bsdus pa*, 236:

> *gdams ngag kyang ma lus pa bla ma rtsa mi nyid kyis bla ma dpal la gnang ste / khong gis bod nas gser srang bco brgyad bla ma la 'bul du btang ba la / rtsa mi'i zhal nas / yang na 'bul ba che ste / nged gnyis ka rnal 'byor pa yin pas 'di ltar mi dgos / yang na chung ba yin te nga rgya gar gyi mi chen zhig la / kho bod kyi mi chen zhig gis 'bul ba yin zhes zhal ta yang mdzad skad /.*

(*rgya gar gyi paṇḍita thams cad kyi gtsug gi nor bu ltar bzhugs*) and that he placed himself over Abhyākara in terms of tantric practice. Hence, we might argue that Rtsa mi Lo tsā ba viewed himself as having a threefold identity: he was born a Tangut, educated as a Tibetan, and taught like an Indian scholar and adept.

Undoubtedly no one we have known so far in Tibetan and Tangut history parallels Rtsa mi Lo tsā ba claiming to have this threefold identity. And his career is embodied by the identity that signals certain power relations between Tangut and Tibet that are dramatically different from those we see later in the century. For example, while the destination of the later Tanguts in the pursuit of Buddhism was primarily Tibet, Rtsa mi Lo tsā ba chose to study in India. Also, different from the later Tanguts who took Tibetans as their masters, Rtsa mi Lo tsā ba instead recruited Tibetan students. In a word, in the eyes of Rtsa mi Lo tsā ba, there was no such thing as "Tibetan Buddhism" that was so charming that it could captivate him and make him bow down to the feet of Tibetan masters. There were only Tibetan masters captivated by him. Therefore, in spite of his reputation in Tibetan history, he almost fell entirely out of the scope of the dynamics in the formative period of the integrative Inner Asian imperial history. This, of course, may also explain why his name rarely appears in the Tangut texts available to us.

However, upon closer examination, the superficial alienation of Rtsa mi Lo tsā ba from the bigger picture of the later patterns belies his underlying significance in the rise of Tibetan Buddhism in the Tangut State. As discussed in detail later in this chapter, those Tibetans who were familiar with him – Lama Zhang and 'Jig rten mgon po – were the very founders of the Bka' brgyud subsects that were to exert remarkable religious influence within the Tangut realm in the late twelfth century to the early thirteenth century. Hence, the career of Rtsa mi Lo tsā ba, although not falling into the theme of the grand sonata of the rise of Tibetan Buddhism in the Tangut State, did form a mellifluous prologue that echoed well the development later in that opus.

2. First Tibetan Scriptures Translated: The Message of the *Pañcarakṣā*

To date, the earliest datable Tangut translation of a Tibetan text is the *Aparimitāyurjñānasūtra*.[196] A postscript appended to a block print of the Tangut translation (#812), which was made by Empress Dowager Liang[197] and Emperor Qianshun for a religious gathering where ten thousand copies of the sutra were distributed, is dated to 1094.[198] Hence, the translation must have been done not long before that.[199] While this year predates the formative period of the integrative Inner Asian imperial history for more than three decades, the translation appears to be more of an exception rather than a representative work of the early period of the rise of Tibetan Buddhism in the Tangut State. An important reason for this is that not a single other Tangut translation of a Tibetan text can be dated to an early date as such. Furthermore, the translation was likely done due to the extreme popularity of the scripture among the Tibetans in the Dunhuang area that continued from the Imperial Period of the Tibetan Empire[200] rather than a result of its transmission from the Tibetan Plateau.

---

[196] For a detailed study of the Tangut translation of the sutra, see Sun, *Xixiawen "Wuliangshou jing" yanjiu*, 20–26; 167–223. The text has been identified as a translation from Tibetan based on the Tibetan style terms contained in it.

[197] This is the later Empress Dowager Liang from the Liang family, who was the mother of Qianshun. She is to be distinguished from the former Empress Dowager Liang, who was the mother of Bingchang 秉常 (1061–1086).

[198] For the postscript, see Nie, *Xixia Fojing xuba yizhu*, 19–22.

[199] To say the translation was made not long before 1094, when the postscript was made, is because the colophon of the sutra says it is "supremely translated" ([illegible]) by Empress Dowager Liang and Qianshun. See Sun, *Xixiawen "Wuliangshou jing" yanjiu*, 167–168. So, the translation must at least have been completed during the reign of Qianshun.

[200] For the popularity of this sutra in Dunhuang, see Dotson, "Misspelling 'Buddha,'" 129–131. There over 1,600 Tibetan copies of the sutra from Dunhuang collected in the British Library.

However, the context against which the sutra was translated and distributed is closely related to our concerns about the beginning of the formative period of the integrative Inner Asian imperial history. As I have noted in Chapter Two, Section 2.4, Pure Land Belief constitutes a crucial factor in Tangut State Buddhism. The wish for rebirth in the Pure Land was strongly expressed in a number of postscripts made by the royal family.[201] Hence, the *Aparimitāyurjñānasūtra*, which centers around the rebirth in the Pure Land, undoubtedly falls into that category. But it is more than just the belief. We know that both the short and long *Sukhāvatīvyūha Sutra*s had already been translated from Chinese into Tangut.[202] But a major characteristic of the *Aparimitāyurjñānasūtra* that distinguished it from these two sutras is that it contained a *dhāraṇī* repeated dozens of times. The *dhāraṇī* is said to have not only the efficacy of enhancing the possibility of rebirth in the Pure Land but also to have the power of bringing worldly benefits. And this feature of the *Aparimitāyurjñānasūtra* is underscored in the postscript made by the Empress Dowager and Qianshun:

> It is definite that the life of the common people would be end early; [but,] if one chants the *dhāraṇī*-spell, one will be able to attain a longer life. Having encountered sudden sickness or other disasters, reciting and copying it will naturally obviate the miseries.[203]

---

[201] Sun, *Xixiawen "Wuliangshou jing" yanjiu*, 8–11.

[202] They should have been translated together with the other texts in the Chinese canon when the Tangut State was first established. And the short *Sukhāvatīvyūha Sutra* was also translated during the reign of Bingchang (r. 1068–1086), attested by the colophon in a block print version (#7564). See Sun, "*Foshuo Amituo jing* de Xixia yiben," 25–26.

[203] Nie, *Xixia Fojing xuba yizhu*, 19:

> [illegible]

Therefore, it is no exaggeration that the *dhāraṇī* contained in the sutra served as the most important reason for its translation and publication. We should also not forget that the Liangzhou Stele was erected in 1094, the same year when copies of the *Aparimitāyurjñānasūtra* were distributed. This was a period when the Tangut State was experiencing extreme political difficulties both due to the internal conflicts between the emperors and the Liang family and external threats from the Northern Song. The frequent religious activities during this period can be interpreted as a response to the crises. However, a tradition of translating Tibetan texts was thus started, and many more scriptures similar to the *Aparimitāyurjñānasūtra* would be translated from Tibetan into Tangut in the years to come.

It is possible, perhaps even probable, that during the later period of the reign of Qianshun[204] another important Buddhist scripture, the *Pañcarakṣā* or the *Five Protective Sutras* ([illegible],

[204] The main clue for determining the date of the translation is the statement that appears in the colophon of the translation, "supremely translated by Ŋwe mji, the Emperor of Perpetual Peace" ([illegible]). However, scholars are not unanimous about the identity of this Emperor of Perpetual Peace. Nie Hongyin and An Ya identify him as Qianshun, whereas Kychanov, Li Fanwen and Cui Hongfen identify him as Renxiao. For this debate, see An, *Xixiawen "Shouhu daqian guotu jing" yanjiu*, 6–8, Cui and Wen, "Xixia Huangdi zunhao kaolue," 12. I agree here with Nie's and An's proposition that the Emperor of Perpetual Peace should be Qianshun because Renxiao later revised the translation, and it would be unusual for an emperor to revise a translation made during his own reign. The major evidence held by Li and Cui is that a piece of stele saying "Emperor of Perpetual Peace" was discovered from the tomb of Renxiao. However, the way I see it is that this does not necessarily indicate that Renxiao was the Emperor of Perpetual Peace. It is of course possible that the original stele was one praising his father Qianshun's achievements. There are some other reasons to support the equivalence between Qianshun and the Emperor of Perpetual Peace, which are worth an independent study and are thus not detailed here. To say that the translation was made in the later period of Qianshun's reign is based on two reasons. First, the regent, Empress Dowager Liang (d. 1099), is absent from the colophon. Second, the author of the preface greatly praises the achievements of the emperor, which likely refers to Qianshun's success in fending off the Northern Song and incorporating Tsong kha into the Tangut State. In any case, 1173 is the *terminus ante quem* for the translation because one manuscript (#562) of the *Mahāsāhasrapramardinī* is dated to that year (Kychanov, *Katalog Tangytckix byddiyckix pamyatnikov Institut Boctokovedeniya Pocciyckoy Akademii Hayk*, 423).

hereafter the *Five Sutras*)[205], was translated from Tibetan into Tangut.[206] It includes five independent sutras, namely, the *Mahāpratisarā*, the *Mahāsāhasrapramardinī*, the *Mahāmāyūrī*, the *Mahāśītavatī*, and the *Mahāmantrānusariṇī*.[207] However, it is often transmitted as one group of texts. The *Five Sutras* is intended to be used for very pragmatic purposes. The *dhāraṇī*s contained in the sutras contain strong apotropaic power that can protect people from misery and hardship, and bring them benefits. As Lewis states, "All the texts in the *raksa* literature promise both merit and worldly blessings as a result of the proper recitation of the specified passages."[208] The *Five Sutras* became an extraordinarily popular scripture in the Tangut State, which is attested by the copious printed texts and manuscripts that were discovered in Khara-Khoto. Its translation was later revised during the reign of Renxiao. And it is evident that its popularity continued until the later period of the Tangut State as a colophon of one version states that it was printed by a private publisher in 1196.[209]

A significant piece of textual material related to the Tangut *Five Sutras* is a preface written by a minister Tshji khjiw (< Qi Qiu 齊丘?), under the command of the Tangut emperor. The

---

[205] For a general introduction to the scripture, see Lewis, *Popular Buddhist Texts from Nepal*, chap. 6. These texts should probably be regarded more precisely as *dhāraṇī*s. Or, according to the major recensions of the Tibetan canon, they should be regarded as tantras. However, since both the Tangut and Tibetan titles call them sutras ([illegible], *mdo*), I will keep that term. Two of the five Tangut texts have now been studied in detail. See An, *Xixiawen "Shouhu daqian guotu jing" yanjiu* and Zhang, *Xixiawen "Da suiqiu tuoluoni jing" yanjiu.*

[206] Again, the conclusion that it was translated from Tibetan rather than Chinese is drawn on the basis of the comparison between the Tangut translation and the Tibetan and Chinese texts. Not only all the term in the Tangut translation are Tibetan style terms, but all the narratives are identical with the Tibetan rather than with the Chinese versions. See notes 229 and 231.

[207] These names vary slightly in different versions of the texts. The names I used here are those recorded in Lewis, *Popular Buddhist Texts from Nepal*, 129. Also, the order of the five also varies on difference occasions. I will not delve into the details here.

[208] Lewis, *Popular Buddhist Texts from Nepal*, 126.

[209] Nie, *Xixia Fojing xuba yizhu*, 134–137.

preface can be divided into four parts. The first part is a general description of Buddhism and praise for the Buddha and his teachings. The second part is a brief history of Buddhism, especially how the Buddhist texts were translated and spread in China. The third part is a summary of the contents of the five sutras and the benefits of chanting the *dhāraṇīs* contained in them. The last part is a praise of the Tangut emperor and a postscript. The preface is an excellent lens through which we might view the context against which the early Tangut translations of Tibetan texts were made. Therefore, I have translated the preface in full below:[210]

Preface to the *Five Sutras*

> I, the ignorant one, have heard that the teaching of the Venerable Awakened One has ten thousand variations but is yet identical in all cases, and it guides all kinds of beings. It is difficult to have the primordial realization of the wonderful and truthful statements [of the Buddha] on the basis of sharp intelligence, and how could one assess the extremely profound meaning by means of a dull faculty? [But,] the power of skillful means and the resourcefulness [of the Buddha] is inconceivable. [By means of] explaining one vehicle[211], he includes one thousand dimensions. If it [=his teaching] is condensed, then it is applied to a particle; when it expands, it reaches the ten directions. Similar to a vast ocean, it does not have limits; just like the sky at night, how could its boundary [i.e., just like the boundary between the sky and the earth] be clarified?

[210] For a Chinese translation of it, see Nie, *Xixia Fojing xuba yizhu*, 76–83.

[211] The "one vehicle" here might refer to the Huayan Perfect Teaching (*yuanjiao* 圓教) doctrine, which had already taken root in the Tangut State by this time. The sentence later, "If it [=his teaching] is condensed, then it is applied to a particle," exemplifies the Huayan teaching that one particle contains all the worlds.

Toward the end of the State of Zhou[212], the Tathāgata appeared in the West. When the kings of the Han[213] first flourished, [Kāśyapa] Mātaṇga[214] arrived in the East. In accordance with the dream at night[215], lucid words were transmitted. The *pattra* script[216] was translated; the uneducated and the perplexed were guided and taught. When the excellent scriptures appeared at one time, the tradition of the teaching would perpetually spread for ten thousand [times] afterward.[217]

Previously, our Buddha transcended beyond the suffering of being drowned in the suffocating ocean and saved [beings] from being burned in the burning house.[218] Fully endowed with a compassionate mind, he made prayers. For the benefit of the sentient beings, he established the *Five Sutras*. Among them, it is the *Mahāsāhasrapramardinī Sutra* that says: when the Tathāgata was staying on the Vulture Peak[219], the monks[220] came to Jeta[221] Grove.[222] King Ajātaśatru[223] of the country of Magadha gave precious jewels and made offerings venerably. At that time, the earth shook; the smoke covered the clouds; there were fierce winds, roaring thunder, rain with hail, and flashing lightning; the light of the sun and the

---

[212] I.e., the Zhou dynasty (1046 BCE–256 BCE). If we follow the "dotted record," which is popular in the East Asian Buddhist traditions, for the dating of the historical Buddha, then his Nirvana would be placed in 486 BCE or 483 BCE, which accord the account here.

[213] I.e., the Han dynasty (202 BCE–220 CE). It is interesting that the Tangut uses "king" (*njij*[2] [illegible] < Ch. *wang* 王) to denote the rulers of the Han dynasty. The author seems to intentionally downplay the legitimacy of the Chinese rulers. This appellation here is in direct opposition to the "emperor" (*ŋwər*[1] *dzjwɨ*[1] [illegible] < Ch. *huang di* 皇帝) that the author uses later in the preface to address the Tangut ruler.

[214] I.e., She Moteng 攝摩騰, one of the very first Indian Buddhist monks who came to China.

[215] This is the locus classicus of how Buddhism first came to China. It is said that Emperor Ming (57 CE–75 CE) of the Han, having dreamed the golden person, sent envoys to India to ask for Buddhist transmissions.

[216] As it is made clear later in the preface, the *pattra* script is nothing but Sanskrit written on *pattra* leaves.

[217] For this classical narrative of how Buddhism was introduced in China, see Zürcher, *The Buddhist Conquest of China*, 22.

[218] I.e., the burning house parable in the Lotus Sutra. The Buddha is like the father who tries to save the children – the sentient beings – who are attached to playing in a burning house.

[219] [illegible], "vulture-heap-mountain," Tibetan style term reflecting *bya rgod phung po'i ri*.

[220] [illegible] *phji*[2] *khjiw*[2] (< *biqiu* 比丘), Chinese style term.

[221] [illegible] *śjɨ*[1] *tow*[1] (< *shiduo* 逝多), Chinese style term.

[222] The Tibetan text does not specify Jeta Grove but just "forest where many trees appeared" (*shing ljon pa rab tu snang ba'i nags tshogs*). The Tangut translation of the sutra says, "great forest" ([illegible] [An, *Xixiawen "Shouhu daqian guotu jing" yanjiu*, 30]). Hence, the author of the preface obviously made a mistake about the place.

[223] [illegible] *·ja śja*[1] *śjɨ*[2] (< *asheshi* 阿闍世), Chinese style term.

moon were obstructed, and the glint of the stars was hidden. Our Buddha, using his divine eyes, saw all the anxieties and fears of the people.[224] The *Mahāmāyūrī Sutra* says: at that time, the Venerable One was staying in Jeta Grove which was close to the city of Śrāvastī. A monk named Svāti, who was a beginning student of the Vinaya discipline, having cut down the tree, was preparing the bath water. From within a rotten wood, a poisonous snake suddenly came out and bit the person, instantly hurting his finger.[225] The *Mahāśītavatī Sutra* says: at that time, when the Venerable One was staying in the cemetery, the Four Heavenly Kings first came at night. Because the *yakṣas*[226], *gandharvas*[227], *kumbhāṇḍas*[228], *nāga*s hurt the people, he spoke the teaching of repentance.[229] The *Mahāpratisarā Sutra* was asked by the Brahman and was spoken by the Venerable One.[230] Clinging to the chant of the spell, one attains all that is wished. As for the *Mahāmantrānusariṇī Sutra*, the true words of the Venerable One were held by the king of Brahmā.[231] One can eliminate the demons and make all kinds of wishes established [on the basis of this sutra]. Now, these five *dhāraṇī*s[232] posit various teachings. They are of different representations but are of one vehicle; they are [spoken] according to the audience but have an identical entity. The numinous spell has extensive qualities, and it can command the heavenly kings. Endowed with magical power, it crushes all ghosts. If a person holds on to it and chants the spell of the sutra, then he will tame all evil

---

224 This passage and the four others that follow are not direct quotes from the sutras but are paraphrases of the episodes of the sutras. For the corresponding passage of this episode in the Tibetan text, see *Bka' 'gyur* 90, 176–178. See also Lewis, *Popular Buddhist Texts from Nepal*, 141.

225 For the corresponding passage of this episode in the Tibetan text, see *Bka' 'gyur* 90, 256–258. See also Lewis, *Popular Buddhist Texts from Nepal*, 148.

226 [illegible], "harm-giving," Tibetan style term reflecting *gnod sbyin*.

227 [illegible], "odor-eating," Tibetan style term reflecting *dri za*.

228 [illegible], "pouch-pot," Tibetan style term reflecting *grul bum*.

229 For the corresponding passage of this episode in the Tibetan text, see *Bka' 'gyur* 90, 423–424. See also Lewis, *Popular Buddhist Texts from Nepal*, 151. A major difference between the Tibetan text of this sutra and the Sanskrit and Chinese texts in that Rāhula, the Interlocutor of the Buddha, never appears in the former. And many other differences exist. See Sonoda, "*Daikanrindarani Mahāśītavatī* ihon ni tsuite."

230 For the corresponding passage of this episode in the Tibetan text, see *Bka' 'gyur* 90, 371–382. See also Lewis, *Popular Buddhist Texts from Nepal*, 134–140.

231 For the corresponding passage of this episode in the Tibetan text, see *Bka' 'gyur* 90, 457–471. See also Lewis, *Popular Buddhist Texts from Nepal*, 153. There are many differences between the Tibetan and the Sanskrit texts. For example, in the Tibetan text the Buddha preached in Śrāvastī, whereas in the Sanskrit text the Buddha preached in Vaiśālī. See Sonoda, "*Daigomyōdarani Mahāmantrānusāriṇī* beppon ni tsuite."

232 [illegible] *thow*^{1} *lo*^{1} *nji*^{1} (< *tuoluoni* 陀羅尼), Chinese style term.

spirits and be free from all suffering and misery. The types of welfare[233] like these are many, and how could one include and explain them all?

The imperial authority of the current emperor controls the nine marsh pools[234], and his virtuous deeds are similar to those of the three peaceful [periods][235]. He has practiced the great institutions of the previous emperor and has achieved extensive feats at present. He venerates the three jewels and benefits ten thousand subjects. In order to obtain the supreme Buddhist scriptures, he, by means of making the prayer reverentially, invited the monks from the Vulture Peak and quickly translated the *pattra* Sanskrit script. He makes it spread in the tainted world and make it perpetually benefit the perplexed people. The following prayer is made: Those who cultivate virtue will have their virtuous roots grow and reach the other shore; those who practice evil will have their evil minds pacified and attain enlightenment. I, the subject Tshji khjiw, have only been trained a little bit in literary skills and have not yet understood the doctrines of Buddhism. Without daring to disobey the imperial order, I composed the preface. When I ponder on it with my own mind, my fear cannot be pacified. While my words are unpolished, I have humbly offered them in accordance with any thoughts the Noble Lord has.[236]

---

[233] [illegible] *phu*^{1} *tow*^{1} (< buduo 部多, Skt. *bhūta*), Chinese style term.

[234] I follow the understanding of Nie, *Xixia Fojing xuba yizhu*, 82, n. 24 here that [illegible] (lit. "nine waterways") is a Chinese style term reflecting *jiugao* 九皋. Here, the "nine marsh pools" means the emperor's authority is far-reaching.

[235] I understand the "three peaceful [periods]" ([illegible]) here as referring to the reigns of Yao 堯, Shun 舜, and Yu 禹, the three earliest sage kings.

[236] #41, frame 2, line 1–frame 4, line 7:

[illegible]

[illegible]

The first important observation from the preface is that the text was translated at a time when Chinese Buddhist influence was still dominant. Although the author Tshji khjiw claims that he does not know much about Buddhism, he evidently has a basic knowledge of it. And his knowledge was clearly derived from the Chinese tradition. The statement, "[By means of] explaining one vehicle, he includes one thousand dimensions," reflects strong Huayan influence. The fact that he mentions the burning house parable implies his familiarity with the narratives in the Lotus Sutra, one of the most influential scriptures in the Chinese tradition. The whole history of Buddhism in the preface, including the famous episode of Emperor Ming of the Han dreaming of the golden person, is about the introduction of Buddhism in China. Also, a large number of terms are Chinese style terms. For example, in his summary of the *Mahāsāhasrapramardinī*, he uses *phji*^{2} *khjiw*^{2} [illegible] (< *biqiu* 比丘) for "monk" and *·ja śja*^{1} *śjɨ*^{2} [illegible] (< *asheshi* 阿闍世) for "Ajātaśatru." Curiously, these two terms are [illegible] ("virtue-arising," *dge slong*) and [illegible] ("un-born-hatred-king," *rgyal po ma skyes dgra*)[237] that typical Tibetan style terms are found in the

---

[illegible]

[237] An, *Xixiawen "Shouhu daqian guotu jing" yanjiu*, 33.

actual translation of the sutra. This seems to tell us that the author never wrote his preface directly on the basis of the translation but on the secondary information he received from other sources about the sutras, where some terms were again framed in the Chinese style. Or he could have read the sutras, but when he wrote the preface, he only tried to reframe the story based on his memory, thus making him change some terms from the Tibetan style to the Chinese style. Indeed, he makes a mistake about the *Mahāsāhasrapramardinī* in stating that the place where the Buddha preached was Jeta Grove, which is not true. He might have confused the place with the Jeta Grove in *Mahāmāyūrī*, especially given that the place in the former is a "great forest." In short, this newly translated scripture does seem to be a bit foreign to Tshji khjiw. And it appears that he feels more comfortable framing it within the context of Chinese Buddhism.

However, we can also see from the preface that Tibetan Buddhist influence is growing among Tangut Buddhists. While some terms Tshji khjiw used in his summary of the *Mahāsāhasrapramardinī* are Chinese style, the term for the Vulture Peak, [illegible] ("vulture-heap-mountain," *bya rgod phung po'i ri*), is in Tibetan style. If it were to be Chinese style, it would be [illegible] (< *jiufeng* 鷲峰). Also, three terms from his summary of the *Mahāśītavatī – yakṣa* ([illegible], "harm-giving," Tib. *gnod sbyin*), *gandharva* ([illegible], "odor-eating," Tib. *dri za*), and *kumbhāṇḍa* ([illegible], "pouch-pot," Tib. *grul bum*) – are obviously Tibetan style terms. If they were to be in Chinese style, they would all be phonetically transcribed.

The essence of the *Five Sutras*, as Tshji khjiw views, is apparently its magical power of the *dhāraṇī*s that may bring worldly benefits, as he says, "The types of welfare like these are many, and how could one include and explain them all?" It is also noticeable that Tshji khjiw devotes a lengthy passage to the description of the disasters that took place in the kingdom of Ajātaśatru, which implies that the *dhāraṇī*s may prevent such miseries from happening at present within the

Tangut realm. In the last part, by listing the emperor's achievements, especially his effort in translating the scripture, Tshji khjiw implicitly connects the great benefit that the *Fives Sutras* may bring to the people to the imperial grace of the emperor. In conclusion, the project of translating the *Five Sutras*, just like the project of translating the *Aparimitāyurjñānasūtra* from Tibetan, was conceived as an integral part of State Buddhism.

Translating *dhāraṇī*s from Tibetan seems to have been an important trend in the early period of the rise of Tibetan Buddhism. In addition to the five sutras, the Tanguts also published the *Uṣṇīṣavijaya-dhāraṇī*, which was translated from Tibetan in 1149. This will be discussed in detail in the next section. The *Avalokiteśvara-dhāraṇī* was published together with the *Uṣṇīṣavijaya-dhāraṇī*. It is likely that the *Sitātapatrā-dhāraṇī* was also translated from Tibetan into Tangut during this time.[238] Finally, the *Mañjuśrīnāmasaṃgīti*, one of the most influential scriptures in the Tangut State, was probably translated from Tibetan not long before 1145.[239] A common feature that all these above-mentioned early Tangut scriptures translated from Tibetan share is that they contain *dhāraṇī*s and mantras, which may enable those who chant them acquire immediate benefits. This feature, as I see, forms the most important incentive for the Tanguts to initiate translating projects of the Tibetan texts because it constitutes a vital cause for the flourishing of the State Buddhism – the *dhāraṇī*s and mantras are powerful instruments for the collective welfare of the state.

3. The Legacies of Jayānanda: Texts and People

[238] A postscript to a newly carved block print version of the *dhāraṇī* in 1185 says the *dhāraṇī* had been very popular but the woodblocks were, at time, already worn out. This suggests the first print might come out several decades ago. For the postscript, see Nie, *Xixia Fojing xuba yizhu*, 91–93.

[239] It is recorded that the Tangut *Mañjuśrīnāmasaṃgīti* was distributed at the religious gathering in 1145. And this is the earliest record we have for the Tangut *Mañjuśrīnāmasaṃgīti*. See Zhang, "Wenben chuanyi yu wenhua liuchuan."

Current evidence shows that very few Buddhists from the Indic world played roles in promoting Buddhism in the Tangut State. The situation is, of course, very different from that of the transmission of Buddhism in early China and in Tibet, where Buddhists from the subcontinent were critical agents. However, Jayānanda, the Kashmirian scholar, stands out as an exception. While he is mostly known in Tibetan intellectual history as one of the key figures who introduced the *prasaṅgika-madhyamaka* philosophical system to the Tibetans,[240] his later career was centered around the Tangut State. As is widely known, Jayānanda first went to Tibet but was likely forced to leave for the Tanguts due to his defeat in a public debate with Phya pa Chos kyi seng ge (1109–1169, henceforth Phya pa) on the subject of Madhyamaka.[241]

In 1149, a grand religious gathering was held by Renxiao, where he distributed more than ten thousand volumes of the *Uṣṇīṣavijaya-dhāraṇī* to the Buddhists within the Tangut realm. The *dhāraṇī* was printed in three languages – Tangut, Chinese, and Tibetan. And Jayānanda acted as an important figure in the translation project.[242] Recently, Alla Sizova, by examining the Tibetan version in detail, further discussed Jayānanda's relevance in transmitting the *Uṣṇīṣavijaya-dhāraṇī* to the Tanguts.[243] In the Tibetan version of the *dhāraṇī* as exemplified by a manuscript version [TX. 126/159] and a block print version [TX. 67 and TX. 63/68], Jayānanda is said to be the person

[240] Vose, *Resurrecting Candrakīrti*, 53–54.

[241] van der Kuijp, "Jayānanda. A Twelfth Century Guoshi from Kashmir among the Tangut," 193.

[242] Many scholars have researched these three versions of the *Uṣṇīṣavijaya-dhāraṇī* that were distributed in 1149. See, for example, Lin, "Xixiayu yi *Zunsheng jing* shiwen", Duan, "Xixiawen *Shengxiang dingzun zongchi gongneng yijing lu* zai yanjiu", Shi, "Zuizao de Zangwen mukeben kaolue", Hamanaka and Sizova, "Imperial Postscript to the Tangut, Chinese and Tibetan Editions of the Dhāraṇī-sūtras in the Collection of the IOM, RAS," and Nie, "Complementary Notes on the Biography of Jayānanda and Dkon mchog seng ge," 75–79.

[243] Alla, Sizova, "Tibetan Translation of the *Uṣṇīṣavijāyadhāraṇīsūtra* Produced in the Tangut Empire" (BuddhistRoad Guest Lecture, February 22, 2023), https://buddhistroad.ceres.rub.de/en/activities/guest-lectures/tibetan-translation-of-the-uiavijayadharaisutra-produced-in-the/.

who "transmitted" (*brgyu'*; read: brgyud) the *dhāraṇī*.[244] And the one who translated the *dhāraṇī* into Tibetan is recorded as 'Gar A na kri ta. This should, in all probability, be Ānandakīrti or Kun dga' grags, with 'Gar as his clan name. As will be discussed below, he was the translator who worked with Jayānanda on the translations of some other texts. In the Tibetan version, Jayānanda's name is prefixed with a title *bghe ne gdzi*, which should be a phonetic transcription of the Tangut *ɣiwej*^{1} *nej*^{1} *dzjo*^{1} [illegible][245] meaning "endowed with [rank of] *nej*^{1} *dzjo*^{1}." The word *nej*^{1} *dzjo*^{1}, which literally means "preserving the ritual" (< Ch. *anyi* 安儀), is the 9th subrank of the 4th rank in the ranking system of the Tangut State.[246] This shows that Jayānanda was already active in the Tangut State before 1149. And he participated in the projects of introducing *dhāraṇī*s to Tangut State Buddhism, a trend discussed in the previous section.

Likely sometime later,[247] Jayānanda participated in another important project of translation, which was the translation of the *Ratnaguṇasaṃcayagāthā* from Sanskrit to Tibetan and then from Tibetan to Tangut.[248] The colophon of the Tangut translation of the sutra lists five persons who did the translation.[249] The first one is Pu nja̱ bu̱ dźju [illegible], the earliest imperial preceptor known to us (see Chapter Two, Section 2.3). He seems to be the editor-in-chief of the project as he

---

[244] My gratitude to Alla Sizova, who kindly shared the Tibetan texts with me, thus allowing me to examine them myself.

[245] Often transcribed phonetically into Chinese as *gui nai jiang* 嚷乃將.

[246] Li, "Xixia guanjie fenghao biao kaoshi," 176, 178.

[247] My chronology here is based on the evidence of the promotion of Xianbei Baoyuan 鮮卑寶源, who translated both the *Uṣṇīṣavijaya-dhāraṇī* and the *Ratnaguṇasaṃcayagāthā* into Chinese. When he translated the former, he was at the rank of *wo ye* 臥耶 (=*wo*^{2} *·jij*^{1} [illegible], the 2nd subrank of the 5th rank); when he translated the latter, he was at the rank of *mei ze* 美則 (= *bji̱*^{2} *dzjɨ*^{1} [illegible], the 12th subrank of the 4th rank).

[248] For a detailed study of the Tangut translation, see Duan, *Xixia "Gongde bao ji ji" kua yuyan duikan yanjiu.*

[249] For the colophon, see Duan, *Xixia "Gongde bao ji ji" kua yuyan duikan yanjiu*, 50.

"examined the meaning" ([Tangut]) of the translation. Jayānanda (Dzaja ·ja ·ja nja dja̱ [Tangut]) is listed in the second place as the one who "proofread the meaning by holding the Sanskrit text" ([Tangut]). Ānandakīrti (·Ja nja dja̱ kjɨ ljɨ̱ tji [Tangut]) translated the Sanskrit into Tibetan ([Tangut]). Zhou Huihai 周慧海 (Tśjiw źjɨr ŋjow [Tangut])[250] translated the Tibetan into Tangut ([Tangut]). And the calligrapher was Ljị tśhjwor ko [Tangut] (< Ch. Li Changguang 李常光?). All of these names, except the calligrapher, are prefixed with their rank titles. Pu nja̱ bu̱ dźju is prefixed with *ŋowr*^{2} *lhə*$^{?}$ [Tangut] (< Ch. *juzu* 具足), the 1st rank; Jayānanda is, as we have seen in the case of the *Uṣṇīṣavijaya-dhāraṇī*, prefixed with *nej*^{1} *dzjo*^{1}; Ānandakīrti is prefixed with *śjọ ?* [Tangut] (< Ch. *muquan* 慕全), the 6th subrank of the 5th rank; and Zhou Huihai is prefixed with *wo*^{2} *·jij*^{1} [Tangut] (< Ch. *yiping* 義平), the 2nd subrank of the 5th rank. All of the four also have religious titles: Pu nja̱ bu̱ dźju is an imperial preceptor; Jayānanda is a state preceptor, and both Ānandakīrti and Zhou Huihai are dharma preceptors.

Prajñāpāramitā literature was an important component of Tangut State Buddhism. In fact, a large portion of all the texts discovered from Khara-Khoto are copies of the Tangut Large *Prajñāpāramitā Sutra*, which was translated from Xuanzang's Chinese translation (T 220). While the *Ratnaguṇasaṃcayagāthā* was translated into Chinese by Faxian 法賢 (d. 1000), it likely did not enter the Tangut State together with other Chinese texts as we have not seen a Tangut translation based on it. Hence, the translation made by the team of the imperial preceptor Pu nja̱ bu̱ dźju was most likely intended to add to the *prajñāpāramitā* literature. Also, it is not impossible that the translation of the scripture is related to the introduction of Gsang phu scholasticism around

[250] For Zhou Huihai, see Dunnell, "Translating History from Tangut Buddhist Texts," 45–47.

the mid-twelfth century (see Chapter Four, Section 2). The *Ratnaguṇasaṃcayagāthā* parallels closely the *Prajñāpāramitā Sutra in Eight Thousand Lines*. And the latter, which also exists in Tangut as a translation from Tibetan,[251] is one of the basic texts in Gsang phu scholasticism.

Again, perhaps sometime later but surely before 1167,[252] Jayānanda once more worked with the imperial preceptor Pu nja̱ bu̱ dźju to revise the short *Sukhāvatīvyūha Sutra*. #6761, a block print of the revised version, preserves a colophon. In the following chart, the Tangut colophon is transcribed on the left, and a translation appears on the right:

[illegible]	Transmitted by:
[illegible]	Imperial preceptor of excellence and awakening, monk, Bu̱ dźju;
[illegible]	State preceptor of the five sciences, monk, Jayānanda;
[illegible]	State preceptor of golden realization, monk, Tsji̱r źjɨr;
[illegible]	State preceptor of ultimate awakening, monk, Źjɨr ·wejr;
[illegible]	Dharma preceptor of harmony, monk, Sji̱j pjɨr;
[illegible][253]	Dharma preceptor of awakened practice, monk, Tśhja źjɨr, etc.

What "transmitted" ([illegible]) here really means is not entirely clear. The text was, of course, already translated during the reign of Bingchang 秉常 (r. 1068–1086). Hence, it should likely mean that the revision was carried out under the collective effort of the team members and thus, the content of the revised text was a product transmitted by the members, probably on the basis of new Sanskrit/Tibetan texts. This project of revision should also undoubtedly be seen as part of State

[251] Kychanov, *Katalog Tangytckix byddiyckix pamyatnikov Institut Boctokovedeniya Pocciyckoy Akademii Hayk*, 266–267. A manuscript (#896) of the sutra is dated to 1152. Hence, the translation of it must predate that year.

[252] Tśhja źjɨr, the last figure lasted in the colophon, was already a state preceptor by 1167. Hence, the project of the short *Sukhāvatīvyūha Sutra* must predate that year. Also, since Tśhja źjɨr's *floruit* postdates Jayānanda, it would not make much sense that he was present in the project of the short *Sukhāvatīvyūha Sutra* but not in the project of the *Ratnaguṇasaṃcayagāthā*, if we place the date of the former before the latter.

[253] Sun, "*Foshuo Amituo jing* de Xixia yiben," 24.

Buddhism since it was the major text in the literature of Pure Land Buddhism, which was promoted by the ruling class.

While there is no question that Jayānanda helped promote Buddhism in the Tangut State, there are two points that remain extremely curious about him. The first point is that although Jayānanda was known as a Sanskritist, the Tanguts never seem to have tried to take advantage of his expertise and make him translate texts from Sanskrit directly into Tangut. The Tanguts insisted on translating texts from Tibetan into Tangut. I assume this is because the Tanguts followed a very pragmatic approach to the translations. Although contemporary scholars tend to hold the Sanskrit text as more reliable than a translation, it would not be the same case for the Tanguts in the twelfth century. For them, translating texts from Tibetan was an established practice born from necessity. And, as noted in Chapter Two, Section 1, the close linguistic relationship between Tangut and Tibetan would greatly facilitate the translation process. The phenomenon of drawing closer to the Tibetan scriptural tradition rather than the Sanskrit one thus marks a salient characteristic of Tangut Buddhism. We will return to the issue again in Chapter Five, Section 7 and in the Conclusion.

The second curious point is that, based on the current available textual material, we have not yet identified anything authored by Jayānanda that was translated into Tangut. Not even a fragment of his magnum opus on *prasaṅgika-madhyamaka*, the *Madhyamakāvatārabhāṣyaṭīkā*, which was translated by Ānandakīrti in the Tangut State,[254] is to date been recovered in a Tangut translation, and the same holds for his *Tarkamudgara*. In fact, when we look at the major Madhyamaka works in Tangut (see Chapter Four, Section 3), they show predominately the

[254] For this translation, see van der Kuijp, "Jayānanda. A Twelfth Century Guoshi from Kashmir among the Tangut," 191–192.

svātantrika-madhyamaka position adopted by the Gsang phu tradition. Hence, it is no exaggeration that Jayānanda, despite being a state preceptor of the Tanguts, had a very limited, if any, philosophical influence on his Tangut audience. Does this then mean Jayānanda was nothing but a rubber stamp or a mascot of the Tangut court?

In order to answer "no" to that question, I suggest we change our perspective and see Jayānanda not as a figure who had extensive and direct interactions with the Tanguts but as a charismatic Indic scholar who had a great influence on his Tibetan audience within the Tangut realm. All the three Tibetan translations he made with Ānandakīrti already mentioned in this section – the *Uṣṇīṣavijaya-dhāraṇī*, the *Ratnaguṇasaṃcayagāthā*, and the *Madhyamakāvatārabhāṣyaṭīkā* – were clearly first and foremost intended for a Tibetan audience, though the former two might also serve as the basis for further Tangut translations. Furthermore, Jayānanda's interaction with his Tibetan audience was not only spontaneous because of their close relationship, but also because his duties assigned by the court. This is evident in the Tibetan translation of the *Uṣṇīṣavijaya-dhāraṇī*, which was distributed at a state-hosted religious gathering. Even the translation of the *Madhyamakāvatārabhāṣyaṭīkā* from Sanskrit into Tibetan might be a state sponsored-project, although the text was likely not translated into Tangut. The colophon to the Tibetan translation preserved in the Beijing edition of the text contains the following passage:[255]

> *'phags pa 'bum gsal brtsegs pa zhes bya ba'i gtsug lag khang chen po'i 'dabs su / gnas brtan chen po su ra sa pa hye na gyon ti shi'i phyag dpe la bris nas / shākya'i*

[255] van der Kuijp, "Jayānanda. A Twelfth Century Guoshi from Kashmir among the Tangut," 192 partially translated the passage three decades ago. However, due to the damage of the text, he says, "I reproduce these lines in the hope that someone else can do more with it than I have been able to."

> *dge slong smon lam rgyal bas gzhan las sbyin par bya ba'i chos su bzhengs nas spyan drangs pa'o* / /[256]
>
> In the vicinity of the temple called "Noble Accumulation of One Hundred Thousand Lights," the great elder, imperial preceptor Su ra sa pa, who wears the black robe[257] wrote it onto a manuscript. Afterward, the monk Smon lam rgyal ba, having established it as a religious book for distribution, retrieved it.

There are two things worth noting here. The imperial preceptor Su ra sa pa, whose identity remains clear,[258] was the one who wrote the translation down. Hence, this was likely also a state-sponsored teamed project involving Jayānanda, Ānandakīrti as well as an imperial preceptor, just like the projects of *Uṣṇīṣavijaya-dhāraṇī*, the *Ratnaguṇasaṃcayagāthā*. The second point is the role played by Smon lam rgyal ba in the production of the text. The expression "established it as a religious book for distribution" (*sbyin par bya ba'i chos su bzhengs*) seems to mean exactly what is advocated by the State Buddhism – printing the text and distributing it to the people of the state. It is, therefore, not impossible that the text in the Beijing edition was derived from a block print prepared by Smon lam rgyal ba.

In short, we might conclude that the Tangut court intentionally put Jayānanda in a position where he could appeal to a Tibetan audience, who, then, would further contribute to the development of Buddhism in the Tangut State. Although the Tanguts do not seem to favor Indic

---

[256] *Bstan 'gyur* 61, 948, n. 899.

[257] "Who wears the black robe" is my temporary solution for the intriguing phrase *hye na gyon*. The word *gyon* here is understood as a verb, "to wear." The word *hye na* is understood as a phonetic transcription of the Tangut [illegible] *gjwi*^{2} *nja̱*^{1}, "black robe." The black robe is an honorary outfit given to esteemed monks; see Han, "*Tiansheng gaijiu xinding lüling* zhong suo fanying de Xixia Fojiao," 85–86. The only problem is that the Tangut word would normally be [illegible], "black-robe," instead of [illegible], "robe-black." But the Tangut way of placing the adjective with a noun is not definite and it is possible to put it after the head noun. Also, the Tibetans could have altered the position of the adjective when transcribing it.

[258] It seems this is a Tibetan nickname rather than a phonetic transcription of a Tangut name. There is a temptation to identify Su ra with Pu nja̱, the first segment of the name of the imperial preceptor Pu nja̱ bu̱ dźju, if we consider *su* as a mistake for *pu* – cursive dbu med Tibetan su and pu are almost indistinguishable. However, this seems to be unlikely. And it much more plausible that Su ra sa pa is a different imperial preceptor from Pu nja̱ bu̱ dźju.

scholars over their Tibetan counterparts, the Tibetans would usually see an Indic scholar like Jayānanda as an authoritative person with whom they could learn well. This tendency is, for example, evident in the story of Rgwa Lo tsā ba mentioned in Section 1. Rgwa Lo tsā ba was somewhat disappointed at first since he planned not to go all the way to India just to study with Rtsa mi Lo tsā ba, who, in his eyes, was just another Tibetan. Jayānanda, not only an Indic-Kashmiri master but also an exceptional scholar in Buddhist philosophy, was supposedly popular among the Tibetans. In fact, it is highly possible when he left Tibet, he did not leave alone but with an entourage of Tibetans, among which Ānandakīrti was undoubtedly one. These Tibetans were likely either followers of his *prasaṅgika-madhyamaka* position or simply admirers of his expertise in Buddhist philosophy. Another possible member of the entourage, Rma bya Byang chub brtson 'grus (d. ca. 1185), was a key figure in transmitting Gsang phu scholasticism to the Tanguts. Rma bya was first a student of Phya pa but was later converted to Jayānanda's philosophical position. His presence in the Tangut State is now attested and we will return to him in Chapter Four, Section 3, and in Chapter Four, Section 3, work no. 15.

Therefore, Jayānanda's career in the Tangut State in the mid-twelfth century left two major legacies: texts and people. Although, for most of the time, in an indirect manner, he helped the Tanguts translate some Buddhist texts into Tangut that we regard as forming a part of State Buddhism. Working mainly with his Tibetan colleague Kun dga' grags / Ānandakīrti, he also translated texts into Tibetan, which was intended for a Tibetan audience within the Tangut State. His second legacy, people, was probably more far-reaching. Jayānanda's charismatic persona as an Indic master and a prominent scholar in Buddhist philosophy attracted learned Tibetan masters from Central Tibet to follow him to the Tangut land. Some of these figures, including Kun dga' grags / Ānandakīrti and Rma bya, were critical in promoting Tibetan Buddhism in the Tangut State.

Not only these figures who went with him, but other Tibetan who were already in the Tangut State were presumably also effectively rallied under the call of him, a state preceptor of the realm. To this end, the Tangut State also achieved another great success in maintaining a multiethnic state by assigning specific religious duties to Jayānanda.

4. Interlude: Local Tangut Buddhist Traditions

As Tibetan Buddhism slowly permeated the Tangut State in the mid-twelfth century, the Tanguts did not only translate Tibetan texts but also started to compose their own indigenous works on Buddhism based on their knowledge of Tibetan Buddhism. However, as pointed out in Chapter Two, Section 2.1, there was never a clear boundary between Chinese Buddhism and Tibetan Buddhism in the minds of the Tangut Buddhists. Therefore, as will be discussed below, when they tried to compose a work on the Tibetan Buddhist tradition, they would nevertheless be influenced by their preexisting knowledge of Chinese Buddhism. Or else, when they set forth to author a treatise on the Chinese Buddhist tradition, they would unwittingly bring their newly acquired knowledge of Tibetan Buddhism into it. So, when they began their own Buddhist enterprise, they creatively but also quite naturally brought the two traditions together, thus resulting in an extraordinarily innovative local tradition. In this section, we will see how two local Tangut traditions grew from a hybridization of Chinese and Tibetan Buddhist influences.

The first is the local Tangut tradition of Mahāmudrā. The Mahāmudrā tradition is an important component of Tibetan tantric Buddhism, particularly of the Bka' brgyud pa school. In Khara-Khoto texts, we find a substantial number of Mahāmudrā texts in either Tangut or Chinese that can be mapped onto the Mahāmudrā tradition in Tibet.[259] However, here, we are dealing with something different, which cannot find its equivalent in the Tibetan tradition.

This local Tangut tradition of Mahāmudrā started with Tśhja źjɨr[260], a Tangut monk who was obviously familiar with the Tibetan tradition and fluent in the Tibetan language. We have seen his name listed as the last one among the masters who transmitted the revised version of the short *Sukhāvatīvyūha Sutra* in Section 3. Therefore, he evidently had the experience of working with Jayānanda and the imperial preceptor Pu nja̱ bu̱ dźju. At that time, likely in the mid-twelfth century, he was only a dharma preceptor. The fact that he was listed as the last person indicates that he was still in his early career. However, by 1167, he was already promoted to state preceptor, and he continued to be successful in his career, which is evinced by the appearance of his name together with his state preceptor title in various colophons. Attested by the colophons, he translated a number of Tibetan tantric texts into Tangut, and he likely translated more. He was still alive in 1184 but probably died before 1189.[261] Tśhja źjɨr was undoubtedly one of the most influential Tangut Buddhists in the twelfth century and was critical in introducing Tibetan Buddhism, especially the tantric traditions, into the Tangut State.

In 1152, when Tśhja źjɨr was wandering in the Tsong kha area, he met a Tibetan master called Diligence (Khu dźjij 𗎗𗢳, Tib. *Brtson 'grus).[262] One night, when Master Diligence was giving a lecture, Tśhja źjɨr was in an audience of more than ten Tibetan Buddhists. That was when

---

[259] See Sun and Nie, *Xixiawen Zangchuan Fojiao shiliao*, chaps. 1–5.

[260] For Tśhja źjɨr, see Dunnell, "Translating History from Tangut Buddhist Texts," 47–49.

[261] Dunnell, "Translating History from Tangut Buddhist Texts," 48.

[262] I have temporarily identified Master Diligence with Rma bya. See Ma, "Introduction to Speculative Thinking," 36–43.

Tśhja źjɨr received the teaching on Mahāmudrā.[263] According to Tśhja źjɨr, Master Diligence was the eighth master and the only Tibetan master in his transmissional lineage of Mahāmudrā. One of the earlier Indic masters in that lineage, the fourth master Maitrīpa, was a typical figure in various Mahāmudrā lineages. But other masters, including the seventh master, "Language-Lord" (Ŋwu̱ djzu 𗏹𗉘, *Vagīśvara?), cannot be identified with certainty.[264] In any case, this transmissional lineage was already different from the mainstream Mahāmudrā lineage in Tibet, which was transmitted from Nāropa to Mar pa Chos kyi blo gros (ca. 1012–1097) and further down to various Bka' brgyud pa masters. Having received the oral transmission from Master Diligence, Tśhja źjɨr wrote down the instruction in Tangut and named it *The Collection of the Ultimate Instruction of the Great Seal* (𗼃𗁦𗆗𗓦𗄈𗤶, henceforth the *Ultimate Instruction*).

We can confidently subsume the *Ultimate Instruction* under the Mahāmudrā tradition because the central concept of the work, "no-thought" (𗅋𗧓), is an equivalent of *amanasikāra*, the core notion of Mahāmudrā.[265] Other key concepts such as the inner heat (𗤻𗏵, Skt. *caṇḍālī*, Tib. *gtum mo*) and essential drop (𗢳𗥤, Skt. *bindu*, Tib. *thig le*) are also typical components in Indo-Tibetan tantric Buddhism. However, it is difficult to conclude that the *Ultimate Instruction* is a record that faithfully translates everything Master Diligence said. The most striking feature here is the literary style of the work. Tśhja źjɨr wrote most of it in beautiful Chinese *pianwen* 駢文 (four-six prose) style, just like most of the sentences we have seen in the *Preface to the "Five Sutras."* This literary style, which never existed in Tibetan literary culture, heavily influenced Tangut

[263] For this episode, see Solonin, "Xixiawen Dashouyin wenxian zakao," 243–247.

[264] Solonin has tentatively identified him with the Newar master Bal po Skye med. See Solonin, "Xixiawen Dashouyin wenxian zakao," 259–261.

[265] Solonin, "Mahāmudrā Texts in the Tangut Buddhism and the Doctrine of No- thought."

literature. It is almost impossible to translate Tibetan – even Tibetan verse – into Tangut *pianwen*. Let us examine the following summary of the qualities of the inner fire in the *Ultimate Instruction*:

> [illegible]? [266]
>
> The fire burns below, which can extinguish the affliction of a hundred kinds of sickness; the medicine flows above, which allows the rise of the magical virtue of ten thousand kinds of happiness. [Since] the old becomes young, how would one's appearance be rivaled by the sun and moon (i.e., the day and the month); [as] the short is made long, how could one's life be matched with the *qian* and *kun*?[267]

Not only do the sentences have to be divided into segments of four and six characters, but a pair of sentences must contain an antithesis. In the first two sentences, "fire" contrasts "medicine"; "burns" contrasts "flows"; below contrasts "above," etc. This phenomenon rarely occurs in Tibetan Buddhist writings, and it is hard to imagine a whole teaching would be put in this way. Especially in the latter two sentences, the "sun and the moon" is made an opposite to the "*qian* and *kun*." The term *qian kun* 乾坤 is clearly a Chinese concept. And "sun, moon, *qian*, and *kun*" (*ri yue qian kun* 日月乾坤) is a set phrase in Chinese literature that indicates the transformational dynamics of the cosmos. Therefore, we can conjecture that Tśhja źjir perhaps never memorized the teaching of Master Diligence and then translated it into Tangut. Instead, he likely first understood the essential meanings of the teaching and then rewrote it so that it could better suit Tangut practitioners' cultural background.

---

[266] Sun and Nie, *Xixiawen Zangchuan Fojiao shiliao*, 315.

[267] The *qian* and *kun* are the two major signs of divination in the Chinese tradition, here translated by Tangut [illegible].

In addition to the Chinese literary style, Tśhja źjɨr's background in Chinese Buddhism is also evident in the *Ultimate Instruction*. Having introduced the masters in his transmissional lineage, Tśhja źjɨr claims that his immediate master, Diligence, gave him the following programming instruction:

> [illegible]
>
> > [illegible]
> > [illegible]
>
> [illegible] [268]
>
> At that time, the master said: anything that moves and anything that subsides are equal in terms of their source; anything pure and anything stained are identical in terms of their nature. [When] the qualities of no-thought manifest, the image in the clear wave appears. Therefore, the following verse was stated:
>
> > [When] thought and thought subsides and subsides, the mind excels and excels,
> > [When] mind and mind excels and excels, the thought subsides and subsides.
> > If there is no thought about subsiding and subsiding, or excelling and excelling,
> > Then the mind and mind, and the thought and thought, would be established as enlightened.
>
> As soon as I, the unintelligent disciple, heard this seal, my body and mind were saturated, and I danced joyfully. It is difficult to illustrate it by netting a golden bird in the sky; it exceeds much more than catching a jade rabbit in the water.

There would be almost no way for the term "clear wave" ([illegible]) to be spoken by a Tibetan tantric master. This term, which renders the Chinese *bocheng* 波澄, is a stock example in Huayan Buddhism, which is used as an analogy to enlightened status. Hence, in the Huayan Chan tradition,

---

[268] Sun and Nie, *Xixiawen Zangchuan Fojiao shiliao*, 302.

there are practices such as the Oceanic Seal of Meditative Stabilization (Haiyin sanmei 海印三昧), which aims at stabilizing the mind like the tranquil surface of the ocean. To this end, Tśhja źjɨr is again not quoting directly what Master Diligence said but is rephrasing it in the context of the Huayan Chan, a tradition already popular among the Tanguts by Tśhja źjɨr's time.

The verse allegedly spoken by Master Diligence is even more curious. It cannot be translated back into anything closer to a Tibetan verse because it would result in a bunch of repetitive *dran pa* and *zhi ba* that do not make much sense. Yet, it could be translated well into a Chinese verse that would sound typical in any Chan text. It would read:

念念寂寂心妙妙，心心妙妙念寂寂。
寂寂妙妙若無念，心心念念正覺成。

I do not suggest this verse in fact appears in any Chinese Chan text. However, the most salient feature here – the use of doubled characters – endows the verse with much Chan flavor. In particular, the phrase "mind and mind" ([illegible] < Ch. *xin xin* 心心) and "thought and thought" ([illegible] < Ch. *nian nian* 念念) appear in Chan texts very frequently. While there is no way for us to know what master Diligence exactly said in the verse, it must be quite different from what is framed by Tśhja źjɨr here. By creatively putting the core concept of Mahāmudrā, in the framework of Chan Buddhism in general, Tśhja źjɨr made a smooth transition from an essentially foreign concept to a familiar foundation in which the Tangut practitioners were already grounded.

The *Ultimate Instruction* does not stand alone as a single text that represents the Tangut local tradition of Mahāmudrā. After the composition of the *Ultimate Instruction*, several Tangut prose commentaries were written on the *Ultimate Instruction*,[269] thus making it a full-fledged tantric tradition with a basic text in a metrical format and commentaries. The Tangut local tradition of Mahāmudrā, which sprouted from the soil of Tibetan Buddhism but was imbued with Chinese Buddhism and culture, was therefore brought into maturity.

The second local Tangut Buddhist tradition we will examine is the tradition of the *Diamond Sutra*. The *Diamond Sutra* was one of the most important sutras ever since the beginning of Tanguts' translation of Buddhist scriptures from Chinese.[270] Until the mid-twelfth century, the study of the *Diamond Sutra* in the Tangut State had been exclusively based on the Chinese tradition. However, with the introduction of Tibetan Buddhism, Tibetan Buddhism elements also begin to accompany the Tanguts' engagement with the *Diamond Sutra*, thus forming a fascinating local tradition. The following two cases will illustrate this important development.

The first case is a Tangut narrative of Kumārajīva (344–413), the Kucha monk who translated the *Diamond Sutra* into Chinese. The narrative appears in a Tangut commentary on the *Diamond Sutra*.[271] Since the Tangut translation of the *Diamond Sutra* was translated from Chinese, it preserves the original colophon indicating it was translated by Kumārajīva into Chinese. Hence, Nẹw dźiej 𗏁𗍫[272], our commentator, includes in his commentary an explanation of the name "Kumārajīva." What is amazing about this explanation is that Nẹw dźiej states Kumārajīva had

[269] See Solonin, *Dapeng zhanchi*, chap. 3. I have also briefly examined one of the commentaries, which is written on #3817. See Ma, "Facheng de 'Qibu liang lun' zai Xixia," 74–75.

[270] For a study of the tradition of the *Diamond Sutra* in the Tangut State, see Arakawa, *Seikabun Konggo kyō no kenkyū*.

[271] For an examination of the narrative, see Solonin, "Textual Evidence for Sino-Tibetan Buddhism in Xixia," 469–475.

[272] Ch. Shanxin 善信. According to Solonin, he was likely a monk in the lineage of the Chan master Tongli Hengce 通理恆策 (1049–1098) of the Liao and he likely flourished after the demise of the Liao in 1125. See Solonin, *Dapeng zhanchi*, chap. 2, § 2.

several different identities in India and Tibet. In particular, he claims Kumārajīva was Dignāga when he was teaching Buddhist epistemology and Kamalaśīla when he was teaching Madhyamaka. He further says Kumārajīva was no one else but Kṛṣṇapāda the junior – his Tibetan name would be Nag po zhabs chung ba - when he was giving instructions in tantric practices in Tibet. And finally – Nẹw dźiej continues – Kumārajīva chose the name Kumārajīva when he went to China to transmit and translate sutras and Buddhist treatises.[273]

Setting aside the ahistorical and fantastic nature of the narrative, what is at stake here is that both Kamalaśīla and Kṛṣṇapāda the junior and their individual activities were unknown in the Chinese Buddhist tradition. Yet they were widely known among the Tibetan Buddhists. Also, while Dignāga was representative of Buddhist epistemology in the Chinese tradition, in Nẹw dźiej's narrative, his name was rendered as [illegible], meaning literally "region-elephant." This is undoubtedly a Tibetan style rendering reflecting the Tibetan *phyogs glang*.[274] We do not know if this narrative of Kumārajīva was a product of Nẹw dźiej's originality or stemmed from other sources. In any case, framing Kumārajīva's life in such a manner allowed him to go beyond the specific identity of a Central Asian monk in China and establish him as a figure who transcends time, place, and the confinement of a single Buddhist tradition. Such an endeavor of constructing the identity of Kumārajīva fuels the tradition of the *Diamond Sutra* with the potential to allow the Tangut Buddhists who were only familiar with the *Diamond Sutra* to greatly expand their horizons and freely link themselves to Indo-Tibetan Buddhist epistemology, Madhyamaka, and tantric practices. In this sense, the function of this narrative of Kumārajīva is like the *matṛka* in

[273] For a translation of the narrative, see Solonin, "Textual Evidence for Sino-Tibetan Buddhism in Xixia," 469–473.

[274] If this were to be a Chinese style rendering, then it would likely be a phonetic transcription of the Chinese name Chenna 陳那.

Abhidharma literature – a simple list of items can potentially bring together an extremely sophisticated system.

The second case of the Tangut local tradition of the *Diamond Sutra* is also a commentary on the *Diamond Sutra*.[275] But in this case, it is a Tangut translation of a Tibetan work. Entitled *The Lamp Commentary That Clarifies the Meaning of the Great Ārya-vajracchedikā-prajñā-pāramitā Sutra* ([illegible], **'Phags pa shes rab kyi pha rol tu phyin pa rdo rje gcod pa mdo sde chen po'i don gsal bar byed pa'i sgron me 'grel pa*, henceforth the *Lamp Commentary*), the author of the work, according to the colophon, is "Dharma Master Su bo̱" ([illegible]). Su bo̱ might be a Tangut phonetic transcription of Sum pa.[276] If that is the case, then Su bo̱ was from the Sum pa area located at the border between today's TAR and Qinghai Province. The fact that his name is prefixed with the title dharma master suggests that he served in the court of the Tangut State. The translator of the text is recorded as Źjir swew [illegible], a Tangut preceptor who appears to have flourished in the late twelfth and early thirteenth centuries.[277]

The tradition of the *Diamond Sutra* never became significant in the Tibetan intellectual history of the Later Diffusion. Hence, it is remarkable that Su bo̱ composed a work in Tibetan on the subject of the *Diamond Sutra*. The *Lamp Commentary* follows in general the structure of Kamalaśīla's commentary on the *Diamond Sutra*,[278] thus indicating Su bo̱'s expertise in the *Diamond Sutra* might be derived from the tradition of the Imperial Period. Strikingly, Su bo̱ also

---

275 For a detailed study of the text, see Li, "Xixiawen *Xianming sheng jingang neng duan zhi shenghui bi'an dajing yi dengju ji yanjiu*."

276 Li, "Xixiawen *Xianming sheng jingang neng duan zhi shenghui bi'an dajing yi dengju ji yanjiu*," 47. The nasal ending *-m* is often dropped in Tangut transcription. Whether *bo* could be *pa* is less certain.

277 For Źjɨr swew, see Dunnell, "Translating History from Tangut Buddhist Texts," 58–64.

278 Li, "Xixiawen *Xianming sheng jingang neng duan zhi shenghui bi'an dajing yi dengju ji yanjiu*," 105–134.

included many elements from the Chinese tradition of the *Diamond Sutra* in his text. In particular, he seems to be heavily influenced by the *Guide to the Meaning of the Diamond Sutra* (*Jingang banruo jing zhi zan* 金剛般若經旨贊, T 2735), which was written by the Tang monk Tan Kuang 曇曠.[279] For example, Tan Kuang's claim that the word "diamond" has ten meanings (*shi yi* 十義), which does not appear to exist in the Indo-Tibetan tradition. Not only is this framework completely inherited by Su bo̱, but the text of Tan Kuang is also paralleled in Su bo̱'s commentary.[280]

We do not know if Su bo̱ composed the commentary after he served the Tangut court. If so, then his motivation for incorporating the Chinese tradition of the *Diamond Sutra* might be similar to that of Tśhja źjɨr in his *Ultimate Instruction* – making it better suited to the intellectual background of his Tangut audience. Yet by translating the text into Tangut, Źjɨr swew introduced the Tangut audience to Kamalaśīla's ideas, of which they likely had no previous knowledge.

What is shared in all three cases discussed in this section is that the Tanguts tried to make a smooth path for Tibetan Buddhism, which was essentially foreign at that time, to enter the existent realm of Tangut Buddhism, which first stemmed from Chinese Buddhism. In a loose sense, this is reminiscent of the Geyi 格義 Buddhism. When Buddhism was first introduced to Chinese people in the first centuries of the first millennium, some translators intended to use concepts in Daoism to translate Buddhist terms to make them more accessible. However, what is different in the case of the Tangut State is that all the hybridization was made within the larger context of Buddhism. This made the process of bringing the Tibetan and Chinese Buddhist traditions a much more natural and effective one. We also realize that the process was not predicated on the random

279 Li, "Xixiawen *Xianming sheng jingang neng duan zhi shenghui bi'an dajing yi dengju ji yanjiu*," 134–150.

280 Li, "Xixiawen *Xianming sheng jingang neng duan zhi shenghui bi'an dajing yi dengju ji yanjiu*," 134–140.

match of both traditions. The way of connecting both traditions was meticulously programmed by the Tanguts. We have seen, for instance, that Tśhja źjɨr creatively reframed *amanasikāra*, the core idea of Mahāmudrā, in the Huayan Chan tradition, which could not only be understood by the Tanguts but could also well reflect the nature of the concept. In this regard, the Tanguts did not only bring both traditions together for the pragmatic purpose of making Tibetan Buddhism accessible, but they innovatively initiated the Tangut local Buddhist traditions, which are essentially coherent and self-sufficient.

5. The Establishment of the Bka' brgyud Hegemony in the Tangut State: Stories of Three Missionaries

Given the local development of Tangut Buddhism in the mid to late twelfth century, one might expect a bloom of the local traditions in the early thirteenth century, when the history of the Tangut State was approaching its end. However, contrary to that assumption, what we really see in the later period of the Tangut reception of Tibetan Buddhism was a strong Tangut adherence to a number of Bka' brgyud masters, who, serving as preceptors in the Tangut State, instructed mainly tantric practices to their Tangut audience. The section, by delineating the careers of three key Bka' brgyud masters in the Tangut State, tries to reveal the internal dynamics that facilitated the establishment of the Bka' brgyud hegemony in the final phase of the rise of Tibetan Buddhism in the Tangut State.

5.1. Yar klungs pa Chos kyi seng ge (1144–1204)

In Tangut sources, there is a figure called "Religious Lion, the State Preceptor who Clarifies Enlightenment" ([illegible], in #7116, etc.). Alternatively, his name is spelled out as "Master ·Ja ljow sjɨ pja Religious Lion" ([illegible], in #821, etc.). Nishida was the first to surmise that the name ·Ja ljow sjɨ pja was probably a Tangut phonetic transcription of the Tibetan Yar klungs pa.[281] Based on this clue, later scholars tried to identify the figure in Tibetan sources.[282] However, the effort had remained inconclusive until a remarkable recent study by Zeng Hanchen, which allows us to conclude on the basis of a relatively solid ground that this state preceptor is Yar klungs pa[283] Chos kyi seng ge, who is also known as Dgyer[284] sgom Tshul khrims seng ge (1144–1204) – we will henceforth refer to him as Yar klungs pa.[285]

Based on Zeng's study, Yar klungs pa's life might be summarized as follows: Yar klungs pa was born to the Dgyer clan in the Yar klungs Valley. Chos kyi seng ge was his name at birth, and Tshul khrims seng ge was his name of religion. When he was 19, he went to study with the Bka' brgyud master Phag mo gru pa Rdo rje rgyal po (1110–1170). After the death of Phag mo gru pa, he studied with Mal ka ba can pa (1126–1211). He obviously also studied with Lama Zhang, which is attested by the fact that he named, in Tangut sources, Lama Zhang as the master who transmitted some tantric teachings to him (#821). In Tshal pa's *Red Annals*, one of Lama Zhang's disciples is called Gu shī Rtogs pa yongs su gsal ba, which matches exactly the Tangut title, the State Preceptor who Clarifies Enlightenment. At the age of 38 (1181), he established Shug gseb Monastery in Snye phu, thus initiating the Shug gseb sub-tradition of Bka' brgyud.[286]

---

[281] Nishida, "Seikago butten mokuroku hensan jō no shomondai," xxxix, n. 21.

[282] See Nie, "Dadumin si kao," 96–98; Dunnell, "Translating History from Tangut Buddhist Texts," 51–54; Sun, "Xixia guoshi Fashizi kao."

[283] Alternatively as Yar klung pa or Yar lung pa.

[284] Alternatively as Gyer or Sgyer.

[285] Zeng "Xixia Juezhao guoshi Fashizi zhi jiaofa laiyuan yu shenfen kao."

[286] See Zeng, "Xixia Juezhao guoshi Fashizi zhi jiaofa laiyuan yu shenfen kao," 181–185.

Notwithstanding Zeng's brilliant study of Yar klungs pa, since Yar klungs pa's activities in the Tangut State are not mentioned in any Tibetan source she used, we are still left with the last piece of the puzzle of reconstructing his life as a state preceptor of the Tanguts. To this end, Ti shri Ras pa's biography has now become an extraordinarily valuable source as it contains some mentions of Yar klungs pa. Therefore, it does not help us further make sure that Yar klungs pa is Religious Lion, the state preceptor, but fleshes out his career in the Tangut State.

According to Ti shri Ras pa'i biography, Yar klungs pa was clearly the most important figure who introduced Ti shri Ras pa to the Tangut court. As we will see later, since Ti shri Ras pa's departure from 'Ba' rom Monastery on the seventeenth day of the eighth month of 1195 for the Tangut State,[287] he had a hard time finding patronage. The person who really helped him at this point was Yar klungs pa, who was obviously already active in the Tangut State by that time. It was in the tenth month of 1196 that Ti shri Ras pa arrived in Dba' rong. We do not know where the place was exactly located. However, it should be in the Tangut realm as Ti shri Ras pa was attending a mourning ceremony for a deceased state preceptor.[288] Some days later, he paid homage to Yar klungs pa, who was residing there in Dkar po Monastery. Yar klungs pa asked about Ti shri Ras pa's teachers and inquired whether he had learned certain tantric invocations (*sgrub thabs*, *sādhana*), including the invocation of religious guardians (*chos skyong*). Ti shri Ras pa said his teachers were Sangs rgyas sgom pa[289] and Lama Zhang and that he had learned the invocations.

---

[287] Ras pa dkar po, *Bla ma rin po che 'gro ba'i mgon po ti shri Ras pa'i rnam par thar pa bzhugs pa'i dbu phyogs lags so*, 102.

[288] Ras pa dkar po, *Bla ma rin po che 'gro ba'i mgon po ti shri Ras pa'i rnam par thar pa bzhugs pa'i dbu phyogs lags so*, 106.

[289] Aka Yel pa Ye shes brtsegs (1134–1194), the founder of Yel pa Bka' brgyud.

Yar klungs pa seemed to be happy with his answers and invited Ti shri Ras pa to stay with him. And they later went together to Yar klungs pa's monastery in Tsong kha.[290]

Having stayed together with Yar klungs pa in Tsong kha for a while, Ti shri Ras pa petitioned Yar klungs pa to go to Liangzhou. And here, Yar klungs pa pointed out that going to Liangzhou was not a good choice for Ti shri Ras pa's career:

> Having said, "Now I am going to Liangzhou[291]," I presented my request [to Yar klungs pa]. In response to that, [Yar klungs pa] said, "The best possible choice is to go to [the capital of] Xia[292]. The medium possible choice is to serve as the court chaplain of Tshar rtse 'dze[293]. The least possible choice is to go to Liangzhou." I asked [Yar klungs pa] not to say that. And I asked to go to Liangzhou no matter what.[294]

---

[290] Ras pa dkar po, *Bla ma rin po che 'gro ba'i mgon po ti shri Ras pa'i rnam par thar pa bzhugs pa'i dbu phyogs lags so*, 107.

[291] Sperling, "Further Remarks Apropos of the 'Ba'-rom-pa and the Tanguts," 8, n. 26, regards the term Tibetan *ling cu* as Lingzhou 靈州, though he mentions R. Stein's earlier identification of *ling cu* to be Liangzhou. I propose that *ling cu* should be Liangzhou instead of Lingzhou. And there are two reasons. First, Lingzhou is very close to the Xia capital on its southeast (see Introduction, fig. 1). Given the narrative of Ti shri Ras pa's biography, *ling cu* is obviously closer to Tsong kha than to the Xia capital. Also, in this passage, Ti shri Ras pa first says he wanted to go to *ling cu*, and then he wanted to go to *byang ngos*, which we know is Liangzhou. Hence, *ling cu* and *byang ngos* should be synonyms. Perhaps *byang ngos* refers to the greater Liangzhou area and *ling cu* refers specifically to the city.

[292] The term *'ga'*, which is a Tibetan phonetic transcription of Xia, does not mean the entire Tangut State. Instead, it means specifically the area of the capital.

[293] Unidentified. Given the context, it is probably a Tangut prince.

[294] Ras pa dkar po, *Bla ma rin po che 'gro ba'i mgon po ti shri Ras pa'i rnam par thar pa bzhugs pa'i dbu phyogs lags so*, 108:

> *da ling cur 'gro byas nas zhu ba phul ba la / rab cig yod pa bhar* [read: *'gar*] *song / 'bring zhig yod pa tshar rtse 'dze'i bla mchod gyis / tha ma zhig yod pa ling cur song gsungs / de skad mi gsungs bar zhu / cis kyang byang ngos su 'gro zhus /.*

We do not know why Ti shri Ras pa insisted on going to Liangzhou and not to the capital. One possible explanation is that Liangzhou had a large Tibetan population and was culturally more Tibetan than Tangut or Chinese, thus allowing Ti shri Ras pa to preach more effectively. But Yar klungs pa obviously knew more about the religio-political culture of the Tangut State. His statement shows that, to have a successful career in the Tangut State, one must be closer to the political center, if not to the emperor himself. While unstated in Ti shri Ras pa'i biography, the main monastic residence of Yar klungs pa in the Tangut State appears to be Dadumin 大度民 Monastery, a state-owned monastery near the capital, which is attested by several colophons.[295] Hence, Yar klungs pa himself was keen on the political culture of the Tangut State. During the following few years, Ti shri Ras pa preached in Liangzhou despite Yar klungs pa's frequent urge that he should be more active in the political center. Finally, in around 1200, by making Ti shri Ras pa his delegate (*sna bo*), Yar klungs pa created an opportunity for Ti shri Ras pa to meet alone with the emperor Chunyou 純祐 (r. 1193–1206) in Ganzhou. The meeting can hardly be said to have been a fruitful one. Because there was no interpreter present (*kha lo rtsa ba med pa*), even though Ti shri Ras pa and the emperor were sitting together on the same piece of silk (*dar cig lhan du bsdad pa*), they had no conversation (*gleng slong ni ma byung*).[296] Despite so, there can be no question that Yar klungs pa was critical in facilitating the success of Ti shri Ras pa's career in the Tangut State.

Ti shri Ras pa'i biography does not mention Yar klungs pa's death in 1204. There seems to be only one more mention of him in around the year 1213, when Ti shri Ras pa had a dream in

[295] Nie, "Dadumin si kao."

[296] Ras pa dkar po, *Bla ma rin po che 'gro ba'i mgon po ti shri Ras pa'i rnam par thar pa bzhugs pa'i dbu phyogs lags so*, 112.

which Yar klungs pa took away a large piece of silk from Ti shri Ras pa and put it in the hand of Gtsang po pa Dkon mchog seng ge (d. 1218/1219) – hereafter Gtsang po pa - immediately before the empowerment given to the emperor Zunxun 遵頊 (r. 1211–1223, see below).[297] The dream seems to imply that Yar klungs pa had Gtsang po pa in mind as his successor in the Tangut State despite his close relationship with Ti shri Ras pa, who had to wait until Gtsang po pa passed away.

As mentioned above, Yar klungs pa's name is widely attested by Tangut Buddhist texts. All of these texts are tantric in nature. Many of them are on Mahāmudrā and the Six Doctrines of Nāropa (*na ro chos drug*).[298] Yar klungs pa's name further appears as Cumajie 粗麻蘗 on a Chinese text from Khara-Khoto called the *Essential Instruction on the Body of the Intermediate State, Zhongyoushen yaomen* 中有身要門 (TK. 327). Cumajie was read as *lamagja* in northwestern Chinese dialect. Hence, in it, *la ma* was Tibetan *bla ma*; and *gja* was Yar klungs pa's clan name Dgyer.[299] The fact that his teaching was also translated into Chinese suggests that he had a Chinese audience in addition to his Tangut followers.

5.2. Gtsang po pa Dkon mchog seng ge (d. 1218/1219)

Gtsang po pa (alternatively as Gtsang so ba/Rtsang so ba) was a disciple of the first Karmapa Dus gsum mkhyen pa (1110–1193). When the Tangut emperor, who can only be Renxiao in this case, invited Dus gsum mkhyen pa to the Tangut court, the latter sent Gtsang po pa on his behalf. Gtsang po pa became an imperial preceptor of the Tangut State and received much wealth

[297] Ras pa dkar po, *Bla ma rin po che 'gro ba'i mgon po ti shri Ras pa'i rnam par thar pa bzhugs pa'i dbu phyogs lags so*, 122.

[298] See Zeng, "Xixia Juezhao guoshi Fashizi zhi jiaofa laiyuan yu shenfen kao," 180–183.

[299] For this identification, see Du and Sun, "Heishuichen wenxian suojian 'Cumajie' kao."

from the Tangut emperors and sent some of it back to Mtshur phu Monastery, his home monastery in Tibet.[300] We do not know exactly when Gtsang po pa arrived in the Tangut State, though it must predate 1193, the year when both Dus gsum mkhyen pa and Renxiao died.

The first mention of Gtsang po pa in Ti shri Ras pa's biography is in an entry that is dated around the year 1200 when Gtsang po pa and Ti shri Ras pa had a chance to meet in Ganzhou.[301] Gtsang po pa and Ti shri Ras pa seem to have formed a close relationship thereafter[302] and worked together for important missions at the order of the emperor.

A major challenge faced by the Tangut State during its later final years was the threat of the Mongols. The Mongols had already launched two unsuccessful attacks against it in 1205 and 1206. Having conquered Qocho, they invaded the Tangut State again in 1209. And this time, they successfully broke the front military towns and surrounded Zhongxing, the capital city. Ti shri Ras pa was summoned by the Tangut emperor Anquan 安全 (r. 1206–1211) to Zhongxing. He arrived in early 1210 and performed apotropaic rituals (*dge sbyor*) together with Gtsang po pa and Dpal chen Shi ri phug pa[303] to repel (*bzlog*) the Mongols. As Dpal chen Shi ri phug pa's foot was not well (*zhabs ma bde*), he only showed up for about ten days. But Gtsang po pa and Ti shri Ras pa continued the rituals ,for another three months or so until the submission of the emperor. A major tactic the Mongols used for attacking the capital was to draw water from the Yellow River to flood the city. And Gtsang po pa and Ti shri Ras pa are said to have performed some rituals of offering

---

[300] Sperling, "Lama to the King of Hsia," 33.

[301] Ras pa dkar po, *Bla ma rin po che 'gro ba'i mgon po ti shri Ras pa'i rnam par thar pa bzhugs pa'i dbu phyogs lags so*, 112.

[302] Some sources mention Ti shri Ras pa became a disciple of Gtsang po pa. See Sperling, "Lama to the King of Hsia," 33. However, this is not explicitly stated in Ti shri Ras pa's biography. The tones in Ti shri Ras pa's biography seem to describe their relationship more like colleagues.

[303] Dpal chen Shi ri phug pa was a missionary sent by his master 'Jig rten mgon po to the Tangut State.

on the fifteenth day of the third month of 1210 that turned the tide of the river and swept away (*phyags*) many Mongol soldiers.[304]

In 1211, Zunxu overthrew Anquan and made himself the emperor. Roughly two years later, in 1213, Zunxu made Gtsang po pa the imperial preceptor. Ti shri Ras pa narrates:

> Later, the king asked the spiritual friend Rtsang so ba for an empowerment and offered him the position of imperial preceptor. Then, I was invited by the king to [the capital of] Xia. Rtsang so ba, the imperial preceptor, and Lhu bi, the state preceptor, and I, the three of us, made consecrated a collection of scriptures the king prepared on the Five-Peak[305] Mountain.[306]

Hence, the passage serves as an important clue for us the determine the date – 1213 – when Gtsang po pa became the imperial preceptor.

Gtsang po pa died in 1218 or early 1219, just after Chinggis Khan resumed his attack against the Tangut State in 1217, and he was buried in Liangzhou. Ti shri Ras pa consecrated his reliquary hall (*gdung khang*) and memorial hall (*lha khang*). Thus, Gtsang po pa served five Tangut emperors, namely, Renxiao, Chunyou, Anquan, and Zunxu. The fact that Zunxu appointed him as

---

[304] Ras pa dkar po, *Bla ma rin po che 'gro ba'i mgon po ti shri Ras pa'i rnam par thar pa bzhugs pa'i dbu phyogs lags so*, 119–120.

[305] The Five-Peak Mountain in the Tangut State, which was essentially the Helan Mountain (Ch. Helan shan 賀蘭山), should be distinguished from the Five-Peak Mountain in Shanxi. The Tanguts called it so due to their faith in the actual Five-Peak Mountain in Shanxi.

[306] Ras pa dkar po, *Bla ma rin po che 'gro ba'i mgon po ti shri Ras pa'i rnam par thar pa bzhugs pa'i dbu phyogs lags so*, 122:

> *phyi nas dge ba'i bshes gnyen rtsang so ba la rgyal pos dbang skur zhus / te zhir mnga' gsol / de nas rgyal pos 'ga' na gdan drangs / rtsang so te zhi dang lhu bi gug shi dang nga dang gsum gyis rgyal pos ri lnga sde zhig bzhengs pa la rab gnas byas /.*

the preceptor for the inaugural empowerment bespeaks that he might be the most esteemed Tibetan preceptor among all the preceptors during his time.

His name is rendered as Ljị ka tśjij [illegible], thus "Jewel Lion," in Tangut. The only work of Gtsang po pa that has so far been identified in the Tangut corpus[307] bears the following title:

> [illegible][308]
>
> *The Clear Explanation of What Is to Be Learned by the Bodhisattvas, together with the Path and Result: The Precious Lamp*

The title can be reconstructed as *Byang chub sems dpa'i bslab bya lam dang 'bras bu dang bcas pa gsal bar bshad pa rin chen sgron me*. The text was translated by Źjɨr swew,[309] the Tangut preceptor who translated the *Lamp Commentary* (see Section 4). The work appears to be on the tantric tradition of the Path and Result *(lam 'bras)*.[310] That many copies[311] of this work discovered in Khara-Khoto bespeaks its popularity among the Tanguts.

5.3. Ti shri Ras pa Shes rab seng ge (1164–1236)

---

[307] Dunnell, "Translating History from Tangut Buddhist Texts," 57, says both Tang. 119 and Tang. 120 are compositions of Gtsang po pa. However, there appears to be no evidence showing that Tang. 119 is authored by him. I suggest that we can only identify Tang. 120 as his work. For a brief examination of the work see Nie, "Complementary Notes on the Biography of Jayānanda and Dkon mchog seng ge," 80–82.

[308] Kychanov, *Katalog Tangytckix byddiyckix pamyatnikov Institut Boctokovedeniya Pocciyckoy Akademii Hayk*, 513.

[309] Kychanov, *Katalog Tangytckix byddiyckix pamyatnikov Institut Boctokovedeniya Pocciyckoy Akademii Hayk*, 513.

[310] Nie, "Complementary Notes on the Biography of Jayānanda and Dkon mchog seng ge," 81.

[311] Kychanov, *Katalog Tangytckix byddiyckix pamyatnikov Institut Boctokovedeniya Pocciyckoy Akademii Hayk*, 513–520, lists 29 manuscript fragments of the work.

While Ti shri Ras pa is often regarded as belonging to the 'Ba' rom Bka' brgyud tradition, he in fact studied with other four major Bka' brgyud masters. In addition to 'Ba' rom pa Dar ma dbang phyug (1127–after 1195), he also studied under Lama Zhang, Yel pa Sangs rgyas sgom pa (1134–1194), Stag lung thang pa Bkra shis dpal (1142–1209/1210), and 'Jig rten mgon po. Hence, it might be said that Ti shri Ras pa was holistic Bka' brgyud figure who was educated by almost all the prominent Bka' brgyud masters of his time. We have already seen in the previous two subsections some episodes of how Ti shri Ras pa made contact with Yar klungs pa and Gtsang po pa during his career. Now, let us focus on some major events related to his sojourn in the Tangut State.

The first time Ti shri Ras pa had the idea of going to the Tangut State is associated with a somewhat incidental event. In early 1193, having paid his last tribute to Lama Zhang, who died in the fifth month of that year, in Skyid shod[312], he returned to 'Ba' rom[313]. At that time, his master 'Ba' rom pa was in poor health. Hence, for one month, 'Ba' rom pa's disciples recited sutras and performing rituals to help 'Ba' rom pa recover. During one session, Ti shri Ras pa had a conversation with a curious person sitting close to him:

> A short, old person with grey hair, who was wearing a yellow robe, a yellow cape, and a felt, upright hat[314], appeared and sat next to me. He asked, "Where did you come from?" I replied, "I come from Rtsi bar in the company of tea merchants." He asked, "How many tea merchants were there?" I replied, "There were many. And there were also silk merchants coming from Mdo smad." He said, "Undoubtedly, the religious king who is called the 'King of Tangut,' a rebirth of

[312] That is, the lower river valley of the Skyid River, which is south to Lha sa.

[313] In today's Gser rnyed District, Nag chu City.

[314] The expression "upright hat" (*zhwa cog cog*), which also appears of similar contexts in other Tibetan texts, is very curious. I suggest it refers to the preceptor hat of the Tangut State. See Chapter Two, Section 3. Further research is necessary to determine the expression's exact reference.

Glang ri thang pa[315], has passed away. Now, it is said that he did not have a son but had a grandson, who took over the kingdom. It is said that, in the twelfth year – according to the calculation – he will also acquire the Chinese State. A Central Tibetan called 'Lama Rgya'[316] bestowed him the empowerment. The preceptor who empowered him, the so called 'Spya[n] [l]nga' Lha chen po,'[317] is called 'Lama Pu rangs pa, the Imperial Preceptor' (Bla ma Pu rangs pa ti zhi). There are also Be 'dul, the State Preceptor, 'Brom Da ra di. Other than those, there are many other Central Tibetans [there]. The merit is great!"

Then, upon my return, when I meditated in the evening, since I remembered those words said by him, I had again and again the idea that I needed to go there. The next morning, having thought that I needed to ask more about it, I looked [for him]. Yet, he did not appear.[318]

The old man here is clearly describing a major event that happened in 1193 in the Tangut State, namely the death of Renxiao and the succession of Chunyou. It appears that the old man did not

---

[315] Glang ri thang pa Rdo rje seng ge (1053–1123) was a Bka' gdams pa monk who studied under Po to ba Rin chen gsal (1027–1105).

[316] There is a strong temptation to identify this "Lama Rgya" with Yar klungs pa, whose clan name is Dgyer.

[317] The term Lha chen po seems to be related to Chunyou's reign title Tianqing 天慶, "heavenly festival."

[318] Ras pa dkar po, *Bla ma rin po che 'gro ba'i mgon po ti shri Ras pa'i rnam par thar pa bzhugs pa'i dbu phyogs lags so*, 97:

> *rgad po se thung ba ral gu ser po zhig gon / phyam tse ser po zhig gon / mgo la phying bu'i zhwa cog cog gon pa zhig byung bas nga'i rtsar bsdad / khyod gang nas 'ongs byas pa la / nga rtsi bar nas ja pa dang 'grogs nas 'ongs zer / ja pa ci tsam snang byas pa la / ja pa mang bar snang / mdo smad nas yong ba'i dar pa yang snang zer / ma dris par mdo smad na mi nyag rgyal po bya ba glang ri thang pa'i sku skye ba yin zer ba'i chos rgyal zhig bzhugs pa mya ngan las 'das / da khong rang la sras med tsha bo zhig yod pa rgyal sar phyung zer / bcu gnyis lon / rtsis byas pa la rgya nag po'i yul yang des 'thob zer / de la bla ma rgya zer ba'i dbus pa zhig gis dbang bskur byas / spya nga lha chen po bya ba de'i dbang bskur mkhan bla ma pu rangs pa ti zhi bya ba yin / be 'dul gug shi bya ba dang / 'brom da ra di bya ba dang / de min yang dbus pa mang po yod / bsod nams che zer /*

> *de nas nub mo mal du phyin nas bsgom tsam na / khos zer ba de rnams dran pas yul der 'gro dgos snyam pa rtog pa la yang yang skyes / nangs par yag par dri dgos snyam nas bltas pas kho mi snang /.*

know the event himself but inferred from that fact that numerous merchants were going to the north perhaps to profit from the enthronement of the new emperor, provided that he knew already that Renxiao had been on his deathbed. The old man seems to be quite well informed about the politics in the Tangut State as he is correct about every point that he makes except that Chunyou should, according to Chinese sources, be a son of Renxiao and not a grandson.[319] An interesting point the old man made is that Renxiao, who was born in 1124, was a rebirth of Glang ri thang pa, who died in 1123. The old man disappeared the next day, which suggests that he might be a guest who had connections with the Tangut State and not a local. Ti shri Ras pa seems to be surprised by his unique garment. We should not forget the yellow robe is an honorary garment given by the Tangut court to esteemed monks.[320] It is a pity that Ti shri Ras pa does not tell us the color of his hat, which, following this track of my hypothesis, could be black (see Chapter Two, Section 2.3). And his disappearance the next morning was then probably because he needed to rush back to the Tangut State as well for the new emperor.

So, driven by this motivation, Ti shri Ras pa left 'Ba' rom for the Tangut State in 1195. However, his journey was first hardly successful as he had a hard time obtaining auspices. During the summer of 1196, when Ti shri Ras pa was in Khams, he was really frustrated about the situation and wrote:

> Someone called Dge bshes Rnga mo ba donated a piece of *dar thong*[321]. Other than that, not even a single donor appeared. Having thought, "It seems I have got nothing

[319] The mistake was made probably because Chunyou was born in 1177, when Renxiao was already at the age 54. But could the Chinese sources be wrong, and the old man was correct?

[320] Han, "*Tiansheng gaijiu xinding lüling* zhong suo fanying de Xixia Fojiao," 85.

[321] What *dar thong* means here is not entirely clear, though it must be related to silk.

at all by going to Khams," I thought about going back to Central Tibet. Then I departed for its foothill, Rag nyag[322].[323]

As discussed above, the tide turned when Ti shri Ras pa encountered Yar klungs pa, probably the "Lama Rgya" mentioned by the old person. Appointed by Yar klungs pa, Ti shri Ras pa started to take charge of monasteries in Liangzhou and Ganzhou. While he did not hold a preceptor title at that time, he was undoubtedly favored by the local Buddhist communities. For example, on the twenty-second day of the second month of sheep year, he was invited to a monastery in Go ra:

> Having been invited to Go ra on the day of the twenty-second, the monastic community there held a grand welcome party. On the twenty-fourth day, having made me sit on a large religious throne that was erected there, more than two hundred monastics requested teaching [from me]. Then, I did not sit on the actual seat. Having sat beside it, I taught the religion and guided the monastics.[324]

---

[322] Near today's Yul shul City in present-day Qinghai Province.

[323] Ras pa dkar po, *Bla ma rin po che 'gro ba'i mgon po ti shri Ras pa'i rnam par thar pa bzhugs pa'i dbu phyogs lags so*, 103:

> *dge bshes rnga mo ba zer ba zhig gis dar thong cha gcig byin / de min ster mi gcig kyang ma byung / nga khams su phyin pas cang mi rnyed par snang snyam pas dbus su log la 'gro snyam nas de shod rag nyag du bzhud /.*

[324] Ras pa dkar po, *Bla ma rin po che 'gro ba'i mgon po ti shri Ras pa'i rnam par thar pa bzhugs pa'i dbu phyogs lags so*, 111–112:

> *nyi shu gnyis kyi nyin par go rar gdan drangs nas dge 'dun gyis bsu ba chen po byas / nyi shu bzhi'i nyin par chos khri chen po brtsigs pa la bzhugs su bcug nas / dge bdun nyis brgya lhag tsam gyis chos zhus / de nas gdan sa dngos su mi bsdad / zur du bsdad nas dge 'dun la chos bshad dang khrid byas /.*

The fact that Ti shri Ras pa chose to sit on the side seems to suggest that the seat belonged to Yar klungs pa, who granted him the opportunity to teach there.

Ti shri Ras pa did not receive a preceptor title even after his meeting with Chunyou around 1200, which, as previously discussed, was not a very successful encounter. Only some six years later did the wheel of fortune turn again. In the first month of 1206, Anquan, an uncle of Chunyou, staged a coup and overthrew his nephew. He proclaimed himself the new emperor of the Tangut State. Ti shri Ras pa has the following very detailed account of what happened in Liangzhou in the third month of that year. On the seventeenth day, Anquan arrived in Liangzhou, obviously to show his subjects there that he was the new emperor. On the nineteenth day, Anquan ascended to the dragon throne and gave appointments to his subjects. Ti shri Ras pa met with Anquan on the twenty-second:[325]

> On the twenty-second, I met with the king. I said the prayer. And the king appointed me to the office of a Chan preceptor (*las ka tsen 'dze*). Then, having said, "Wait for a while," in the evening, he appointed me to the office of a state preceptor. He gave appointments to the thirty-two people of my entourage.[326]

And that was no doubt a key moment for Ti shri Ras pa's career in the Tangut State. Ti shri Ras pa does tell us what he thought might be the reason for his rapid promotion in one single day. We

[325] Ras pa dkar po, *Bla ma rin po che 'gro ba'i mgon po ti shri Ras pa'i rnam par thar pa bzhugs pa'i dbu phyogs lags so*, 115.

[326] Ras pa dkar po, *Bla ma rin po che 'gro ba'i mgon po ti shri Ras pa'i rnam par thar pa bzhugs pa'i dbu phyogs lags so*, 115:

> *nyi shu gnyis la rgyal po dang mjal / smon lam btabs / rgyal pos nga la las ka tsen 'dze byin / de nas en cig sdod zer nas rgong* [read: *dgong*] *kar song tsam na las ka gug shi byin / 'khor sum bcu rtsa gnyis la las ka byin /.*

can, however, conjure that Anquan might want to bring in previously marginalized people to the political center to strengthen his power due to his presumable distrust of those who were close to Chunyou.

Ti shri Ras pa continued to be successful in his career. After the death of Gtsang po pa in 1218 or early 1219, Ti shri Ras pa was appointed as the imperial preceptor by Zunxu, obviously succeeding Gtsang po pa's position. His biography says:

> Then, in the seventh month of the rabbit year (1219), having been invited by the king, I went to [the capital of] Xia. In the eighth month, I gave empowerment to the king. On the twenty-fifth day, I was offered the appointment of the imperial preceptor.[327]

However, being an imperial preceptor during the final years of the Tangut State was not an easy task due to the constant Mongol attacks. And Ti shri Ras pa had, again and again, to perform rituals to stop the Mongols. But Ti shri Ras pa realized that the Tangut State would eventually fall. And he pondered, likely after the Mongol conquest:

> Since the karma of every sentient being will ripen, no one can stop it. Even the Blessed One is not excluded from the ripening of karma. It is not the case that all the Buddhas, Bodhisattvas, and the capable guardians of the religion are not protecting [the state]. Since it is certain that the ripening of every sentient being's karma is experienced, it cannot be stopped. Yet, it was not the case that I was not

---

[327] Ras pa dkar po, *Bla ma rin po che 'gro ba'i mgon po ti shri Ras pa'i rnam par thar pa bzhugs pa'i dbu phyogs lags so*, 127:

> *de nas yos bu lo zla ba bdun pa la rgyal pos gdan drangs nas 'gar phyin / zla ba brgyad pa la rgyal po la dbang bskur byas / nyi shu lnga la ti zhi'i las ka phul /.*

> going to protect it, either. Ever since the emergence of the Mongols, I protected [the state] for twenty-seven years by means of religious guardian.[328]

In 1223, as the Mongol attack intensified, Zunxu, afraid of becoming the last emperor of the Tangut State, decided to abdicate and passed down the throne to his son, Dewang 德旺 (r. 1223–1226).[329] The latter obviously could not turn the tide either and was already on his deathbed in the first month of 1226. And Ti shri Ras pa was called to see him:

> I arrived in [the capital of] Xia on the twenty-eighth day. I empowered the king and taught him religion. Then, after twenty days, the king passed away. I performed the ritual of forty-nine days.[330]

Ti shri Ras pa went to Tsong kha thereafter. While Tsong kha was occupied by the Mongols even before they took the capital, he escaped the final destiny of becoming a captive together with the

---

[328] Ras pa dkar po, *Bla ma rin po che 'gro ba'i mgon po ti shri Ras pa'i rnam par thar pa bzhugs pa'i dbu phyogs lags so*, 129:

> *sems can so so'i las kyi rnam par smin pa yin pas gang gis kyang dgag par mi nus so / / bcom ldan 'das kyis kyang las kyi rnam par smin pa ma gtogs so gsungs / sangs rgyas dang byang chub sems dpa' thams cad dang / chos skyong ba'i srung ma nus pa can thams cad kyis mi srung ba ma yin te / sems can so so'i las kyi rnam par smin pa myong bar nges pas de dgag par ma nus pa yin / 'o na yang ma bsrung ba ma yin / hor byung nas lo nyi shu rtsa bdun chos skyong gis bsrung ba yin /.*

[329] The event is documented in Ti shri Ras pa's biography. See Ras pa dkar po, *Bla ma rin po che 'gro ba'i mgon po ti shri Ras pa'i rnam par thar pa bzhugs pa'i dbu phyogs lags so*, 131.

[330] Ras pa dkar po, *Bla ma rin po che 'gro ba'i mgon po ti shri Ras pa'i rnam par thar pa bzhugs pa'i dbu phyogs lags so*, 132:

> *nyi shu brgyad la ghar [read: 'gar] slebs / rgyal po la dbang bskur chos bstan / de nas zhag nyi shun as rgyal po 'das / zhag bzhi bcu zhe dgu'i dge sbyor byas...*

last emperor Xian 睍 (r. 1226–1227) in the capital. Despite some hardships, he successfully went back to Central Tibet and spent his last years there.

Ti shri Ras pa's works have not yet been identified among Khara-Khoto texts. And this is somehow understandable: Ti shri Ras pa came to the Tangut State at a relatively late point and became only influential among the Tanguts after 1206. This is also probably why we find many Tangut translations of the works of Yar klungs pa, who presumably went to the Tangut land earlier than Gtsang po pa, of whom we have only identified one work so far. We also need to keep in mind that Khara-Khoto is a borderland military town which is far from the capital. Therefore, even if Ti shri Ras pa's works had been translated in the capital, it would take them some time to travel to Khara-Khoto.

The establishment of the Bka' brgyud hegemony in the Tangut State during the final phase of the rise of Tibetan Buddhism was not accidental. At the beginning of this chapter, we have seen how Rtsa mi Lo tsā ba became a cultural hero in the Bka' brgyud school. Rtsa mi Lo tsā ba was regarded by the Bka' brgyud masters as embodying three identities – a Tangut master, a Tibetan master, and a great tantric practitioner, especially in the tradition of Mahākāla. Rtsa mi Lo tsā ba's disciple Rgwa Lo tsā ba had disciples such as Phag mo gru pa, Lama Zhang, and Dus gsum mkhyen pa. And the three figures discussed in this section are all connected to them. Yar klungs pa was a disciple of Phag mo gru pa and Lama Zhang, Gtsang po pa was a disciple of Dus gsum mkhyen pa, and Ti shri Ras pa was a disciple of Lama Zhang and 'Jig rten mgon po, who was further a disciple of Phag mo gru pa. While we do not see these Tibetan figures in the Tangut State mentioning Rtsa mi Lo tsā ba, the latter indirectly shaped their relationship with the Tangut State.

Another factor for the establishment of the Bka' brgyud hegemony is the strong will and the ability of the Bka' brgyud masters to secure patronage. Twelfth-century Tibet saw the affluence of many newly founded religious institutions. However, these institutions also faced intensified competition in getting hold of more land, resources, and followers. While institutions such as Sa skya Monastery had a strong clan structure to support it, most Bka' brgyud lineages did not have that privilege and had to attract external auspices. Sørensen and Hazod suggest, "Two basic factors proved indispensable for their proliferation: the rigorous assertion of authority, divine or worldly, and the ability to attract a steadily growing circle of followers (along with ample patronage)."[331] I would rather see the former as a means to achieve the latter, and the latter as the end that stimulates the cultivation of the former. We have seen how they can be mapped onto the Bka' brgyud figures in the Tangut State. Ti shri Ras pa had made it clear that a major purpose of his journey was to secure patronage. And he felt extremely distressed when he was ignored by the people of Khams. Yar klungs pa, when offering the three different choices to Ti shri Ras pa, was obviously thinking about their different chances of obtaining optimal patronage. And the successes of all three figures were undoubtedly predicated on their capacity to show their religious authority. Yar klungs pa, when interviewing Ti shri Ras pa, asked in particular if he had been trained in the invocation of protective deities. Gtsang po pa was asked by Zunxu to give him the empowerment as a way to enhance his legitimacy. And Ti shri Ras pa worked tirelessly to protect the Tangut State from the Mongol invasion by performing a variety of rituals. Therefore, the ascendency of the Bka' brgyud tradition in the Tangut State was also inextricably linked to its own institutional nature of seeking a strong patron-priest tie.

[331] Sørensen and Hazod, *Rulers on the Celestial Plain*, 11.

Not only appealing to the Tangut emperors, who were obviously interested in State Buddhism, but these charismatic Bka' brgyud masters were also centers of Individual Buddhism because many Buddhists within the Tangut realm attended to and received teachings from them. The many copies of the Tangut translations of Yar klungs pa and Gtsang po pa's tantric teachings support this claim. These Tangut Buddhists, eager for spiritual attainments, were resolute followers of these Tibetan masters, who could lead them to that goal with their powerful tantric instructions. While we have not yet identified any Ti shri Ras pa's work in Tangut translation – nothing seems to be extant in Tibetan either –, his biography tells us much about his popularity among the Buddhists of the Tangut State. As we have seen, in 1199, not long after his arrival in the Tangut State, he was welcomed with much hospitality and was requested to give teachings to more than two hundred monastics.

When examining the careers of the three Bka' brgyud figures, an interesting phenomenon that emerges is how the social networks between the Bka' brgyud figures facilitated their success. This does not necessarily mean they held self-consciously a common Bka' brgyud identity. But, we notice that when Ti shri Ras pa named Lama Zhang as one of his teachers, Yar klungs pa was satisfied with that answer, supposedly because Lama Zhang was also his own teacher. Gtsang po pa, at least according to the biography of Ti shri Ras pa, was a friendly and supportive colleague of Ti shri Ras pa, even though they did not share a common teacher. In fact, when we think more critically about the episode in which Gtsang po pa and Ti shri Ras pa performed months of rituals to fend off the Mongols in early 1210, such smooth cooperation should not be taken for granted. It must have been preceded by their long-term partnership. It is also very likely that the rituals they collectively performed were shared in the larger Bka' brgyud tradition, thus allowing them to work together seamlessly without much rehearsal before. Therefore, I suggest the social networks under a shared Bka' brgyud tradition dramatically strengthened the ties between the individual Tibetans who were foreign to the Tangut land.

In a more general sense, the establishment of Bka' brgyud hegemony also signaled the triumph of Tibetan tantric Buddhism of all the Buddhist traditions in the development of Buddhism in the Tangut State. The sheer number of tantric texts belonging to the Tibetan tradition attests to it. And many of the traditions, such as the Bka' brgyud Mahāmudrā tradition, continued to be practiced by Chinese practitioners in the Yuan, Ming, and Qing periods.[332] On the other hand, most local Tangut traditions, such as Tśhja źjɨr's Mahāmudrā tradition, do not appear to have been passed down to later generations after the demise of the Tangut State.

6. Epilogue: 'Phags pa and His Tangut Audience

The Mongol conquest of the Tangut State in 1227 came with much bloodshed. Not only many Tanguts, but Chinggis Khan himself died during the war. Nevertheless, those Tanguts who survived the catastrophe started to be employed by the Mongols and serve in the Mongol army and government. In particular, the Tangut clergy began to exert its influence over the Mongols and convert some of them to Buddhists.

As the Mongol conquest of China continued, Köden, the second son of Ögedei Khan (1186–1241), was granted the old Tangut realm as his fiefdom in 1229 by his father. While his famous meeting with Sa paṇ in 1247 marks a milestone in the Mongol reception of Tibetan Buddhism, Köden was already familiar with Buddhism prior to it through the Tangut agency. The postscript of a Tangut block print version of the *Sitātapatrā-dhāraṇī*, which is from a private

---

[332] A major witness of the trend is the *Esoteric Collection of the Essential Way of Mahāyana, Dacheng yaodao miji* 大乘要道密集. See Shen, "*Dacheng yaodao miji* yu Xixia Yuan chao suo chuan Xizang mifa."

collection, is an important witness here.[333] While the main text is fragmentary, the postscript was kept intact and reads:

> I, the humble one, have heard that *Sitātapatrā-dhāraṇī*, a magical spell that comes from the crown of the Buddha's head, is an essential seal of the Buddhas and a profound religious treasury. It is hard to assess its power. And its magical quality is unlimited. Therefore, when practicing in accordance with the way of chanting it and holding on to it, or if affixing the writing of it to one's body, or if putting it on the top of a victorious banner, one's death is avoided, one's life increases, one's sickness is cured and removed, one's offspring flourishes, and the evils, disasters, ghosts and spirits cannot inflict any harm. One's house would remain peaceful, and one's country would be pacified. In this life, the serious transgressions one committed would be cleared away, and one's faculty would be pure in terms of the disciplines. When one passes away, one would be reborn in the most pleasant land and reach enlightenment. Every disaster and calamity would be cleared away without remainder; all that one pursues could be fulfilled as one wishes.
>
> Having seen such magical qualities, the monk of the Śākya clan[334], the state preceptor Buddhavajra[335], makes the following great prayer: I wish the crown prince of the emperor, Köden[336], would have his blessing increasing, would have no sickness, and have his life prolonged. Also, I wish the sentient beings would be benefited, their transgressions would be cleared away, and they would attain happiness. Hence, I recruited artisans and carved the woodblock. I made them print one thousand volumes for each in the Tibetan, Tangut, and Chinese languages. And I distributed them to both the monastics and the laypeople. By means of this virtuous power, I only wish that ten thousand years would come to the crown prince of the emperor, Köden, and one thousand autumns[337] would be seen by him. The foundation of the country would be steady and solid, the fortune of the common people would flourish, and all beings of the universe would be enlightened.

---

[333] The block print has been examined by Shi Jinbo together with a Chinese translation of its text. See Shi, "Xixiawen *Da baisangai tuoluoni jing* ji fayuanwen kaoshi."

[334] [illegible], equivalent of *shākya'i dge slong*.

[335] [illegible], Bu dja bja dzjɨ rjar.

[336] [illegible], Ko tja. See discussion below. The crown prince was in fact Güyük (1206–1248), the eldest son of Ögedei Khan, who succeeded his father in 1246. The author of the postscript here obviously tries to elevate Köden's position.

[337] The two phrases in the sentence, "ten thousand years" ([illegible] < Ch. *wansui* 萬歲) and "one thousand autumns" ([illegible] < Ch. *qianqiu* 千秋) are common phrases in Chinese literary culture that indicate an extreme long time.

Humbly distributed and disseminated on the day and in the month[338] of the *jiachen*[339] year of the country of the Great Dynasty[340]. Distributed by the crown prince of the Eastern Stairs[341].[342]

The postscript contains several key pieces of historical information. What we immediately notice is Köden's name appears in it. The Tangut Ko tja [illegible] is a phonetic transcription. While it lacks the nasal ending *-n*, it can be explained by the fact that the nasal ending of a syllable is often dropped in the northwestern Chinese dialect, a linguistic phenomenon that undoubtedly influenced

---

338 The specific day and month are not filled in the block print. They were intentionally left blank to be filled later on the day of the actual distribution.

339 [illegible], a year in the sexagenary cycle of the Chinese calendar. See discussion below.

340 For "Great Dynasty," See discussion below.

341 According to the Chinese tradition, the palace of the crown prince is in the east of the royal palace.

342 I use the transcription of the text from Shi, "Xixiawen *Da baisangai tuoluoni jing* ji fayuanwen kaoshi,"10–11, on the basis of checking it with the photographs of the block print contained in the same article, 9:

[illegible]

[illegible]

[illegible]

Tangut pronunciation as well.[343] Given that Ko tja is the "crown prince," it is also reasonable to identify Ko tja with Köden, whose father Ögedei was the Khagan.

The date in the postscript is presented in an interesting way. It is not indicated with a reign title (*nian hao* 年號). Instead, it uses the *ganzhi* 干支 sexagenary system prefixed by the term "Great Dynasty" (𗏁𗴂), which is a translation of the Chinese *da chao* 大朝. *Da chao*, an equivalent of *yeke* [*mongyol-un*] *ulus*, is the name that Chinese used to refer to the Mongol Empire before the establishment of the Yuan Empire.[344] Since the Mongols did not adopt the reign title until Kubilai used Zhongtong 中統 as his reign title in 1260, combining the term "Great Dynasty" with the *ganzhi* sexagenary system was a usual way to indicate the year in China. Then, since there is only one *jiachen* year between 1206 – the establishment of the Mongol Empire – and 1260, we know the year is 1244.

Finally, the one who wrote the postscript is a state preceptor called Bu dja bja dzjɨ rjar 𗴿𗏹𗍋𗉣𗑠, which is undoubtedly a phonetic transcription of the Sanskrit Buddhavajra. This, however, does not necessarily mean he was from the Indic world, just like Ānandakīrti was not an Indian but Tibetan. The fact that he was prefixed by the expression "monk of the Śākya clan," which reflects the Tibetan *shākya'i dge slong*, bespeaks that he was more likely a Tibetan because the expression often precedes the actual name of religion of a Tibetan monk. If that is the case, then his actual name of religion would be Sangs rgyas rdo rje. His state preceptor title seems also to suggest that Köden inherited the preceptor system in his court.

---

[343] For a similar case, see note 276.

[344] Xiao, "Shuo 'Da chao.'"

In sum, what this postscript tells us is that, in 1244, on behalf of Köden, the state preceptor Buddhavajra or Sangs rgyas rdo rje took charge of a printing project of the *Sitātapatrā-dhāraṇī*. The copies were then distributed to the Buddhists within Köden's realm.

What is exciting about the 1244 block print of the *Sitātapatrā-dhāraṇī* is that it can be examined together with another fragmentary Tangut block print of the same text against the same historical context. This block print, which is collected in the National Library of China, now consists of only three pages of its postscript.[345] But the postscript itself is of great interest. Having extolled the power of the *dhāraṇī*, the rest of the postscript says:

> [The original of the *dhāraṇī*] was obtained from the imperial preceptor Po tjɨj sjij [=*Byang chub ye shes]. The state preceptor Ljị mjij ɣiej translated and disseminated it. Later, the Tangut State was destroyed, and the Great Dynasty was established. During the reign of Köden, the crown prince of the Southern Circuit[346], the monk and state preceptor Tśhja dwewr ɣjị njij [=*Sangs rgyas rdo rje], who was extraordinarily learned in the secret mantras, skilled in practice, and renowned in the world, became the master of Köden. He promulgated the sutra and printed three thousand copies of it and disseminated it around the world. Now, since the printing side of the woodblock is worn and broken, I, the disciple and dharma preceptor Kwo zjwị Źjɨr be, am a direct disciple of the master. I have studied all the [subjects of] Buddhist philosophy[347], and I have learned [lit. heard] much about both the exoteric and esoteric teachings. I made a great prayer, gave away offerings, and newly carved the woodblock. The races [End of the fragment]… [348]

---

[345] The block print has been examined by Shi Jinbo together with a Chinese translation of its text. See Shi, "Liangzhou huimeng yu Xixia Zangchuan Fojiao."

[346] The Southern Circuit ([illegible]) is a military district of the Tangut State. Its headquarters are Liangzhou.

[347] The Tibetan equivalent of the Tangut [illegible] is *mtshan nyid*. It should mean philosophical subjects in this context.

[348] I use the transcription of the text from Shi, "Xixiawen *Da baisangai tuoluoni jing* ji fayuanwen kaoshi," 90–91, with some corrections on the basis of checking it with the photographs of the block print contained in the same article, 90:

[illegible]，[illegible]，[illegible]，[illegible]，[illegible]。
[illegible]，[illegible]，[illegible]，[illegible]，[illegible]，[illegible]
[illegible]。[illegible]，[illegible]，[illegible]。[illegible]，[illegible]

A critical clue in the postscript is the name Tśhja dwewr ɣjɨ njij, "Enlightenment-Diamond," ([illegible]), which is nothing but a translation of the name Buddhavajra in the 1244 postscript. The "three thousand copies" in the latter postscript also aligns well with the "one thousand volumes for each of the Tibetan, Tangut, and Chinese languages"[349] in the 1244 postscript. Hence, the two postscripts refer to two closely related events in which the latter is predicated on the former. The fact that the Tanguts would usually translate the name of religion for Tibetans and transcribe it for Indic masters enhances the possibility that Buddhavajra was a Tibetan bearing the name Sangs rgyas rdo rje. This postscript further makes clear that he was the master of Köden, thus showing Köden was already a Buddhist – and most likely a Tibetan Buddhist – at the time of inviting Sa paṇ to Liangzhou in 1244.

The author of the latter postscript and a disciple of Buddhavajra / Sangs rgyas rdo rje is Kwo zjwị Źjir be. He is clearly a Tangut since he bears the Tangut clan name Kwo zjwị. On the other hand, Źjɨr be, which means "Wisdom-Sun," should be a translation of his Tibetan name of religion, Shes rab nyi ma. Being a dharma preceptor, he wanted to continue his master's enterprise of printing the *Sitātapatrā-dhāraṇī*.

Kwo zjwị Źjir be also tells us the origin of the Tangut translation. He specifies that the translation was done by the state preceptor Ljị mjij ɣiej from the original obtained from the imperial preceptor Po tjɨj sjij. Ljị mjij ɣiej was a state preceptor of the Tangut State. He composed

---

[illegible]，[illegible]。[illegible]，[illegible]，[illegible]，[illegible]，[illegible]。[illegible] [End of the fragment]……

349 Given the very short length of the *Sitātapatrā-dhāraṇī*, it is clear that one copy can only be in one volume.

a Tangut eulogy to Amitābha, which was unearthed from Wuwei (Liangzhou).[350] The imperial preceptor Po tjɨj sjij was likely a Tibetan whose name of religion was Byang chub ye shes. Therefore, the prints made by both Kwo zjwị Źjɨr be and his master Buddhavajra / Sangs rgyas rdo rje were based on the translation from the Tangut period.

The postscript unfortunately lacks a date, which is presumably in the missing ending part of it. But judging from the expression "during the reign of Köden," it appears that Köden had already passed away at the point when Kwo zjwị Źjɨr be prepared his block print. Also noticeable is the fact that Kwo zjwị Źjir be still calls the Mongol Empire the "Great Dynasty" but not the "Great Yuan." Hence, it likely predates 1271. All in all, the project of Kwo zjwị Źjɨr be and the composition of the postscript should likely fall between 1251–1271.

What these two postscripts of the Tangut *Sitātapatrā-dhāraṇī* show is a trend in the Tangut period carried to the Mongol period. As we have seen in Section 2, translating, printing, chanting, and distributing the *dhāranī*s was an essential practice of Tangut State Buddhism. Since these *dhāraṇī*s could potentially bring collective welfare to the state, they were extensively introduced to the Tangut State on the basis of their Tibetan versions at the beginning of the formative period of the integrative Inner Asian imperial history. And the *Sitātapatrā-dhāraṇī* was one of the *dhāraṇī*s translated into Tangut during that period. Manifestly, Köden, despite a Mongol conqueror of the Tangut land, followed the spirit of State Buddhism and promulgated the *Sitātapatrā-dhāraṇī*. The ethos of wishing for the great fortune of the ruler, the people, and the state in the 1244 postscript is completely identical to that of the postscripts of the *dhāraṇī*s from the Tangut period. Based on the fact that 1244 was the year Köden sent the invitation to Sa paṇ and asked him to go to Liangzhou, Shi Jinbo pointed out that the 1244 print of the *Sitātapatrā-dhāraṇī* might be a wish

[350] See Yu, "Wuwei cang 6749 hao fojing *Jingtu qiu sheng li Fo sheng zan ji* kaoshi."

for the success of their meeting that followed and the preparation for Sa paṇ's arrival.[351] And such a wish is exactly what the *dhāraṇī* has the potential to fulfill. The popularity of the *Sitātapatrā-dhāraṇī* continued into the Yuan period. The famous Yuan translator Shes rab dpal (Ch. Shaluo ba 沙囉巴, 1259–1314) again translated the *Sitātapatrā-dhāraṇī* into Chinese (T 976).[352]

The 1247 meeting between them indeed came as a success for both parties. The Mongols thus started to control Tibet, and the Sa skya school established its hegemony in Tibet. After the deaths of Köden and Sa paṇ, a new alliance formed between 'Phags pa, the nephew of Sa paṇ, and Kubilai. 'Phags pa was first granted the title of state preceptor by Kubilai in 1260 and was promoted to imperial preceptor in 1270, thus becoming the first imperial preceptor of the Yuan Empire. The patron-priest relationship between the Tangut emperor and Bka' brgyud masters was, after a brief interim period, now transformed into the relationship between the Mongol emperor and Sa skya masters. Consequently, tantric teachings belonging to the Sa skya tradition were introduced to the practitioners within the Mongol realm, including the Tanguts. A few years ago, the first volume of a Tangut tantric text entitled *The Realization of Hevajra: A Wish-Fulfilling Jewel* ([illegible]) emerged in a manuscript from a private collection. It turned out the text was a Tangut translation of 'Phags pa's *Kye rdo rje'i mngon par rtogs pa yid bzhin gyi nor bu*, which was composed in 1258.[353] The Tangut translation shows that 'Phags pa had a Tangut audience who were eager to follow his tantric teachings.

---

351 Shi, "Liangzhou huimeng yu Xixia Zangchuan Fojiao."

352 To say he translated the "again" is because the was translated into Chinese during the Tangut period by Zhenzhi 真智 (T 977). The Chinese version printed by Buddhavajra/Sangs rgyas rdo rje was likely Zhenzhi's translation. For a study of Zhenzhi's translation, see Sun, "Zhenzhi yi *Foshuo Da bai sangai zongchi tuoluoni jing* wei Xixia yiben kao."

353 For a detailed study of the Tangut text, see Li, *Xixiawen "Xijingang xianzheng ruyi bao" kaoshi yu yanjiu.*

A major contribution 'Phags pa made to Mongol culture was his invention of the 'Phags pa script in 1269, a writing system used for the Mongol language. In Tenri Central Library, Tenri University, Japan, there is a curious sample of the 'Phags pa script (see fig. 1).[354] This block print fragment, which can be dated to the Yuan period, bears two scripts, the 'Phags pa script and the Mongol script. When both scripts appear in a line, they write the same thing. The content of the text is the *Mahāsāhasrapramardinī*, one of the *Five Sutras*. The base of the text should be written in the Mongol script since the first two lines in the fragment do not have the corresponding text in the 'Phags pa script. The 'Phags pa script, which is more accurate in indicating the phonetic value, appears to have been used as a phonetic aid. This is supported by the fact that the first two lines are narrative and the latter three lines are the actual *dhāraṇī*.

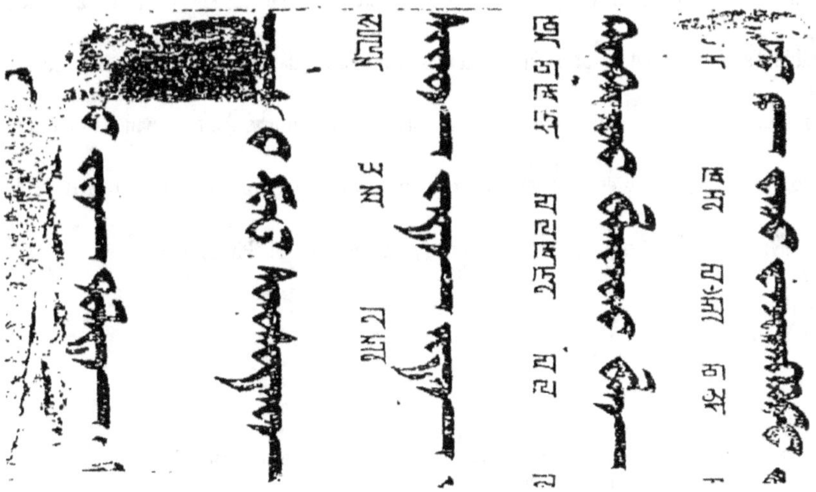

[354] For a study of the fragment, see Zhaonasitu and Niu, "Menggu wen – Basiba zi Wu shouhushen dacheng jing shou hu daqian guotu jing Yuan dai yinben canpian kaoshi."

Figure 1. Fragment of a block print of the Mongol translation of the *Mahāsāhasrapramardinī* in both 'Phags pa and traditional Mongol scripts. Tenri Central Library, Tenri University, Japan.[355]

We remember that the *Five Sutras* was one of the first scriptures translated from Tibetan into Tangut. And the *Five Sutras* served as an important component of Tangut State Buddhism. Hence, here, we see again a continuity from the Tangut period to the Yuan period. And the 'Phags pa script acted as a catalyst for the assimilation of the *Five Sutras* in the Mongol Buddhist tradition. It should also be noted when the fragment was discovered, it was placed between the pages of Tangut Buddhist scriptures.[356] This tells us the Mongol translation of the *Five Sutras* circulated in a group of Buddhists that also contained Tanguts.

'Phags pa died early at the age of forty-six in 1280. But his influence among the Tanguts did not wane. Recently, Sun Bojun uncovered a Tangut translation of 'Phags pa's work and the translation was done after 'Phags pa's death. Most likely dated to 1293,[357] the text is also the latest datable Tangut translation of a Tibetan text and the latest datable Tangut text of a block print. Identified again from the collection of the Tenri Central Library, the text, which is entitled *The Lotus Rosary of the Blessed One Whose Gnosis and Life Are Unlimited: Words of Praise* ([illegible]), is evidently a translation of 'Phags pa's *Bcom ldan 'das tshe*

---

[355] Photograph from Zhaonasitu and Niu, "Menggu wen – Basiba zi Wu shouhushen dacheng jing shou hu daqian guotu jing Yuan dai yinben canpian kaoshi," 42.

[356] Zhaonasitu and Niu, "Menggu wen – Basiba zi Wu shouhushen dacheng jing shou hu daqian guotu jing Yuan dai yinben canpian kaoshi," 38.

[357] In theory, the *guisi* year documented in the colophon can refer to 1293, 1353, 1413, etc., as long as it postdates 'Phags pa's composition of the work in 1258. However, since the group of people, especially the translator, were obviously heavily influenced by 'Phags pa's ideas, the date of the translation cannot be too late. Another clue is that the Tangut text was discovered in a jar together with fragments of the Tangut Buddhist canon published in 1302. Hence, it is more reasonable to date the translation to 1293.

dang ye shes dpag tu med pa la bstod pa'i tshig padmo'i phreng ba.[358] 'Phags pa's eulogy, composed in 1258, is dedicated to the *Aparimitāyurjñānasūtra*, which, as we have seen in Section 2, is the very first datable Tangut translation of a Tibetan text.

The colophon of the Tangut translation has the following sentence:

> [illegible]。[359]
>
> Composition completed by 'Phags pa[360], the imperial preceptor, who teaches correctly the scriptures and reasoning[361], on the eighth day of the *lousu*[362] month of the *wuwu*[363] year.

This sentence is somewhat at variance with the texts' colophon in the Tibetan original:

> *'phags pa zhes bya bas sa pho rta'i*[364] *lo dbyu gu'i zla ba'i tshes brgyad la sbyar ba'o / /*[365]
>
> Composed by 'Phags pa on the eighth day of the *dbyu gu* month of the earth-male-horse year.

---

358 There are two differences between the titles. 1. While the Tibetan has "life and gnosis" (*tshe dang ye shes*), the Tangut has "gnosis and life." 2. While the Tibetan title puts "lotus rosary" (*padmo'i phreng ba*) in the subtitle, the Tangut puts it in the main title.

359 Sun, "Tianli tushuguan cang Basiba 'zangtan' *Dacheng wuliangshou zongyao jing*," 105, frame 1C, lines 5–7.

360 [illegible], Phja sjɨ pja.

361 [illegible] is clearly a Tangut equivalent of the Tibetan *lung dang rigs pa*.

362 [illegible] < *lousu* 婁宿, the Chinese name for one of the twenty-eight lunar mansions, corresponding the Tibetan *tha skar/dbyu gu*, or the Sanskrit Āśvina. It refers to the seventh month. See discussion below.

363 [illegible] < *wuwu* 戊午, the name of one year in the Chinese *ganzhi* sexagenary cycle, corresponding the Tibetan earth-male-horse year.

364 The Sde dge version of the text has *stag gi* instead of *rta'i*, which is in Zhwa lu and Lu phu versions. This, then, poses a very interesting case of how a Tangut translation may aid us in determining the date of the composition of its Tibetan original. If we read stag instead of rta, then we would misplace of the composition of the date in 1278.

365 'Phags pa, *Tshe dpag med kyi stod pa padmo'i phreng ba*, 207.

Several differences between the two passages are worth noticing. First, 'Phags pa is entitled "imperial preceptor" in the Tangut translation, which is not seen in the original. This is understandable, since 'Phags pa only became the imperial preceptor in 1270. Furthermore, the presentations of the year and month are different in both passages. The nomenclature used in the Tangut translation is from the Chinese calendar, which obviously aims at accommodating the cultural background of the Tangut audience. But the Tangut terms correspond well with the Tibetan terms. The *wuwu* year is the equivalent of the earth-male-horse year, which can only be 1258. And the *lousu* month is an equivalent of the *dbyu gu* month, both of which refer to the seventh month.

Then, having made a prayer in a verse, the colophon of the Tangut translation continues:

> The one who aspired to make the translation is ·O gju̱, the monk and dharma preceptor of the virtuous ornament in Śjã djɨj[366] Monastery of Ganzhou[367]. Translated in the chamber of the dharma master Bia tśhja tśhja, which is in the lecture hall of Śjã djɨj Monastery. Translated into Tangut on the fifteenth day of the month of the magical feet[368] in the *guisi*[369] year by the translator-in-chief Lji̠ dźjow gju̱ me̱ Tow. The one who aspired to produce the woodblock is the donor and preceptor ·Jow tśhja gju̱.[370]

---

366 [illegible] < *chan ding* 禪定.

367 [illegible] *kã tśjiw*.

368 [illegible] < *shen zu* 神足, namely the first month.

369 [illegible] < *guisi* 癸巳, a year in the *ganzhi* sexagenary cycle. It should most likely correspond the year 1293. See also note 357.

370 Sun, "Tianli tushuguan cang Basiba 'zangtan' *Dacheng wuliangshou zongyao jing*," 105, frame 1C, lines 10–15:

[illegible]

So, the translation was made likely in 1293. While the Tanguts in general followed the Chinese calendar, in this case, they likely followed the Tibetan calendar since the fifteenth day is the day of Amitābha, which aligns with the theme of the text.

Among all the persons listed here, the one of great interest is the translator-in-chief Ljɨ̣ dźjow gju̱ me̱ Tow [illegible]. Tow [illegible] is a Tangut clan name and Ljɨ̣ dźjow gju̱ me̱ [illegible] is his name in religion. Among the four characters of his name of religion, *ljɨ̣* and *dźjow* are Tangut equivalents of Tibetan *dkon mchog* and *rgyal mtshan*; *gju̱* and *me̱*, on the other hand, are Tangut equivalents of Tibetan *dpal* and *bzang po*. Hence, his full name of religion in Tibetan should be Dkon mchog rgyal mtshan dpal bzang po. The ending *dpal bzang po*, which is a Tibetan equivalent of the Sanskrit *śrībhadra*, is a typical part of the name of religion in the Sa skya tradition ever since Sa paṇ, who inherited as a part of his name *śrībhadra* at his ordination from his Kashmirian teacher Śākyaśrībhadra.[371] Therefore, Ljɨ̣ dźjow gju̱ me̱ Tow is very likely a Tangut monk ordained in the Sa skya tradition. In fact, he could well be a direct disciple of 'Phags pa himself, given the historical context of the translation.

We also notice that the translation was done on the basis of a collective effort. ·O gju̱ was the organizer and ·Jow tśhja gju̱ was the patron. The fact that Ljɨ̣ dźjow gju̱ me̱ Tow is called the "translator-in-chief" means that he was likely accompanied by other people in his team of

[371] The full name of religion of Sa paṇ is Kun dga' rgyal mtshan dpal bzang po, and the full religious name of 'Phags pa is Blo gros rgyal mtshan dpal bzang po.

translation. ·O is no doubt a Tangut clan name and ·Jow tśhja gju̠ could also be a Tangut.[372] And the translation was done in Ganzhou, one of the most important cities of the old Tangut State. These all show that even after 'Phags pa's death, he still had a strong presence in his Tangut audience, who continued to value his teachings.

Thus we see another continuity from the Tangut period to the Mongol period with the case of 'Phags pa's Tangut audience – the charismatic Tibetan preceptor served as a center of Tanguts' Individual Buddhism. Before it was Yar klungs pa and Gtsang po pa whose Bka' brgyud teachings were popular among the Tanguts. Now, it was 'Phags pa whose compositions of the Sa skya tradition appealed to the Tanguts. But there is also a major difference between the two periods. The Bka' brgyud masters in the Tangut State served primarily the Tangut audience. For 'Phags pa, the Tanguts were only one of the many groups of people who needed his service. 'Phags pa's main concern was presumably the Mongols. However, he was obviously also influential among the Uyghurs since his Uyghur disciple Puṇyaśrī translated some Tibetan tantric texts belonging to the Sa skya tradition into Uyghur.[373] We should also not forget that some tantric works of 'Phags pa himself and other Sa skya masters were translated into Chinese.[374] In this regard, 'Phags pa was indeed facing many different audiences from different ethnic regions of the Yuan Empire. This is, then, further related to the transition from the prototypical Inner Asian empire to a mature empire. We will return to this in the Conclusion.

---

[372] ·Jow is often the Tangut equivalent of the Chinese surname Yang 楊. But many Tanguts also used the surname Yang due to their adoption of Chinese culture, just like the Tangut emperors would also use the Chinese surname Li 李. For example, the Yang family flourished in Puyang 濮陽, Henan , during the Yuan period was Tangut.

[373] Elverskog, *Uygur Buddhist Literature*, 110–113.

[374] Shen, "*Dacheng yaodao miji* yu Xixia Yuan chao suo chuan Xizang mifa," 262–269.

Thus, in this chapter, we start to detail the Tanguts' engagement with Tibetan Buddhism on the basis of the Tangut *Aparimitāyurjñānasūtra* distributed in 1094 and concluded with the translation of 'Phags pa's praise verse in most likely 1293. The two centuries witnessed a profound revolution of the Buddhist Complex and the establishment of the Sino-Tibetan Buddhist Complex, which shaped the religious landscape of the Yuan, Ming, and Qing empires.

Chapter Four: The Tangut Assimilation of Gsang phu ne'u thog Scholasticism

1. Gsang phu ne'u thog Scholasticism

Founded by Rngog Legs pa'i shes rab in 1073, Gsang phu Monastery to the south of Lhasa was undoubtedly a pivotal point in facilitating the later diffusion of Buddhism.[375] Rngog Lo, a nephew of Legs pa'i shes rab, studied in India (*rgya gar*) and Kashmir (*kha che*), translated and revised many texts in the triad of the seventeen years of his life.[376] After the major direct disciples of Rngog Lo were abbots of Gsang phu, Phya pa inherited the abbotship and greatly developed the tradition established by Rngog Lo in the twelfth century. Gsang phu scholasticism that formed and developed over roughly a century from Rngog Lo to Phya pa and his disciples[377] influenced later Tibetan intellectual culture to no small extent. One should not be surprised to perceive traces of Gsang phu scholasticism in the Bka' gdams school in general, in the Sa skya school, and, of course, also in the Dga' ldan or Dge lugs school that arose centuries later.

The term "scholasticism is highly relevant to our discussion of the Gsang phu tradition in the Tangut State and thus needs some clarification. Despite being a term that is contextually European, José Cabezón argued for it as a general and cross-cultural category in the history of philosophy, particularly in his effort to subsume the relevant practices of Tibetan Buddhism under that concept.[378] For Cabezón, the essence of scholasticism is predicated on the relationship

---

[375] For general information on Gsang phu ne'u thog Monastery's significance in the Later Diffusion, see Nishizawa, "gSang phu ne'u thog," and Hugon, "Enclaves of Learning, Religious and Intellectual Communities in Tibet."

[376] For Rngog Lo's career, see Kramer, *The Great Tibetan Translator*.

[377] I here follow Nishizawa's periodization of the Gsang phu tradition, see Nishizawa, "Sanpu kyōgaku no rekishiteki tenkai ni kansuru ichi kōsatsu."

[378] See Cabezón, *Buddhism and Language* and Cabezón, *Scholasticism*.

between rationality and spirituality, as he states, "scholasticism, whether monastic or not, is concerned with reconciling the rational and the experiential aspects of human religiousness," and "reasoning and systematicity, far from being incompatible with personal religious experience, are the very prerequisites for spiritual realization and action."[379] Hence, a remarkable characteristic of scholasticism is that it entails a soteriological goal dependent upon the means of reason. In this regard, scholasticism is different from tantric practices in general, many of which are intentionally designed as irrational and devoid of reason.[380] It is also the opposite of the central spirit of Chan Buddhism, which views the tendency of conceptualization as detrimental.[381] But on the other hand, the means cannot supersede the goal and rationality cannot cancel the ultimate spiritual significance. Otherwise, scholasticism would not be tenable just like how "an interest in knowledge for its own sake" would hinder the development of ancient Chinese logic.[382]

A typical characteristic of Gsang phu scholasticism is the soteriological use of the "neither one nor many" argument. While emptiness is the ultimate status that a Buddhist practitioner would like to experience, in Buddhist scholasticism it is also something one needs to prove first in order to make it a justifiable pursuit. Śāntarakṣita (8th c.) center stages this argument at the very outset of his *Madhyamakālaṃkāra*, thereby using the inferential method of Dignāga and Dharmakīrti: all phenomena are empty of their intrinsic nature because they are neither one nor many. This

---

379 Cabezón, *Buddhism and Language*, 19.

380 See Wedemeyer, *Making Sense of Tantric Buddhism*, esp. chap. 4. Understanding Tantric Buddhism through connotative semiotics, Wedemeyer, *Making Sense of Tantric Buddhism*, 123–124 claims: "Similarly, in the ritual context of the *sādhana*–calling as it does for the practitioner to renounce her rational, discursive knowledge of her own ordinary and limited personality–connotative semiotics are used as a more direct, mystifying mode of signification than ordinary rhetorical suasion."

381 See McRae, *The Northern School and the Formation of Early Ch'an Buddhism*, 246–247. This is not to say that one should wrestle with conceptualization arduously, which would potentially reinforce that tendency. It is more important to let it flow naturally without directing oneself toward it.

382 I am here quoting Cabezón's citation of Wing-tsit Chan's comment; see Cabezón, *Buddhism and Language*, 19.

formulation later became an extensively discussed subject in the Gsang phu tradition. The Gsang phu masters tried to figure out how this argument could play out as a valid one and what philosophical implications the argument entailed. For example, Phya pa argued that we can understand the property to be proven (*bsgrub bya'i chos*) in this argument as something resulting from the affirming negation (*ma yin dgag, prayudāsa*); other Gsang phu masters such as Gro lung pa Blo gros 'byung gnas (late 11th to early 12th century, henceforth Gro lung pa) and Rgya dmar ba Byang chub grags (late 11th to early 12th century, henceforth Rgya dmar ba) suggested that it can only be something resulting from the non-affirming negation (*med dgag, prasajyapratiṣedha*).[383] Consequently, Phya pa *establishes* an idea of the absence of intrinsic nature, but Gro lung pa and Rgya dmar ba, while they would accept the fact of the absence of intrinsic nature, they do not hold that this entails an affirming idea of it. The disagreement would, of course, generate very different understandings of the "neither one nor many" argument and could potentially influence the individuals' mental state – a more or a less conceptual one – when approaching the notion of phenomena being empty of an intrinsic nature

Another salient feature of scholasticism might be described as a tension between a structured tradition and the intellectual agency. This is hinted by Cabezón[384] but only is made clear by Georges Dreyfus, who says, "Thus, rather than discuss scholasticism as revolving around the relation between faith and understanding, revelation and reason, I discuss scholastic practices as being concerned with the relation between authority and interpretation. I believe the most

[383] Hugon, "Proving Emptiness," esp. 62–66, 73. The affirming negation and the non-affirming negation are a common pair of concepts used in Buddhist philosophy. While I have tentatively labelled them so in English, it would be in fact extremely hard to translate them aptly. While the latter would be the mere negation, the former would mean affirming *x* by stating "*x* is not non-*x*." An example of the former would be "the fat Devadatta who does not eat during the day." It does not necessarily mean Devadatta eats during the night, but it does affirm the fat Devadatta.

[384] Cabezón, *Buddhism and Language*, 20–21, second point.

distinctive feature of scholasticism to be its emphasis on interpreting the great texts constitutive of the tradition within the confines of its authority, using the intellectual tools handed down from previous generations."[385] There are three elements to be noticed in this exposition: 1. there is a stable tradition that sets the limits of the discussion; 2. there is the agency that can interpret the tradition within the limits; 3. the interpretation is made so by using certain available intellectual tools over times. And it is a tension between 1. and 2. with 3. as the adhesive.

An example of this tension in Gsang phu scholasticism is the ways in which different masters viewed the relationship between the Two Truths (*bden pa gnyis*, *satyadvaya*) of Madhyamaka. In the second chapter of Rgya dmar ba's *Analysis of the Essence of Madhyamaka*, *Dbu ma de kho na nyid rnam par dpyod pa*, he discusses the "meaning of the compartmentalization [of the Two Truths]" (*dbye ba'i don*).[386] He first presents the following four possibilities of the relationship between the two truths:

a. There is no compartmentalization at all (*dbye ba gtan med pa*).

And, if there is [compartmentalization] (*yod na*), then—

b. They are different entities (*ngo bo tha dad pa*).
c. They are compartmentalized properties of the same entity (*ngo bo gcig la chos kyi dbye ba*).
d. They are compartmentalized in the sense of the mere negation of being unicity (*gcig pa bkag pa tsam gyi dbye ba*).

---

[385] Dreyfus, *The Sound of Two Hands Clapping*, 11.

[386] Rgya dmar ba, *Dbu ma de kho na nyid rnam par spyod* [read: dpyod] *pa*, 2b1–5a8.

Having presented the possibilities, Rgya dmar ba quickly excluded positions *a* and *b* by citing the explanation from the *Saṃdhinirmocanasūtra*.[387] Then, he provides a lengthy discussion of why position *c*, which is held by a certain Dge bshes pa[388], should be rejected. And, finally, he takes position *d* as what he approves of. However, Dge bshes pa's position was later again followed by Phya pa.[389]

The tradition is clearly that the Two Truths are in this way compartmentalized and that consequently one cannot say that they are not all different. Thus, *a* should be easily excluded. What is implicitly entailed here is also that there should be no more than Two Truths, which would equally go counter to the limit set by the tradition. Position *b* can be viewed as more or less out of the limit, too, since it can be rejected easily by the *Saṃdhinirmocanasūtra*. In contrast, *c* and *d* are the places where the agency of Gsang phu masters takes effect. Both *c* and *d* would fit in with the tradition and can both be argued. Hence, while being harnessed by the tradition, they could gallop well on the plain of reasoning. Notwithstanding these two factors, the most interesting fact of this list of the four possibilities, which serves as a heuristic tool, is that different Gsang phu philoosphers have put it to use it in different ways. It is evident that the same list is also used in their analysis of the compartmentalization of direct perception and inference. Thus, the list

---

[387] See *Bka' 'gyur* 49, 16–19. According to the sutra, there would be four mistakes if the defining characteristic of the conditioned phenomena (*'du byed kyi mtshan nyid*) and the defining characteristic of the ultimate (*don dam pa'i mtshan nyid*) were to be indistinct: 1. All immature, ordinary individuals would see the truth (*byis pa so so'i skye bo thams cad bden pa mthong ba yin par yang 'gyur*); 2. The defining characteristic of the ultimate would also be included in the defining characteristic of the thorough affliction (*don dam pa'i mtshan nyid kyang kun nas nyon mongs pa'i mtshan nyid du gtogs par 'gyur*); 3. There would be no differentiations between the [varieties of] the defining characteristic of the conditioned phenomena (*'du byed kyi mtshan nyid thams cad kyang bye brag med pa*); 4. The ultimate cannot be pursued (*don dam pa yongs su 'tshal bar yang mi 'gyur*) apart from the ways of seeing (*mthong ba*), hearing (*thos pa*), differentiating (*bye brag phyed pa*), and conceptualizing (*rnam par shes pa*), which are applied to the conditioned phenomena.

[388] Dge bshes pa could be either just Khyung Rin chen grags or a faithful follower of Khyung. See Hugon, "Wonders *in margine*," § 3.2.2.

[389] Hugon, "Wonders *in margine*," 138–139.

becomes a subject-free, all-encompassing heuristic tool that can effectively aid the analysis of any given two related entities in a Buddhist context. Another tool like this is the triad of the definiens (*mtshan nyid*), the definiendum (*mtshon bya*), and the definitional basis (*mtshan gzhi*), which was brought to its maturity by Phya pa.[390] These tools provide a powerful conceptual framework for the Gsang phu masters to engage in sophisticated inquires of the traditions.

The subject of Gsang phu scholasticism consists of four fields of study on the most general level. The first one concerns the *prajñāpāramitā* or "transcendent insight" literature represented mainly by the *Abhisamayālaṃkara* of Maitreya/Asaṅga and indirectly by the Five Treatises of Maitreya (*byams chos sde lnga*). The second centers around the Madhyamaka tradition established by the Three Eastern Svātantrika Teachers (*rang rgyud shar gsum*), namely, Jñānagarbha (early 8th century), Śāntarakṣita, and Kamalaśīla (late 8th c.). The third field involves *pramāṇavāda* or Buddhist epistemology and logic with a focus on the Seven Treatises of Epistemology and Logic (*tshad ma sde bdun*) of Dharmakīrti. These three subjects are essentially about speculative thinking and serve as the main fields for philosophical inquiry. The fourth and last subject is termed the "subject of practice" (*spyod phyogs*), which would include primarily *Bodhisattvacaryāvatāra* and *Śikṣāsamuccaya* literature.[391] The division of the subjects is already evident in Rngog Lo's works.[392] Not all Gsang phu masters are specialized in all four subjects. Rngog Lo's student 'Bre Shes rab 'bar and his student Ar Byang chub ye shes seem to have more expertise in the first subject, whereas Khyung Rin chen grags, another student of Rngog Lo and his student Rgya dmar

---

[390] This is argued by Hugon, "The Origin of the Theory of Definition and Its Place in Phya pa Chos kyi seṅ ge's Philosophical System."

[391] For the division of the four subjects, see Nishizawa, "gSang phu ne'u thog," 347–348.

[392] In Rngog lo tsā ba's biography written by his disciple Gro lung pa, 43 works are listed. Among them, nos. 1–13 would fall into the first subject; nos. 14–19 and nos. 23–27 the second; nos. 28–43 the third; and nos. 20–22 the fourth. See Kramer, *The Great Tibetan Translator*, 109–113.

ba appear to be primarily scholars in the second and third subjects. There is no doubt, however, that Phya pa was once again a great scholar in all four subjects, attested by his extensive writings on them.[393]

An issue that must be addressed at this point is the relationship between Gsang phu scholasticism and the Bka' gdams pa tradition in general. There is no question that all those who are trained exclusively in the Gsang phu monastery should be counted as Bka' gdams pa since Legs pa'i shes rab, the founder of the monastery, was a student of Atiśa. However, while a large number of Bka' gdams pa from other monasteries would also be trained in the same scholastic tradition, we cannot say that Gsang phu scholasticism is nothing but the essence of the Bka' gdams school because it cannot cancel the independent status of many other sub-traditions among the Bka' gdams and, as a consequence, it cannot deconstruct its own uniqueness among the Bka' gdams school either. Hugon concluded in her examination of Gsang phu scholasticism, "Clearly, however, the 'philosophical turn' promoted by the second abbot, rNgog Blo ldan shes rab, was not in phase with the usual orientation of other proto-bKa' gdams pa and bKa' gdams pa centres."[394] Vose, upon his appraisal of Rgya dmar ba's *Analysis of the Essence of Madhyamaka*, holds a similar idea, "If we understand Kadampa in a narrow sense, as Dromtön's 'children,' Sangpu would seem to have little to do with it. Even if we expand the sense to something like 'Atiśa-inspired traditions,' Kadampa may have a tenuous relationship with Sangpu, given the disparities between Atiśa's and Ngok Loden Shérap's respective intellectual emphases."[395] Separating Gsang phu scholasticism initiated by Rngog Lo and the Bka' gdam traditions more immediately influenced by Atiśa is also

[393] See the catalog of his writings in the *Collected Writings of the Bka' gdams School* (Dpal brtsegs bod yig dpe rnying zhib 'jug khang, *Bka' gdams gsung 'bum phyogs sgrig thengs dang po'i dkar chag*, 16–18).

[394] Hugon, "Enclaves of Learning, Religious and Intellectual Communities in Tibet," 306.

[395] Vose, "Absemce and Elimination," 152.

the tendency of the Tibetan historiography before the canonization of the four schools of Tibetan Buddhism. For example, in the *Red Annals*, Kun dga' rdo rje has the following narrative for the "lineage of the Bka' gdams pa" (*bka' gdams pa'i brgyud pa*):

> While he [=Atiśa] had many students from India and Tibet, the principal of his spiritual sons in Tibet were the three: Khu, Rngog, and 'Brom.[396] From among them, 'Brom ston pa Rgyal ba'i 'byung gnas, the forefather of the Bka' gdams, was a layman relying upon the Bye ma lung pa of Gnams[397] from Stod lungs, and he established the Ra sgreng monastery. While he had many spiritual sons, the three brothers were Phu chung ba Gzhon nu rgyal mtshan, Po to ba rin chen gsal, and Spyan snga Tshul khrims 'bar. Adding Kham pa lung pa[398], they were known as four. Phu chung ba did not take students.[399]

The passage provides an overview from Atiśa to the initial offspring of the Bka' gdams school. We notice while Kun dga' rdo rje does include Rngog Legs pa'i shes rab as one of the main students of Atiśa, and only 'Brom ston pa is regarded as "the forefather of Bka' gdams." After this passage, Kun dga' rdo rje then proceeds to narrate three sub-lineages of Bka' gdams, namely, the "lineage of scripture" (*gzhung pa'i brgyud pa*) initiated by Po to ba, the "lineage of essential instructions" (*man ngag pa'i brgyud pa*) initiated by Spyan snga Tshul khrims 'bar, and the

---

[396] These are Khu ston Brtson 'grus gyung drung (1011–1075), Rngog, and 'Brom ston.

[397] What *gnams* means here is unclear.

[398] This is Sgang Shākya yon tan (1023–1115). For him, see *Deb sngon*, 346; Roerich, *The Blue Annals*, 283–284.

[399] Tshal pa, *Deb ther dmar po*, 61:

> *de la slob ma rgya gar dang bod du mang du byon kyang / bod du sras kyi thu bo khu rngog 'brom gsum / de'i nang nas bka' gdams kyi mes po 'brom ston pa rgyal ba'i 'byung gnas / stod lungs pa gnams kyi bye ma lung pa / rten dge bsnyen te / ra sgreng dgon pa btab / de'i sras mang du byon kyang / ska mched gsum ni / phu chung ba gzhon nu rgyal mtshan / po to ba rirnon chen gsal / spyan mnga' tshul khrims 'bar te / kham pa lung pa dang bzhir grags / phu chung pas slob ma ma bsten no /.*

"lineage of the stages of path" (*lam rim pa'i brgyud pa*) initiated by Nag tsho Lo tsā ba Tshul khrims rgyal ba (1011–after 1064), another student of Atiśa. Only after these three sections does Kun dga' rdo rje begins to discuss the lineage of the Gsang phu monastery. This scheme implies that the Gsang phu tradition should not be superimposed on the lineages derived from 'Brom ston and the "lineage of the stages of path" associated with Nag tsho Lo tsā ba. A similar scheme also appears in 'Gos Lo's *Blue Annals*, where the lineages associated with Atiśa and those with Rngog Lo are treated independently.[400]

On the other hand, Gsang phu scholasticism was seminal in the development of the scholastic traditions in schools other than the Bka' gdams. Since he was seventeen years old, Bsod nams rtse mo (1142–1182), the second patriarch of the Sa skya monastery, studied under Phya pa for eleven years until the latter's death in 1169 with training in *prajñāpāramitā* and Buddhist epistemology.[401] Known as one of the major students of Phya pa, Bsod nams rtse mo was trained in Gsang phu scholasticism. Later, Sa paṇ studied with Mtshur ston Gzhon nu seng ge, a renowned Gsang phu master of his time, for several years before meeting with Śākyaśrībhadra and his entourage.[402] The fact that Sa paṇ's magnum opus, *Epistemology: Treasury Reasoning*, *Tshad ma rigs pa'i gter*, rejects Phya pa's general epistemological position and calls for a return to what we might call a more conservative understanding of Dharmakīrti's thinking[403] reveals his strong familiarity with Gsang phu epistemology (*tshad ma*, *pramāṇa*).

---

[400] *Deb sngon*, 297–425.

[401] Ngag dbang kun dga' bsod nams, *Sa skya'i gdung rabs ngo mtshar bang mdzod*, 64.

[402] Jackson, *The Entrance Gate for the Wise*, 26.

[403] For this philosophical turn, see Hugon and Stoltz, *The Roar of a Tibetan Lion*, 96–100.

Furthermore, a number of key early Bka' brgyud figures also received scholastic training from Gsang phu masters. For example, Dus gsum mkhyen pa and Phag mo gru pa Rdo rje rgyal po (1110–1170) were both students of Rgya dmar ba and Phya pa.[404] While the Bka' brgyud school did not significantly develop Gsang phu scholasticism intellectually, it did institutionally assist in maintaining the Gsang phu Monastery. Notwithstanding its glory in intellectual achievements, the Gsang phu Monastery had a hard time consolidating its monastic power and keeping the integrity of its institutions. The most notable event here is the schism between the upper college (*gling stod*) and lower college (*gling smad*) of the monastery in the late 12th century.[405] Also, since an increasing number of famous Gsang phu masters decided to establish their own colleges elsewhere rather than staying in Gsang phu.[406] In response to this development, several Bka' brgyud sub-schools invited Gsang phu masters to establish colleges among their monasteries to enhance their sustainability as well as boost the scholastic training in their traditions. A famous instance here is the Gsang phu master 'Jam dbyangs Shākya gzhon nu, who was invited to Tshal gung thang to establish Chos 'khor gling college in 1308. He served for six years and then returned to Gsang phu Monastery and became her sixteenth abbot for another twenty-seven years[407] – a case not so different from an academic career today. Therefore, in the fourteenth century, Gsang phu Monastery had already become institutionally intertwined with the Bka' brgyud school. And, consequently, its scholastic tradition was well assimilated into the Bka' brgyud learning.

---

[404] For Dus gsum mkhyen pa, see *Deb sngon*, 565; Roerich, *The Blue Annals*, 475. For Phag mo grub pa, see *Deb sngon*, 655; Roerich, *The Blue Annals*, 555.

[405] See van der Kuijp, "The Monastery of Gsang-phu ne'u-thog and Its Abbatial Succession from ca. 1073 to 1250," 112–114. While the lower college was the old structure of the monastery, the upper college was a new institution split from it.

[406] For example, Sa paṇ studied with Mtshur ston not in Gsang phu but in Rkyang 'dur in upper Nyang River valley.

[407] Sørensen, and Hazod, *Rulers on the Celestial Plain*, 230–231.

And finally, the early Dga' ldan masters were of course followers of Gsang phu scholasticism. But we should notice here the influence of Gsang phu scholasticism was mainly an indirect one from the Sa skya tradition. Tsong kha pa (1357–1419) and his two principal direct disciples were all trained at Sa skya Monastery and Tsong kha pa was heavily influenced by the Sa skya scholar Red mda' ba Gzhon nu blo gros (1349–1412). It is not surprising to see that the Gsang phu scholastic tradition, having been developed by Sa paṇ and his followers in the reappraisal of Gsang phu masters' ideas and interpretations of especially Dharmakīrti, once again evolves in the debates between rising Dga' ldan scholars and the defenders of the Sa skya tradition such as Stag tshang Lo tsā ba Shes rab rin chen (1405–1477).[408]

Thus, it might be argued that Gsang phu scholasticism an undeniably profound influence on shaping Tibetan Buddhist thought as we understand it to be today. And now, we know that it also contributed to the formation of Tangut Buddhism.

2. The Transmission of Gsang phu Scholasticism to the Tangut State

It is thanks to the efforts of Solonin – he was the first to systematically identify a group of non-tantric, doctrinal Tangut texts as belonging to the Bka' gdams traditions – that we gained an idea of the doctrinal extent of these texts. His endeavor remained a preliminary one, since he was unable at the time to delve deeper in the actual contents of most of these texts.[409] It now turns out that most of the texts, together with many others, should be considered more precisely as vessels of Gsang phu scholasticism. A descriptive catalog of the texts is provided in Section 3. But let us

[408] For an introduction to the debates, see The Yakherds, *Knowing Illusion*.

[409] See Solonin, "Dīpaṃkara in the Tangut Context (Part One)" and "Dīpaṃkara in the Tangut Context (Part 2)."

first attempt the answer the following question: How did the Gsang phu scholastic tradition end up in the Tangut State?

The only direct evidence here is Rma bya's physical presence in the Tangut State in the late twelfth century, which has been briefly mentioned in Chapter Three, Section 3. As the colophon of the Tangut translation of his *Ornament that Clarifies the Introduction to Speculative Thinking* ([Tangut script], **Rtog ge la 'jug pa gsal bar byed pa'i rgyan*, see work no. 15 in Section 3) indicates, he resided in Tha dwewr [Tangut script] (< Dajue 大覺) Monastery in Mount Mati (馬蹄) in Liangzhou and presumably had Tangut students. His work itself is a treatise on Buddhist epistemology that closely follows the Gsang phu "summary" (*bsdus pa*) style. It is probable that he also introduced many other Gsang phu texts to the Tanguts.

Other pieces of evidence, despite indirect, are also telling. A major agent in transmitting Gsang phu scholasticism to the Tangut State seems to have been a monastic community in Tsong kha that was closely associated with the Gsang phu monastery. In the *Red Annals*, it says:

> [Rngog Lo] made Buddhist Teaching shine like the rising sun. None of those who were involved in studying the philosophical systems from Central Tibet, the borderlands,[410] the upper and lower Mdo (*mdo stod smad*), Tsong kha in the East, and Chinese Tangut[411], etc., had not become his students or grand-students (*ring slob*).[412]

---

[410] The term *lho bal*, which generally means "barbarians," is often seen in Dunhuang texts. More specifically, it usually means borderland people that are not Chinese. Sometimes it also means Khotanese. See Richardson, "Bal-po and Lho-bal."

[411] The expression *rgya mi nyag* can be understood either as "China and Tangut" or "Chinese Tangut." I regard the latter as more reasonable not only because there is no evidence showing any Chinese figure related to him but also because the trisyllabic combination of *rgya mi nyag* would parallel well the trisyllabic combination of *shar tsong kha* (qualifier + place name). This would, of course, also trigger the huge issue of how the Tibetans at that time viewed the ethnic boundaries between peoples. But it is out of the present scope of investigation.

[412] Tshal pa, *Deb ther dmar po*, 67:

The passage does not only confirm the connection between the Gsang phu Monastery and the Tangut State, but demonstrates the connection between the monastery and Tsong kha. Another source that supports the connection is an open letter Rngog Lo wrote to the monastic community in Tsong kha. This versified letter, entitled *Open Letter: A Drop of Elixir* (*Spring pa'i yi ge bdud rtsi thig le*) mainly discusses some philosophical systems and his own take on various philosophical issues.[413] The colophon of the letter is of great interest:

> The end of *Open Letter: A Drop of Elixir*, sent by the monk Blo ldan shes rab to the monastic community of the three districts (*ru gsum*) of Tsong kha, [whose members include] the old teacher Shes rab grags, etc.[414]

Therefore, a close tie between Gsang phu Monastery and the monastic community in Tsong kha existed. The fact that the monks in Tsong kha were the addressee of the philosophical message bespeaks that the community was intellectually guided by the Gsang phu Monastery.

As I have noted in Chapter Two, Section 1, the incorporation of Tsong kha into the Tangut State was a milestone in the Tangut reception of Tibetan Buddhism. It is not hard to imagine that these Tibetan monks in Tsong kha facilitated the transmission of Gsang phu scholasticism. Hence, we might say, after the historical event in 1137, there was a Tibetan monastic community within the Tangut realm that most probably followed the Gsang phu scholastic tradition.

---

bstan pa nyi ma shar ba ltar gsal bar mdzad / dbus gtsang / lho bal / mdo stod smad / shar tsong kha / rgya mi nyag la sogs kyi grub mtha' 'dzin pa slob ma / ring slob tu ma gyur pa med /.

[413] For a study of this open letter, see Kano, "Goku Roden sheirapu cho *Shokan kanro no shizuku*: Kōtei text to naiyō gaikan."

[414] Kano, "Goku Roden sheirapu cho *Shokan kanro no shizuku*: Kōtei text to naiyō gaikan," 13: *dge slong blo ldan shes rab kyis rga ston shes rab grags la swogs pa gtsong kha ru gsum gyi dge 'dun la spring pa'i yi ge bdud rtsi thig le zhes bya ba rdzogs sho / /.*

The history of Rwa sgreng Monastery documents that the monastery sent dozens of its members to the Tangut State for the purpose of receiving patronage from the Tangut emperor.[415] We do not know exactly what teachings they offered. It is of course not impossible that they preached Atiśa's teachings other than those developed by the Gsang phu tradition. But judging from what we currently see in the Tangut texts, Bka' gdams contents that are not connected to Gsang phu are rare. For example, the literature on the stages of the path (*lam rim*) has not been seen in the corpus. When Ti shri Ras pa first arrived in the Tangut realm, he was also invited by a Bka' gdams figure Lha rje Sman chung for one month and "stayed with the Bka' gdams there."[416]

We should also not forget the Bka' brgyud masters, who played a vital role in the dissemination of especially Indo-Tibetan tantric teachings to the Tanguts. We have seen how some early Bka' brgyud figures, including Dus gsum mkhyen pa and Phag mo gru pa, are closely related to Gsang phu scholasticism in Section 1. And, among the four figures discussed in Chapter Three, Section 5, Gtsang po pa was a student of Dus gsum mkhyen pa; Yar klungs pa was a direct disciple of Phag mo gru pa; and the teacher of Ti shri Ras pa, 'Jig rten mgon po, was also a direct disciple of Phag mo gru pa. While there is no record that they ever actively promoted Gsang phu scholasticism in the Tangut State, it would not be surprising that they actually did so. Granted that their primary interest might be tantric practices, but to draw a strict line between a scholar and a practitioner is irrelevant for that time. Master Diligence mentioned in Chapter Three, Section Four, for instance, was famous both for his expertise in scholastic traditions and his skills as a Mahāmudrā practitioner. Hence, these Bka' brgyud masters might have also instructed the Tanguts

---

[415] Iuchi, *An Early Text on the History of Rwa sgreng Monastery*, 28–30.

[416] Ras pa dkar po, *Bla ma rin po che 'gro ba'i mgon po ti shri Ras pa'i rnam par thar pa*, 109: *der bka' gdams pa rnams kyis* [read: *kyi*] *nang du bsdad pas /*.

in Gsang phu scholastic subjects, in which they likely were trained at their individual monasteries back home.

3. A Descriptive Catalog of Texts Related to Gsang phu Scholasticism in the Tangut Language

The following catalog presents what I have identified so far among the Tangut texts as belonging to Gsang phu scholasticism. All textual items are incomplete fragments of manuscripts or blockprints. The catalog encompasses the first three of the four subjects of Gsang phu scholasticism discussed in Section 1. Work nos. 1–3 are on *prajñāpāramitā*; nos. 4–7 are on Madhyamaka; nos. 8–16 are on Buddhist epistemology.

No. 1. [Tangut][417]

Tang. 101 (#5130, #6449)

Tib. *Shes rab kyi pha rol tu phyin pa'i man ngag gi bstan bcos mngon par rtogs pa'i rgyan*

The #6449 is a fragmentary blockprint of the Tangut translation of the Tibetan version of the *Abhisamayālaṃkāra*. The text only covers the beginning verses (Chapter I, vv. 1–14b, 26c–41b) of the work. It starts with the Tangut phonetic transcription of the Sanskrit title: [Tangut] [Tangut]□□ [Tangut] [Tangut] [Tangut] [Tangut] (*P[jɨ]-rjar nja̠ pja rjar mji tja ˙wu pja* ? ? *śja-s[jɨ] tja ˙ja bji sja mja ˙ja ˙ja lã-ŋ[ə] kja̠ rjar nja mja*, i.e., *Prajñāpāramitā upadeśa śāstra abhisamaya alaṃkāra nāma* with no sandhi involved). Then we have the Tangut title, which is

[417] This is the title that appears in #6449. The title in #5130 is slightly different. See below. Notably, [Tangut] is [Tangut] in #5130, though they are both supposedly translations of the Tibetan *man ngag*.

followed by the authorship statement: "Composed by the Venerable Maitreya" ([illegible]).

The statement is further followed by a proofreading statement:

> [illegible]
>
> "Supremely proofread by Ŋwe mji, the Honest, Gentle, Virtuous, and Respectful Emperor Who Follows the Heaven and Illuminates the Way, Who Shows the Martial and Promotes the Civil, Who Skillfully Plans and Wisely Ponders, Who Cultivates the Righteous and Eliminates the Evil".

The title of the emperor is the most common one for Emperor Renxiao.[418] So, the text was proofread at least once before 1193 and was translated earlier than this proofread edition.

The issue with #5130 is more complex. This is a fragmentary manuscript that has already become the object of scholarly pursuit for some time primarily because of its highly informative colophon.[419] The colophon indicates that it was copied in 1216 from a block print version. And the block print version itself contains the following information: this text was translated by Vidyākaraprabha and Bande Dpal brtsegs, revised by Amaragomin and Rngog Lo. This is obviously the colophon of the Tibetan text that the Tangut translator directly translated into the Tangut version. The intriguing part of the text is that the colophon seems to indicate the text is in fact a Tangut translation of Haribhadra's commentary on the *Abhisamayālaṃkāra* instead of the basic text of Maitreya because the Tibetan translation of that commentary lists exactly those four figures and their duties as such.[420] The colophon of the basic text in Tibetan translation, on the

[418] For the imperial titles of the Tangut emperors, see Cui and Wen, "Xixia Huangdi zunhao kaolue."

[419] See Nie, "E cang 5130 hao Xixiawen Fojing tiji yanjiu" and Ma, "Xixiawen *Shenghui bi'andao yaomen jiaoshou xianqian jie zhuangyan lun quan song* yi kao."

[420] This is also Nie's identification (Nie, "E cang 5130 hao Xixiawen Fojing tiji yanjiu," 50, n.2).

other hand, lists only Amaragomin and Rngog Lo as the translators.[421] Granted, the fragmentary text itself contains only verses, which are from chapters one and eight, without a commentary. But we cannot rule out the possibility that the scribe decided to only copy the verse part for the purpose of memorization. This assumption can in fact be supported by the somehow strange title recorded at the end of the manuscript: [illegible], which means "the verses that clarify the treatise of the *Prajñāpāramitā-upadeśa-śāstra-abhisamaya-alaṃkāra*." Due to the ambiguous syntax at the end, I assume we can alternatively read it as "the verses of that which clarifies the treatise of …" If so, then these would be the verses taken from the commentary.[422] But we cannot be sure of this. In any case, since #5130 only contains verses, I have temporarily subsumed it under the same text number.

Even if #5130 contains indeed the verses of the basic text, the version of the block print that was accessible to our scribe is not the version of #6449. The following is a comparison between Chapter I: vv. 5–7 in both versions with the Tibetan canonical version:

#5130	#6449	Tibetan Basic Text
[illegible][1][illegible], [illegible]。 [illegible], [illegible]。	[illegible][1][illegible], [illegible]。 [illegible], [illegible]。	*/ rnam kun mngon rdzogs rtogs pa dang /* */ rtse mor phyin dang mthar gyis pa /* */ skad cig gcig mngon rdzogs byang chub /* */ chos kyi sku dang de rnam brgyad /* (5)
[illegible], [illegible], [illegible][2][illegible], [illegible][3][illegible],	[illegible], [illegible], [illegible][2][illegible], [illegible][3][illegible],	*/ sems bskyed pa dang gdams ngag dang /* */ nges 'byed yan lag rnam bzhi dang /* */ sgrub pa yi ni rten gyur pa /* */ chos kyi dbyings kyi rang bzhin dang /* (6) */ dmigs pa dag dang ched dang ni /*

[421] But, of course, we do not know if they also based themselves on the basic text translated in the Imperial Period by Vidyākaraprabha and Bande Dpal brtsegs.

[422] Note also that Haribhadra's commentary is called *Sphuṭārthā* (Tib. *Don gsal*).

[illegible][4][illegible],	[illegible][4][illegible],	*/ go cha 'jug pa'i bya ba dang /*
[illegible],	[illegible],	*/ tshogs ni nges par 'byung bcas rnams /*
[illegible][5][illegible],	[illegible][5][illegible],	*/ thub pa'i rnam kun mkhyen pa nyid /* (7)[425]
[illegible]。[423]	[illegible]。[424]	

The variants are not significant enough to make the two versions dramatically different. But, in terms of the closeness to the Tibetan canonical version, #5130 is better, especially in [2], [4], and [5]. This phenomenon serves as a piece of evidence that supports #5130 to be the translation of the basic text. The argument can be further enhanced by the comparison between #5130 and #5179 (see work no. 2).

No. 2. [illegible]

Tang. 101 (#4722, #5164, #5179, #8329)

Tib. *Shes rab kyi pha rol tu phyin pa'i man ngag gi bstan bcos mngon par rtogs pa'i rgyan ces bya ba'i 'grel pa.*

Haribhadra's *vṛtti*-commentary on Maitreya's *Abhisamayālaṃkāra* (D 3793). All four items are incomplete manuscript fragments. #4722, #5164, and #5179 lack their beginnings. #8329 lacks its end. #4722 and #5179 are the first volume of the Tangut translation; #5179 and #8329 are the fifth volume. I have preliminarily examined #5179. The comparison between the Tangut

[423] #5130, frame 3, lines 1–6.

[424] #6449, frame 5, lines 22–27.

[425] *Bstan 'gyur* 49, 4.

translation and the Tibetan text shows the translation follows closely Rngog Lo's revised translation of the work.

The Tanguts obviously translated the basic text and the commentary independently, as the Tangut translations for the basic text and the commentary are quite different. We will still use the same verses as an example:

#6449	#5179	Tibetan Verse Text in the Commentary
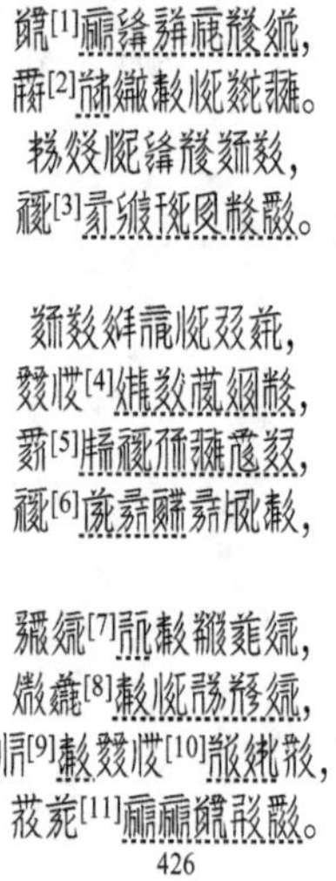 [426]	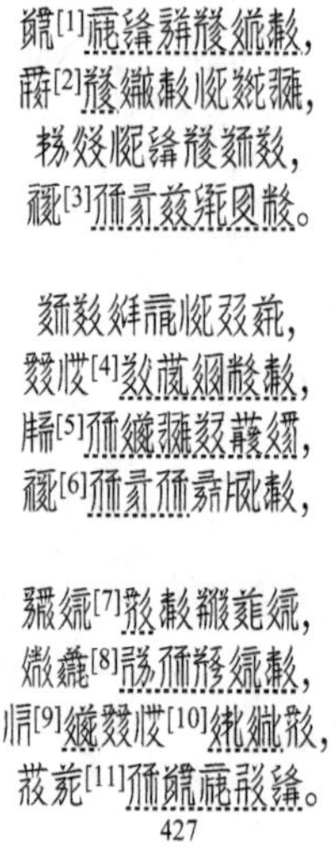 [427]	*/ rnam kun mngon rdzogs rtogs pa dang /* */ rtse mor phyin dang mthar gyis pa /* */ skad cig gcig mngon rdzogs byang chub /* */ chos kyi sku dang de rnam brgyad /* (5) */ sems bskyed pa dang gdams ngag dang /* */ nges 'byed yan lag rnam bzhi dang /* */ sgrub pa yi ni rten gyur pa /* */ chos kyi dbyings kyi rang bzhin dang /* (6) */ dmigs pa dag dang ched dang ni /* */ go cha 'jug pa'i bya ba dang /* */ tshogs ni nges par 'byung bcas rnams /* */ thub pa'i rnam kun mkhyen pa nyid /* (7)[428]

While these three verses are completely identical in the Tibetan translations of the text and the commentary, they are rather different in the Tangut translations. While none of these differences are in any sense dramatic, there are two features worth noticing. The text after nos. 1 and 4 of

[426] #6449, frame 5, lines 22–27.

[427] #5179, frame 6, lines 13–19.

[428] *Bstan 'gyur* 52, 212.

#5179 end with the conjunctive [Tangut], reflecting Tibetan *dang*. But [Tangut] is missing in both cases in #6449. The text after nos. 3 and 11 of #6449 end with the linking verb [Tangut], which reflects Tibetan *yin*. But [Tangut] is missing in both cases in #5179, which better reflects the Tibetan text. When taking #5130 into consideration as well, we realize it aligns with #6449 in all four places but is different from #5179. In view of these observations, we can draw a tentative conclusion that the Tanguts had two ways of translating the verses of the *Abhisamayālaṃkāra*, namely, one of the basic text and the other of the commentary, though the verses in these Tibetan translations identical.

Why, then, does the Tangut translation of the text move away from the Tibetan original while the system of the commentary does not do so from the Tibetan commentary text? If we exclude the possibility that the Tibetan basic text the Tanguts had was quite different from what we see today, then I suppose this has to do with the nature of the basic text. When reading and memorizing the basic text independently, it is ideal that the meaning of the verses should be as clear as possible. By adding the linking verb [Tangut], the system of the basic text makes it clear that it is the end of a section.[429] We also notice that, in [8], a conjunctive phrase is inserted between [Tangut][Tangut] (*go cha*, "armor") and [Tangut][Tangut][Tangut] (*'jug pa'i bya ba*, "that which is engaged"). The same applies to #5130. But such a conjunctive phrase is unseen in the Tibetan text. The translator of the basic text might have intentionally added it for the purpose of clarity because [Tangut][Tangut][Tangut][Tangut][Tangut][Tangut], the phrase in 5179, might be taken as meaning "the deed of engaging with the armor." Inserting the phrase makes it clear that these are two items. In contrast, the translator of the commentary could be more faithful to the verse text since the prose part would provide an explanation.

---

[429] I.5 is the end of listing the eight subjects of the *Abhisamayālaṃkāra*; I.6–7 are a list of the items contained in the first subject *sarvākārajñatā* (*rnam kun mkhyen pa nyid*) among the eight.

No. 3. [Tangut characters]……

Tang. 98 (#4593)

Tib. **Shes rab kyi pha rol tu phyin pa'i bshad pa gsal ba…*?

While the title can be translated as *Clarification…Commentary on the Prajñāpāramitā*, it is a commentary on the *Abhisamayālaṃkāra* and includes a topical outline in the text itself. While we can take [Tangut characters] as one phrase meaning "clarification…explanation," there seems to be at least one character missing at the end due to the damage of the manuscript. Nishida supplies [Tangut character], "mirror," at the end,[430] which is possible. [Tangut characters] would then seem to be a translation of the Tibetan *gsal gyi me long*, "clear mirror," which is a popular subtitle in Tibetan literature. The author is unknown though he undoubtedly postdated Ar Byang chub yes shes. Because at the end of the manuscript, it indicates "the fifth [volume]" ([Tangut characters]) and because the text is incomplete, we can suppose that this work had at least six volumes in its Tangut translation. Rngog Lo's viewpoints are cited for multiple times and Indian masters such as Haribhadra ([Tangut characters]) and Vimuktisena ([Tangut characters]) are also cited. A series of other Tibetan names also appear in the text. While some remain mysterious, we recognize names such as ·Jar [Tangut characters], who can be reasonably identified as Ar [Byang chub ye shes]. Ar Byang chub ye shes was a disciple of 'Bre Shes rab 'bar, who was the most important disciple of Rngog Lo tsā ba that developed his teachings on the *Prajñāpāramitā*.

[430] Nishida, "Seika yaku butten mokuroku," 34.

No. 4. [illegible]

Tang. 197 (#865, #866); Tang. 296 (#2531)

Tib. *Bden pa gnyis la 'jug pa.*

This is Atiśa's *Satyadvayāvatāra* which Solonin and Liu Kuowei Liu have studied closely and is related to the Bka' gdams pa tradition in general.[431] Our main concern here is whether and how the text is related to Gsang phu scholasticism in particular. According to Solonin and Liu, it is clear that #865 and #866 are parts of a translation of Atiśa's work in the translation made by Rgya Brtson 'grus seng ge and Atiśa himself.[432] However, #2531 is distant from the version that ended up in the Tibetan canon and should be regarded as translated from a different version of the Tibetan text that may not have been authored by Rgya and Atiśa.[433] Given that we know for sure that #2531 is a translation of the basic text of the *Satyadvayāvatāra* and not verses taken from other works,[434] it is, then, not impossible that the Tibetan original of #2531 was a new/revised translation of the *Satyadvayāvatāra*, which circulated mainly within the Gsang phu tradition. Even if the translation was not made by Rngog Lo,[435] it could have been done by another Gsang phu master.

---

[431] See Solonin and Liu, "Atiśa's *Satyadvayāvatāra* (*Bden pa gnyis la 'jug pa*) in the Tangut Translation."

[432] Solonin and Liu, "Atiśa's *Satyadvayāvatāra* (*Bden pa gnyis la 'jug pa*) in the Tangut Translation," 124–127. Rgya Brtson 'grus seng ge was one of the Tibetans who invited Atiśa but was unfortunately died on the way back to Tibet. For him, see Vitali, "Glimpses of the History of the Rgya Clan with Reference to Nyang Stod, Lho Mon and Nearby Lands (7th-13th Century)," 13–14.

[433] Solonin and Liu, "Atiśa's *Satyadvayāvatāra* (*Bden pa gnyis la 'jug pa*) in the Tangut Translation," 125.

[434] The colophon says [illegible] (*dji*^{2} *pã*^{1} *kja̱*^{1} *rjar*^{1}) [illegible], thus "composed by Dīpaṃkara[śrījñāna, i.e., Atiśa], the great master of the Western World."

[435] The list of works translated by Rngog Lo does not include the *Satyadvayāvatāra*; see Kramer, *The Great Tibetan Translator*, 54–70.

The possibility that the text belongs to the Gsang phu curriculum is enhanced when we look for an entry-level textbook for Madhyamaka in the Gsang phu tradition. For *prajñāpāramitā*, such a textbook is evidently the *Abhisamayālaṃkāra*; for Buddhist epistemology and logic, the textbook is obviously the *Nyāyabindu* (see work no. 9 in this section and Chapter Five). If we exclude the *Satyadvayāvatāra* from the Gsang phu tradition, then there will be virtually no entry-level textbook, and students would go directly to higher-level texts such as work nos. 5–7, which is unreasonable. The supposition is further supported by the content of #2531. The text is written in a notebook, which contains other philosophical texts; it is probably important to point out that in that notebook a précis of the *Nyāyabindu* is preceded by the *Satyadvayāvatāra*.[436] Since I will argue for the important position of the *Nyāyabindu* in Gsang phu scholastic training in the next chapter, it is quite possible that this notebook serves as a collection of the basic texts that are studied in the Gsang phu tradition of scholarship.

According to Solonin and Liu, there are additional Tangut texts that are in fact commentaries on the *Satyadvayāvatāra*.[437] Having examined more closely these texts, we will gain a deeper understanding of the place of the *Satyadvayāvatāra* in Tangut Buddhism.

No. 5. [Tangut characters]

Tang. 367 (#4372)

Tib. **Rngog lo tsā bas bshad pa'i tshul bden pa gnyis gyi don gyi zin bris*[438]

---

[436] Solonin and Liu, "Atiśa's *Satyadvayāvatāra* (*Bden pa gnyis la 'jug pa*) in the Tangut Translation," 127–132.

[437] Solonin and Liu, "Atiśa's *Satyadvayāvatāra* (*Bden pa gnyis la 'jug pa*) in the Tangut Translation," 125.

[438] The exact meaning of the word [Tangut character] (< Chin. 記, lit. "notes") in Tangut literature awaits appraisal, because it can have literally several meanings, including notes, biography, and epitaph (Li, *Jianming Xia Han zidian*, 645); however, it is clear that it is at least a genre of commentarial literature. Another hypothesis is any text bearing the word is a Tangut indigenous composition. But this cannot be proved at the moment. Therefore, in this section, I have tentatively used *zin bris*, "notes" in Tibetan, to reconstruct [Tangut character] throughout this section.

The Tangut title can be construed to mean *Notes on the Meaning of the Two Truths—According to the Explanation of Rngog Lo tsā ba*, and this is reflected in my reconstruction of the Tibetan title. The manuscript lacks a beginning and is somewhat fragmentary, but there is enough to enable us to get a sense of its contents. Rngog Lo has summary of and a commentary on Jñānagarbha's *Satyadvayavibhaṅga*.[439] This Tangut text could be to be a series of notes on the commentary in which we also find a topical outline that gives the reader an idea of the architecture of the text, and it often mentions Rngog Lo by name. Further study will no doubt be illuminating!

No. 6. [illegible]
Tang. 169 (#889, #5032)
Tib. *Dbu ma de kho na nyid* [*rnam par*] *dpyod pa*.

This is probably a translation of another recension of Rgya dmar ba's *Analysis of the Essence of Madhyamaka*, *Dbu ma de kho na nyid rnam par dpyod pa*. I have provided a detailed preliminary analysis of the text elsewhere.[440] I concluded in my earlier paper although the Tangut text is a translation of a work by Rgya dmar ba, it is not based on our current, unique Tibetan witness of a work with the same title of which we have a manuscript in thirty-one folios.[441] The Tangut translation and the manuscript version of the Tibetan text overlap about 50% in terms of

---

[439] See Kramer, *The Great Tibetan Translator*, 111, work nos. 16–17.

[440] See Ma, "Unveiling Gsang phu Madhyamaka Thought in Xixia."

[441] There are now several pieces of scholarship on the Tibetan version. See, for example, Hugon, "Wonders *in margine*." See also the project "The *dBu ma de kho na nyid* of rGya dmar ba Byang chub grags (12th c.)" started by Pascale Hugon and Kevin Vose in 2017. https://www.oeaw.ac.at/ikga/forschung/tibetologie/materialien/the-dbu-ma-de-kho-na-nyid-of-rgya-dmar-ba-byang-chub-grags-12th-c.

their contents, but the other 50% are different in various ways. For example, a large number of the verses that are present in the Tibetan manuscript are missing from the Tangut translation. Interestingly, what are there and what are missing do not seem to be random because almost all the introductory verses that set up the outline for the following sections are present, while all the concluding verses that summarize the meaning of the previous sections are missing. We could surmise that the Tibetan version is closer to Rgya dmar ba's original composition and the Tangut version is an adaption because the Tanguts judged those summarizing verses as unnecessary. But we could equally say the Tangut version is more faithful to the primitive status of the text and the Tibetan manuscript embodies a later stage of the text with more than one textual layer because the "missing verses" could also be interpreted as the verses later added as a mnemonic device. On the sentential level, while in most cases it is the Tibetan version that contains more information, we also see places where the Tangut version provides critical phrases and sentences that are otherwise unseen in the Tibetan version. Hence, the decisive evidence for supporting either the Tibetan or Tangut precedent is not available at the moment. Further research is necessary to settle the issue.

A fascinating feature of the Tangut manuscripts (especially #889) is that they contain notes that correspond to the notes in the Tibetan manuscript. The basic text of Rgya dmar ba's work contains very many philosophical positions whose holders are either listed as "someone" (*kha cig*) or simply left with no indication at all. Therefore, to effectively make sense of the philosophical positions, the user of the Tibetan manuscript wrote down notes to identify these positions as belonging to Rngog Lo and other Gsang phu masters such as Khyung Rin chen grags, Gangs pa She'u Blo gros byang chub, and Rgya dmar ba himself. Strikingly, notes like these are also present in the Tangut manuscripts. The Tangut notes use a phonetic transcription of a part of the name of the figure plus the affix 𗪙, "master," to identify the holder of the philosophical position. For example, Rngog Lo would be identified in the note as [Tangut] *ŋwə*^{1} *dzjij*^{2}, thus "Master Rngog." These Tangut notes are obviously not translations of the Tibetan notes. For example, in one place, the Tibetan note says, "Khyung and Lo tsā ba [=Rngog Lo]" (*khyung lo tsa*), but the Tangut note says, "Rngog and Khyung" ([Tangut] *ŋwə*^{1} *khjow*^{2}).[442] Therefore, these Tangut notes were likely taken in the classroom during a lecture, just like the Tibetan notes were taken so.

No. 7. [Tangut]

Tang. 225 (#883)

Tib. *Kun rdzob don dam bden gnyis kyi don bsdus pa'i zin bris*?

The Tangut title means *Notes on the Summary of the Two Truths of the Conventional and Ultimate*. I have preliminarily examined this text and concluded that it is a précis of Rgya dmar ba's work that figures above under work no. 6.[443] Although we do not know if the Tangut text is a translation or an indigenous composition, the *Summary of the Two Truths of the Conventional and Ultimate* is likely nothing but Rgya dmar ba's work because the first verse that appears in the manuscript is almost identical with the second verse of Rgya dmar ba's *Analysis of the Essence of Madhyamaka*, which is the introductory verse that sets forth what he intends to do in six chapters of his work. Of the five occurrences of Tibetan names in the Tangut manuscript, one is Rngog Lo, and the other four are all Rgya dmar ba,[444] thus further attesting its relevance to this Tibetan author.

---

[442] If the Tangut text were to be a translation of the term *lo tsa ba*, then it would use the phonetic transcription [Tangut] *lu*^{2} *tsja*^{1} *wa*^{1}.

[443] Ma, "Unveiling Gsang phu Madhyamaka Thought in Xixia," Section 7.

[444] Cited either as [Tangut], "Master Bodhi-Known" or simply [Tangut], "Master Known," thus a translation of Rgya dmar ba's religious name Byang chub grags.

Also noticeable is the scribe's colophon that is preserved at the end of manuscript #883. Following the Chinese calendar, it says that he completed his work on the twenty-seventh day of the seventh month (September 4th) of 1222, thus some 5 years before the Mongol conquest of the Tangut State. The year 1222 is then also the *terminus ante quem* for the reception of Rgya dmar ba's ideas of Madhyamaka in the Tangut State. But, of course, the actual introduction of his ideas was presumably earlier.

No. 8. [Tangut script]

Tang. 232 (#4363, #832), Tang. 233 (#5609), Or.12380/2145.

Tib. *Rigs pa'i thigs pa zhes bya ba'i rab tu byed pa.*

This is the Tangut translation of Dharmakīrti's *Nyāyabindu-prakaraṇa*, which I have studied in great detail elsewhere.[445]

No. 9. [Tangut script]

Tang. 231 (#826, #861, #863, #5022)

Tib. **Rigs pa'i thigs pa'i tshig don gsal bar byed pa.*

The English translation of the Tangut title is *Clarification of the Meaning and Words of the Nyāyabindu*. In Chapter Five of this dissertation, I offer a detailed introduction to this work and its place in the Gsang phu tradition, which also includes a fully annotated integral translation.

---

[445] See Ma, "The *Nyāyabindu* in Tangut Translation."

No. 10. [illegible]

Tang. 234 (#5951)

Tib. *Rigs pa'i thigs pa don dang po'i dpyod pa'i zin bris*?

The title means "Notes on Analysis of the First Section of the *Nyāyabindu*." This text does discuss direct perception (*pratyakṣa*), the topic of the first chapter of the *Nyāyabindu*. Rngog Lo's name is cited many times in the text.

No. 11. [illegible]

Tang. 234 (#873)

Tib. *Rigs pa'i thigs pa don gsum pa'i dpyod pa'i zin bris*?

The title means "Notes on Analysis of the Third Section of the *Nyāyabindu*." Kychanov's catalog records this text and work no. 10 under the same entry. But it seems reasonable to treat them differently since the titles of the two do not indicate one commentary on two chapters but two commentaries. And although work no. 10 and work no. 11 are both manuscripts, they were obviously written by different hands. Also, curiously enough, based on the remains of this text, we do not see it comments, at least not overtly, on the inference for others, which is the topic of the third chapter of *Nyāyabindu*. More study is necessary for determining both the relationship between work no. 10 and work no. 11 and their relations to the larger tradition.

No. 12. [illegible]

Tang. 230 (#834)

Tib. **Tshad ma nam mkha' rgyal mtshan* [*gyi*] *man ngag*?

The title means "The Essential Instruction of the Space Victorious Banner [=Nam mkha' rgyal mtshan?] on Epistemology." Kychanov recorded three fragments under this title (#834, #835, #890).[446] However, both #835 and #890 should be under the title of work no. 13 (see below). I have not seen the only fragment (#834) under this title. But judging from its title, it should be the basic text of work nos. 13–14.

The author of the work is unknown. I suspect the term "space victorious banner" ([Tangut characters]) stands for the Tibetan religious name Nam mkha' rgyal mtshan. Yet it is difficult to come up with anyone linked with the Gsang phu tradition bearing that name. Notably, there is another text that bears the strange name "space victorious banner" in its title. And this is *The Essential Instruction of the Space Victorious Banner in Forty Sections* ([Tangut characters], #871), which is about the ethical conduct prescribed by Atiśa and is similar to some small pieces in Atiśa's *Miscellaneous Teachings* (*Chos chung brgya rtsa*). Since the *Essential Instruction of the Space Victorious Banner on Epistemology* and the *Essential Instruction of the Space Victorious Banner in Forty Sections* have dramatically different subjects, the term "space victorious banner" does not seem to indicate anything related to the nature of the text. Instead, it is more plausible that it is a personal name. We can alternatively take it as a signature subtitle of the author, just like the signature "Ornamental Flower" (*Rgyan gyi me tog*) contained in almost every subtitle of Bcom ldan rig[s] pa'i ral gri, a.k.a. Dar ma rgyal mtshan (1227–1305), but it does not form a reasonable semantic segment. All

---

[446] Kychanov, *Katalog Tangytckix byddiyckix pamyatnikov Institut Boctokovedeniya Pocciyckoy Akademii Hayk*, 550–551.

in all, it is most likely the instruction given by a person called and so is the *Essential Instruction of the Space Victorious Banner in Forty Sections*.

No. 13. [Tangut]

Tang. 230 (#835, #890)

Tib. **Tshad ma['i] man ngag zin bris*?

The title means "Notes on the Essential Instructions of Buddhist Epistemology." It is a work on Buddhist Epistemology with the topical outline delineated. It is presumably a commentary on work no. 12, as the general convention of the text is that it first quotes from a "text" ([Tangut]) and then explains it. The author of the text is unknown. We cannot rule out the possibility that the text was composed by a Tangut. Rngog Lo is often referred to in the text. I observe two other curious names, which should indicate Indian masters. The first one is "Master Ornament" ([Tangut]). This most likely refers to Prajñākaragupta, the scholar who composed the *Ornament of the "Pramāṇavārttika"* (Skt. *Pramāṇavārttikālaṃkāra*). The second name is "Master Noble Virtuous Divinity" ([Tangut]). Philologically speaking, this seems to reflect Tibetan 'Phags pa Dge ba'i lha. Based on this, the only Indian master we can possibly think of is Kalyāṇadeva, who composed a commentary on Śāntideva's *Bodhicaryāvatāra*. However, it would be a little bit unnatural to ascribe Kalyāṇadeva to someone who is skilled in epistemology. In the text, the viewpoint of "Master Noble Virtuous Divinity" is presented as regarding the means of knowledge as something without which one ultimately disintegrates all phenomena and makes one realize emptiness.

Both fragments lack the beginning. The available part of the work begins with explaining some important points of the inference for oneself and the inference for others. Then, it explains the three types of correct logical reason. Further, it explains the types of pseudo-logical reasons. Following that, it demonstrates the use of examples. Finally, it discusses why emptiness, the ultimate truth, is what should be assessed by means of knowledge. The structure, in general, seems to be based on the structure of the *Nyāyabindu*.

No. 14.

Tang. 236 (#912)

Tib. * *Tshad ma*[*'i*] *nam mkha' rgyal mtshan man ngag sgo lcags 'byed pa*?

The title means "Unlocking the Essential Instruction of the Space Victorious Banner [=Nam mkha' rgyal mtshan?] on Buddhist Epistemology)." The author is unknown. And we cannot rule out the possibility that the text was composed by a Tangut. Like work no. 13, this text is also supposedly a commentary on work no. 12. The convention is the same. It first quotes several phrases from the "text," and then explains them. Obviously, some of the quoted passages in both works are identical, thus indicating they are most probably commentaries on the same basic text. The sequence of topics presented in the work is the same as that of work no. 13. And while it also lacks a beginning, it covers more topics and includes most of the topics related to direct perception. However, this work is much more succinct than work no. 13, it only very briefly discusses most topics, and because of its conciseness, it does not cite any scholar's viewpoint.

That being said, it is still possible to determine its relation to the Gsang phu scholastic tradition. The most striking fact is that the text has abundant traces of "text re-use," an important custom in the Gsang phu tradition.[447] For example, the Tangut text has the following sentence:

> [illegible]，[illegible]，[illegible]。[448]
>
> The definition of the mere sensory cognition is, having relied on the sense faculty, the dominant condition, being able to perceive the cognitive object.

Interestingly, in 'Jad pa's *Essential Nature*, there is a sentence that has almost the same meaning:

> *dbang po'i mngon sum tshad ma'i mtshan nyid ni bdag po'i rkyen dbang po gzungs can la rten nas skyes shing gzung don la ma 'khrul ba'i stobs kyis sgro 'dogs gcod byed ces bya ba'o /*[449]
>
> The definition of valid sensory perception is being born on the basis of having relied on the apprehender—sense faculty, the dominant condition, and, through the force of being non-erroneous with regard to the apprehended object, eliminating the superimposition.

Not only are their meanings similar, but many words and even particles used in the sentences are equivalents. For example, [illegible] is the Tangut equivalent for *ni*; [illegible] is for *bdag po'i rkyen*; [illegible] is for *dbang po*; [illegible] is for *la*; [illegible] is for *brten*, etc. Of course, the places where they are different are also significant. For example, "superimposition" (Tib. *sgro 'dogs*) is not present in the Tangut text. This is likely because the concept of superimposition as a criterion for determining whether an episode of awareness is knowledge or not only became vital in Phya pa's works. And 'Jad pa, a

---

447 Pascale Hugon, "Text Re-use in Early Tibetan Epistemological Treatises," 453–491.

448 #912, frame 1, lines 12–13.

449 *Tshad bsdus*, 165.

post-Phya pa figure, was also heavily influenced by Phya pa's thoughts. Yet the Tangut text is probably a reflection of the pre-Phya pa tradition, just like work no. 9.

No. 15. [illegible]

Tang. 314 (#5073, #5112, #5801, #7905)

Tib. **Rtog ge la 'jug pa gsal bar byed pa'i rgyan.*

The title means "The Ornament that Clarifies the Introduction to Speculative Thinking." Since my detailed study of this work has been published elsewhere,[450] The author is Rma bya. And the work, whose Tibetan original is not yet available, is a typical Gsang phu "summary" (Tib. *bsdus pa*) and follows in general the structure of Phya pa's *Tshad ma yid kyi mun sel*. The text is valuable as it is the only witness of Rma bya's thoughts on Buddhist epistemology that we currently have.

No. 16. [illegible]

Tang. 235 (#4851, #5923, #5933)

Tib. *Tshad ma yid kyi mun sel*

My preliminary examination of the work was published elsewhere.[451] Using English, I will discuss some essential points related to the text here. This is an extremely intriguing text for which we can, without even looking at the content, almost reconstruct the Tibetan title as Phya pa's

---

[450] See Ma, "Introduction to Speculative Thinking."

[451] See Ma, "Xixia yi *Zhengli chu yi zhi an* chu tan."

famous work on *pramāṇa*, *Epistemology—Dispelling the Mind's Darkness*, *Tshad ma yid kyi mun sel* (henceforth *Epistemology*).[452] However, it remained inconclusive because of the Tangut text. By closely examining the content, I identified this text with Phya pa's *Tshad ma yid kyi mun sel*. The three available textual items of the work all lack beginnings. Based on the endings of them, we know they are the fourth, fifth, and sixth volumes of the Tangut translation. The following is a comparison between the end of #4851 and the corresponding passage in the Tibetan text:

> [illegible]。[illegible]。[453]
>
> *mthong yang bdag gcig*[a] *ma yin par bsgrub pa ni tha snyad tsam bsgrub pa yin no / sha pa'i rnam pa gzhan du mthong ba med pas ga la mtshungs /*[454]
>
> [a] Ms. gchig.

Curiously, while the Tibetan sentence quoted above is located somewhere towards the end of chapter two of the work, the Tangut text ends abruptly after this sentence with the colophon title [illegible], "The Fourth Volume of the *Tshad ma yid kyi mun sel*." In this case, the Tangut "volume" does not translate Tibetan *le'u*, which means "chapter" in this context. Therefore, the Tangut volume seems to be rather arbitrarily designated not only because they do not reflect the Tibetan chapters but also because they end in the middle of a passage like this one. The next Tibetan sentence that follows the above quoted lines is *gnod byed yod pa ni / shing snang pa na*

---

[452] For the process of identification, see, for example, Nishida, "Seika yaku butten mokuroku," 45, translated the Tangut title into Japanese which was picked by Kano, *Buddha-Nature and Emptiness*, 208, who tentatively identified as Phya pa's *Tshad ma yid kyi mun sel*, which then found its way in Hugon and Stoltz, *The Roar of a Tibetan Lion*, 41.

[453] #4851, frame 22, lines 11–12.

[454] *Epistemology*, 39a6.

sha pa the tshom.... We observe a similar way of ending the sixth volume of the Tangut translation (#5933):

> [illegible]，[illegible]，[illegible]。[455]
>
> *the tshom za ba rtags kyi skyon ma yin pas nges pa la rnam par gcad par bya ba med pas mtshan nyid ma yin no /*[456]

The last sentence of this volume is located in the middle of the fourth chapter of the Tibetan original. Although this time, the Tangut text does close in tandem with a Tibetan passage, the ending is still somehow flawed in terms of coherence as this passage is the second topic under a general heading that contains three topics.

To account for this randomness, I assume we need to view the intention of the editors of the Tangut texts from a quantitative perspective rather than a qualitative one. The strict enforcement of the cutoff could be based on a rigid limit of the length of a volume. We do not know whether the measure of the length is based on the counting of the Tangut characters or the Tibetan syllables. But it is obvious that every volume of this work would cover a relatively equal span of the text, while the distribution of the lengths of the five chapters is quite unequal (The fourth chapter takes more than one-third of the work). A simple calculation may prove this. For the total 192 pages of the published Tibetan manuscript[457], the first four volumes occupy about 78 pages, thus making one volume about 19.5 pages if we calculate the mean value. The first six volume spends about 115 pages, yielding about 19.2 pages for the mean. The fact that these two

---

[455] #5933, frame 14, lines 13.

[456] *Epistemology*, 57b10–58a1.

[457] *Epistemology*, 435–626 (in modern pagination).

results are very close supports this hypothesis. Based on this, we could even deduce the total number of volumes translated for Phya pa's *Epistemology*, which is 10 (192 ÷ 19.2 = 10).

We do not know why this quantitative measurement was carried out faithfully. A clue would be from the translation projects in the early Later Diffusion period when translators were sometimes paid based on the number of groups of syllables (*bam po*)[458] they translated. It is possible to conjure a similar episode for the Tanguts. It should also be noted that in the manuscripts of this text, we see a large number of interlinear notes and annotations, which imply the actual application of this text for extensive training on Buddhist epistemology.

This list is by no means exhaustive. Judging from the titles and colophons provided in other catalogs, we can surmise that there are many more texts that would be attributed to the Gsang phu tradition. But their natures can only be determined after carefully analyzing their contents. Hence, I have not included every possible text here. Besides, we should not forget the Tibetan texts excavated in Khara-Khoto. Kano Kazuo, for example, has identified one text from the British Library to be Rngog Lo's *Summary of the Meaning of the Uttaratantra*, *Rgyud bla ma'i bsdus don*.[459] The IOM in St. Petersburg obviously possesses many more unpublished Tibetan texts that may further shed light on the issue of Gsang phu scholasticism in the Tangut State.

4. Gsang phu Scholasticism and the Structure of Tangut Buddhism

Having discussed some salient features about the Gsang phu tradition in the Tangut State, we now realize that, as detailed in Chapter Three, the rise of Tibetan Buddhism was heavily

[458] van der Kuijp, "Some Remarks on the Meaning and Use of the Tibetan Word *bam po*," 131–132.

[459] Kano, "Rngog blo ldan shes rab's Topical Outline of the *Ratnagotravibhāga* Discovered at Khara Khoto."

predicated on the fact that the strong transformative power of Tibetan Buddhist tantra fulfilled both the soteriological goal pursued by individuals, that is, Individual Buddhism, as well as the collective welfare of the State in the sense State Buddhism. Thus, it appears prima facie that the scholastic approach was only a trivial or perhaps even an irrelevant issue in adoption of Buddhism. How then should we make sense of it against the context of the profound religious transformation of the Tangut State? Or can we even make sense of it?

To answer these questions, let us first examine several features of the Tangut texts of Gsang phu scholastic subjects. The first notable feature is that almost all texts are manuscripts. This is remarkable when we compare them to texts of other subjects. We have seen in Chapter Two, Section 2.4, that most texts of State Buddhism are block prints since they are intended for mass distribution. About half of the Tangut Chan texts are also block prints. For example, in the four textual items of the Tangut translation of the *Preface to the Collection of Chan Sources*, *Chan yuan zhu quan ji du xu* 禪源諸詮集都序, of Zongmi listed by Kychanov, two are manuscripts and two are block prints.[460] Some other Chan works, such as the intriguing *Collection of the Accordance of Condition* (𗌭𗗙𗆗, *Sui yuan ji 隨緣集)[461], only have block print texts. A portion of the Tangut texts of Tibetan tantric Buddhism is also block print. The most famous case would be the Tangut translation of the *Saṃpūṭatantra* the text of which was based on the Tibetan translation of ’Gos Lo tsā ba Khug pa lhas btsas (11th c.).[462]

[460] Kychanov, *Katalog Tangytckix byddiyckix pamyatnikov Institut Boctokovedeniya Pocciyckoy Akademii Hayk*, 465–466.

[461] Kychanov, *Katalog Tangytckix byddiyckix pamyatnikov Institut Boctokovedeniya Pocciyckoy Akademii Hayk*, 584. For a study of the work, see Solonin and Zhang, "The Tangut Text of *Suiyuan ji* and the History of Chan Buddhism in Xixia."

[462] For a study of the work, see Sun, *Xixiawen "Jixiang bianzhi kouhe benxu" zhengli yanjiu*.

A reasonable explanation for the scarcity of Tangut printed texts of Tibetan scholastic subjects, I suppose, is the lack of a market. These texts are obviously not suitable for distribution at a religious gathering as they are not really powerful objects for merit accumulation. We know that some people in the Tangut State had their private printing houses and printed Buddhist texts for commercial purposes.[463] But they clearly did not see the project of printing these texts on scholastic subjects as profitable. Thus, people such as the user of #5130 (work no. 1) had to make a manuscript copy from an older printed version. And some of the texts might never have been printed ever since their translation or composition.

Another feature is that most of these manuscripts contain annotations, and some of these are quite extensive like the ones in the manuscripts of works nos. 6, 15, and 16 (see fig. 1). This phenomenon of extensive annotation is rarely seen in Tangut texts that deal other subjects such as tantric instructions, etc. What it tells us, I suppose, is that the manuscripts of scholastic subjects were used in classroom settings where either students were taking notes or the teacher was teaching from a manuscript of a certain work on which he had scribbled his notes. So, the Tangut translators or students must have an informant providing them with all the identities of those unidentified "some" or "someone" ([illegible], **kha cig*) in the main text. Hence, the notes should be viewed as a real-time product resulting from classroom instruction. And when we proceed further with this analysis, it is evident that we are not talking about any classroom in general but the classroom in monasteries due to the nature of these texts. The audience should therefore be monastics. The evidence that effectively supports the assumption is that the "owner of the manuscript" ([illegible]), if recorded,

[463] This kind of activity is attested by publisher's colophons. See Nie, *Xixia Fojing xuba yizhu*, 16–17.

usually bears a religious name. For example, both the owners of manuscripts #834 (work no. 12) and #890 (work no. 13) both have [illegible], "jewel,"[464] as a part of their names.

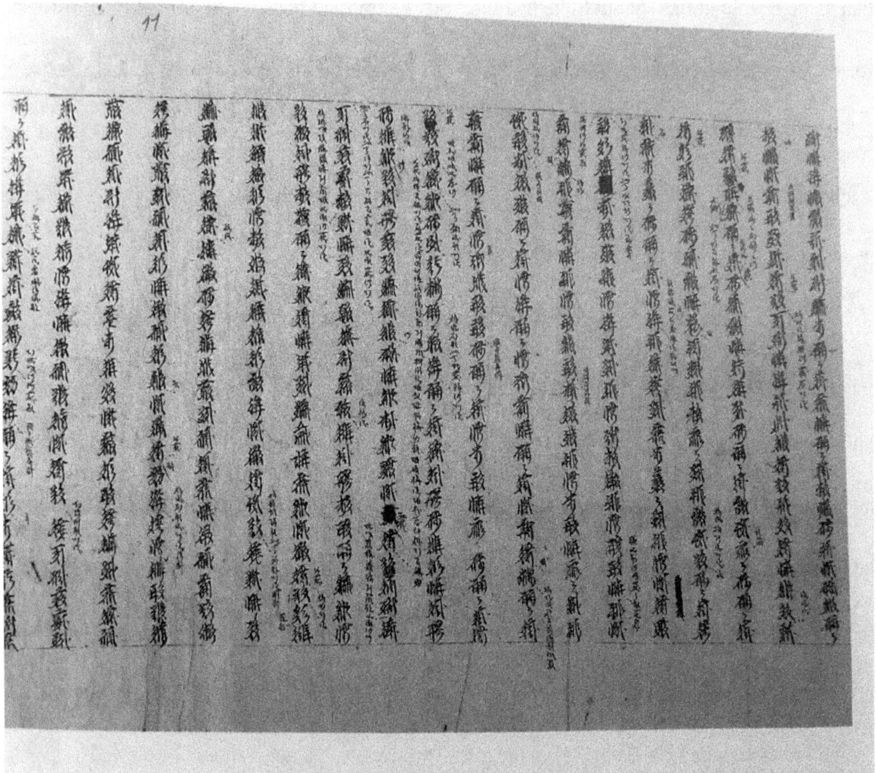

Figure 1. The ending part of #5933. Institute of Oriental Manuscripts, Russian Academy of Sciences, St. Petersburg.[465]

The next feature, although only shown in one case, is significant. Manuscript fragment #2516 contains two fragments whereby the beginning and the end are missing. The first fragment

---

[464] This could mean that if they had a Tibetan master, the master might have *dkon mchog* as part of his name in religion. For example, this could remind us of the imperial preceptor Gtsang po pa Dkon mchog seng ge, whose name is partly translated as [illegible], "dkon mchog," in his Tangut name.

[465] Photo from ECMS 28, plate 3.

is a work on a philosophical subject which is followed by a tantric text. The first is a work on Gsang phu Buddhist epistemology, whose content remains to be identified.[466] Surprisingly, the text is followed by a *sāadhana* of Vaiśravaṇa. This might suggest that the study of a philosophical subject does not preclude the study of tantric work, and this precisely what we also find in late Indian and Tibetan Buddhism.

Finally, as some colophons of manuscript nos. 1, #5130 and 7, #883) of the work that we discussed in Section Three already indicate, these manuscripts were in general copied during the very end of Tangut State. This means that the rise of Tibetan tantric Buddhism never replaced the study of scholastic and philosophical subjects. The practice of engaging in both of them continued until the end of the Tangut State.

In sum, we can assume that the intended audience and users of these philosophical texts were mainly monastics. And thus the circulation of these works was very likely quite restricted. As the *Tiansheng Legal Code*[467] prescribes, Tangut monks need to be trained in certain Buddhist subjects before getting promoted. While the *Tiansheng Legal Code* does not list names of works that pertain to what I have called Gsang phu scholasticism – it does list, for example, the *Avataṃsakasūtra* and the *Humane King Sutra*, as titles – it is very likely that in the late twelfth century, these works were incorporated into the curriculum. Also, monks who studied the scholastic subjects did not distance themselves from tantric practices. Exoteric and esoteric contents formed a consistent whole in their training, which continued until the very end of the Tangut State.

[466] I have briefly discussed the text in Ma, "The *Nyāyabindu* in Tangut Translation," 783–784.

[467] See Introduction and Chapter Two, Section 2.3.

Therefore, it is not the case that Gsang phu scholasticism is irrelevant to the rise of Tibetan Buddhism in the Tangut State, which is primarily a story about the ascendency of Tibetan tantrism. Instead, the Tangut assimilation of the Gsang phu tradition of philosophical analysis was an integral part of that process. I suggest, in some ways, this inclusion also facilitated the success of tantrism. Tantric movements, which are at times rebellious,[468] can potentially cause disturbance within the preexistent political structure. This is apparent in the case of King Ye shes 'od (947–1019/1024) of the Gu ge Kingdom, who, in an edict around 990, criticized some tantric practitioners in Tibet who did not follow the monastic rules.[469] Ye shes 'od prohibited "such false teachings," and what he offered to "these misguided *tāntrikas* was normative exoteric Buddhism – the moral truths of cause and effect, a gradual path of self-improvement, generosity, and laboring for the welfare of others."[470] I would hypothesize that by implementing a required scholastic curriculum in the Tangut State within the monastic institutions, the later Tangut rulers, if they did so, did it to prevent a decentralization of their religio-political authority. It is obvious that Ye shes 'od's intentional avoidance of the uncensored tantric teachings did not bring his kingdom a full victory. As Dalton concludes, "Yeshe Ö's ambitious project fell short. For centuries, his Gugé Kingdom would remain strongly dedicated to monastic Buddhism, but it would never achieve anything approaching the glory of the early Pugyal Empire."[471] While the Tangut State did not

---

[468] A typical example of this is the emergence of siddhas. Davidson summarizes, "The siddhas' goal was individual dominion over the sorcerers, the Vidyādharas, and the gods themselves, those divinities by whose authority the overlord rules. The siddha traditions also imported a politics of dominion and control, but for the benefit of the single siddha and not necessarily for the betterment of the surrounding community"; see Davidson, *Indian Esoteric Buddhism*, 337.

[469] See Dalton, *The Taming of the Demons*, chap. 4. For a study of the edict, see Karmay, *The Arrow and the Spindle*, 3–16.

[470] Dalton, *The Taming of the Demons*, 97, 105.

[471] Dalton, *The Taming of the Demons*, 102.

have an achievement comparable to the Tibetan Empire either, its religio-political structure was maintained steadily until the final Mongol conquest.

On the other hand, institutionalization seems inevitable for the long-term success of tantric Buddhism. Although the tantric movement might start with individual effort, at a certain point, it will become institutionalized.[472] This is what we see in the case of Tibet – multiple transmissional lineages such as those from 'Brog mi Lo tsā ba (ca. 992–1074) and Mar pa Lo tsā ba (?1012–1097?), which started in the early eleventh century, were turned into various monastic institutions in the late eleventh century, thus ensuring a continuing institutional basic of the esoteric teachings.[473] The Tangut courts may have based themselves on such a model from early on, thereby perhaps appointing state-controlled monasteries as critical nodes for promulgating Tibetan tantric Buddhism, thus effectively transforming the whole realm into the new religious ideal. Such an endeavor of bringing together philosophical training and tantric practice to a single institutional basis stands then in sharp contrast to the rulers of the later empires of China and Inner Asia, who confined the teachings mainly within the circle of the royal family. This difference further demonstrates the important dynamics in shaping the historical development from the prototypical empire, the Tangut State, to the mature Inner Asian empires of the Yuan and Qing.

---

[472] Wedemeyer rejects the notion that Buddhust tantra initially was the enterprise of individuals. He argues that tantric Buddhism was at the very beginning rooted in Buddhist institutions. He says, "Unlike previous models my interpretation suggests communities deeply integrated into the intellectual, institutional, and social structure of prior Buddhist traditions"; Wedemeyer, *Making Sense of Tantric Buddhism*, 202.

[473] See Davidson, *Tibetan Renaissance*, chap. 7, esp. 274–275.

Chapter Five: A Preliminary Study of

The Clarification of the Words and Meaning of the Nyāyabindu

This chapter falls into two parts. The first part contains some general remarks about the text and its witnesses, its importance for Buddhist epistemology, its place in Tangut Buddhism, and other aspects that facilitate the understanding of second part which consists of a partial annotated translation of the beginning of the text.

PART ONE: INTRODUCTION

1. The Purpose of the Study

This chapter presents a preliminary study of the first volume[474] of *The Clarification of the Words and Meaning of the Nyāyabindu* ([illegible], **Rigs pa'i thigs pa'i tshig don gsal bar byed pa*, henceforth *Clarification*), which has been recorded as work no. 9 in Chapter Four, Section 3. An important question we must tackle before going into the translation is, as many would ask, in what way is my study of a text in Buddhist philosophy related to the whole discussion of the rise of Tibetan Buddhism in the Tangut State. This is undoubtedly a justifiable question in many respects. First, the text provides us with almost no historical information about how Tibetan Buddhism was transmitted to the Tangut land. Apart from its extremely succinct colophon, the text contains no personal names, place names, dates, or events of any sort that allow us to investigate that very history of transmission. Not only that, but the text is also, above all, a product of

---

474 What is currently available is only the first volume. See Chapter Four, Section 3 and Chapter Five, Section 2.

speculative thinking, which means it does not deal with Buddhist ethics, rituals, medical science, arts and crafts, etc., subjects that may in one way or the other inform us about the social history of Tangut Buddhism.[475] Quite the opposite, the text engages in philosophical discussions that are essentially devoid of a tangible spatial or temporal context due to the very nature of its subject. And, given that Buddhist epistemology is one of the least "Buddhist" subjects in Buddhism, it seems even more difficult to connect it to the main concerns in this dissertation, which are all about Buddhism. Furthermore, the text is a Tangut translation of a Tibetan treatise rather than a Tangut indigenous composition. Although its original is not extant, we cannot say that the text reflects much Tangut local creation on account of its reception of Tibetan Buddhism. Hence, we are also unable to take it as a Tangut intellectual product resulting from that very history.

The lack of historical sources such as the *Blue Annals* in the case of Tibet poses the biggest obstruction to any endeavor of forming a rich historical narrative for the rise of Tibetan Buddhism in the Tangut State. By collecting pieces of historical information from colophons, paleographical materials, and biographical accounts, we can try to push that effort of building up a historical narrative much as we can. This is what I have attempted to do in Chapter Three. However, there should be an alternative way of studying the history, namely, to make sense of the documents of that very history. And this is the task I conceive for myself in this chapter. While the text examined here does not tell us anything *about* the history, it is itself a piece *of* the history. By reading the text, we endeavor to put ourselves in the very historical moment in which our fellow Tangut readers engaged in the same text. In such a process, we do not learn the history on the basis of

[475] For example, canonical works on the rules and regulations to be followed by the clergy and the laity, that is, *vinaya*, have become important sources in recent scholarship of the social history of early Buddhism. See Clarke, *Family Matters in Indian Buddhist Monasticisms*. Ritual texts, on the other hand, may reflect how Buddhism is practiced in a given social context. For example, a ritual text of human sacrifice from Dunhuang bespeaks the possible violence practiced during that period. See Dalton, *The Taming of the Demons*, chap. 3.

being instructed by something external; instead, we experience the history reflexively through the contact with our reading experience of the document belonging to that history. Indeed, this is what I personally feel as a long-term companion of Khara-Khoto texts – they speak to me as witnesses of the history, and I appear to be carried to the time of their existence when reading them. This privilege is probably enjoyed only by those textual sources that are not intended to be written as history. We should also keep in mind that the extremely arcane philosophical content in the text for any reader who has little or no background in the subject would look equally foreign to its Tangut readers.

The possible path of "experiencing" the history has thus endowed my work with some significance: the Tangut text has to be accessible to a modern audience in order to bridge the past and the present. For those who do not read Tangut, we now have the option to read the English version; for those who are not familiar with the philosophical language, we can now refer to the annotations for explanations. Therefore, I believe my primary undertaking here is to make sense of the text and make it an approachable document of history.

Making sense of the text grants us another opportunity of looking into the history. While the text does not tell us what its history was diachronically, it can at least tell it synchronically. By probing into the content of the text as well as relating it to other Tangut Buddhist texts, we are able to come up with an understanding of the kind of curriculum of Tibetan Buddhist scholasticism the Tanguts engaged in, especially the curriculum of Buddhist epistemology and logic. Moreover, in terms of intellectual history, since we already know the text is a sample from the Gsang phu scholastic tradition, we can try to figure out what particular ideas the Tanguts judged as worth learning in comparison with those they excluded. And those ideas they embraced, then, might become what shaped the Tanguts' intellectual world of Tibetan Buddhism. Contextualizing the text in Tibetan intellectual history thus sheds light on the Tangut's particular way of assimilating that tradition. These issues will be discussed mainly in Section 8.

The content of this text within the larger Gsang phu tradition also means we can have a more comprehensive understanding of the intellectual history of the early phase of the Later Diffusion in Tibet in that it adds another piece of the puzzle to this tradition since the Tibetan original of the text appears not to be extant. This is another great strength of Tangut-Tibetan Studies, which has so far not been specifically addressed.[476] As we will see, this text serves as a crucial exemplar of the interim thoughts on Buddhist epistemology and logic between Rngog Lo and Phya pa, which is unfortunately missing from the Tibetan texts that are currently available. We will turn to this later in Section 7. Granted, the potential of the text to showcase Tibetan intellectual history does not seem to be immediately linked to our pursuit of the rise of Tibetan Buddhism in the Tangut State. Yet, that is only true if we confine ourselves to the regional studies of Tangut. From a more transregional perspective, the significance of this text in the study of Tibetan intellectual history and the point addressed in the last paragraph are evidently two sides of the same coin. Without making sense of the position of the text in the Gsang phu scholastic tradition, an evaluation of the reception of these ideas in the Tangut State is impossible. On the other hand, an explicit pursuit of the ideas in the Tangut State will of course also implicitly reveal the structure of them in the Gsang phu tradition.

The study also aims at laying the foundation for our future exploration of the other similar Buddhist philosophical texts in Tangut. The paucity of our knowledge of the scholastic language in Tangut is in sheer contrast with the abundance of the textual material written in that language, which has been partially shown in Chapter Four, Section 3. As I have argued elsewhere, to

[476] For some remarks on this question, see Ma, "Introduction to Speculative Thinking," 4–6.

effectively engage in the research of a certain genre of text, the readers cannot merely claim that they have learned the language but have to be sure that they have mastered the specific type of language germane to that genre.[477] For example, the triad of definition / definiens ([Tangut], *mtshan nyid*), definiendum ([Tangut], *mtshon bya*), and definitional basis ([Tangut], *mtshan gzhi*) in the Tangut language exists in the texts belonging to the Gsang phu tradition as well in Sa paṇ's *Epistemology: Treasury of Reasoning* and its many commentaries. To this end, the study of the text is also a specimen for linguists to further investigate the syntax and lexicon of the Tangut language. While the task of advancing our knowledge of the language might be better done with the textual criticism of a Tangut translation and its Tibetan original, like work no. 16 in Chapter Four, Section 3, the text in question here should not be excluded from the list of ideal candidates. Although the original of the text is not available, many other Tibetan texts that contain terms, sentences, and passages parallel to those in this text are available. This is demonstrated in Section 6. We can thus reconstruct the Tibetan of many of the words and phrases in the Tangut text and make sense of some long and complicated sentences. I have therefore reconstructed as many as possible to allow linguists in Tangut and scholars in Tibetan Studies to keep track of the translation.

This is, I believe, the very first time a Tangut text of Buddhist philosophy of this length has been translated into English.

2. Manuscripts

The Tangut translation of the *Clarification* has four fragmentary manuscript witnesses, namely, #861, #862, #863, and #5022. For our convenience, we will name them M1–M4. The

[477] See Ma, "The *Nyāyabindu* in Tangut Translation," 781.

Tangut title of the work appears at the very beginning of M1 (see fig. 1) and at the concluding lines of M2–M4. Based on their shared titles, Gorbacheva and Kychanov decided in their 1963 catalog of Tangut texts that they belonged to the same work and numbered it as Tang. 231.[478] However, all the titles in these manuscripts are followed by the phrase "upper volume" (𗼃𗣼), thus indicating that all of them only represent the first part of the whole work. Nishida, in his 1977 catalog, assumes that the work might be translated from Tibetan and refers to the canonical Tibetan translation of Jinamitra's *Nyāyabindupiṇḍārtha* as its possible original.[479] We now know it is indeed translated from Tibetan, but the specific identification should be set aside.[480] In his 1999 catalog, Kychanov further provides details of the formats and sizes of the four manuscripts. In addition, he identified the information of the author recorded in the colophon in M1 as well as the scribe's colophon in M2.[481] In the most recent catalog of Hui Hong and Duan Yuquan, they only briefly describe the work and basically follow Nishida's assumption.[482]

---

[478] Gorbacheva and Kychanov, *Tangutskiye rukopisi i ksilografy*, 108.

[479] Nishida, "Seika yaku butten mokuroku," 45.

[480] I have discussed this briefly in Ma, "The *Nyāyabindu* in Tangut Translation," 790, n.3.

[481] Kychanov, *Katalog Tangytckix byddiyckix pamyatnikov Institut Boctokovedeniya Pocciyckoy Akademii Hayk*, 502–503.

[482] Hui and Duan, *Xixia wenxian jieti mulu*, 212.

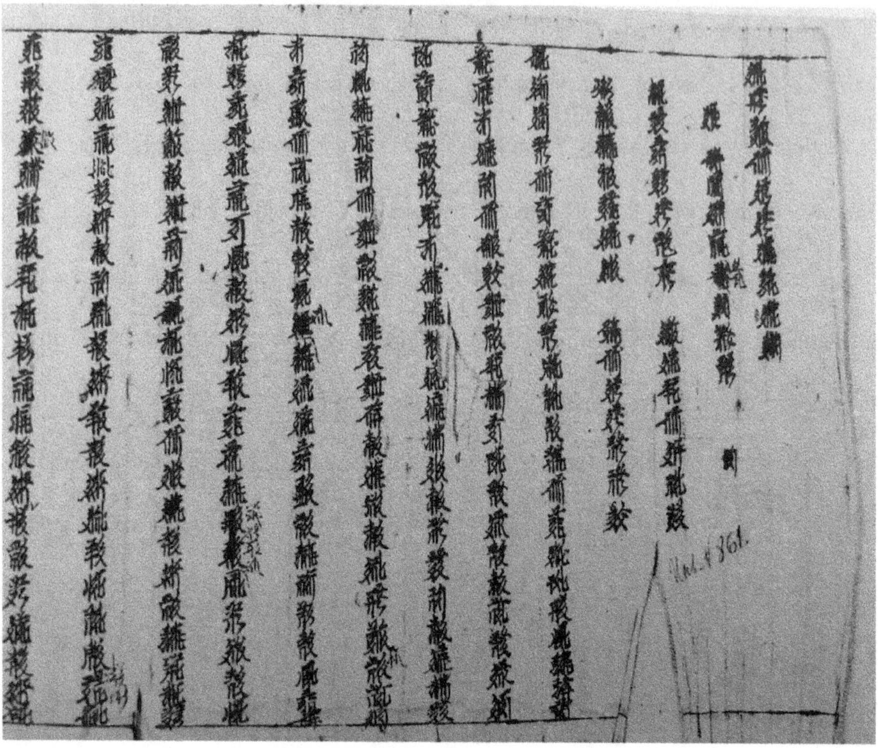

Figure 1. The beginning of M1 (#861). Institute of Oriental Manuscripts, Russian Academy of Sciences, St. Petersburg.[483]

We will discuss the authorship statement in M1 in Section 3. Here, let us examine the scribe's colophon at the end of M2. The last two characters are hardly legible and there seem to be more characters that are now missing due to the break in the manuscript. Still, the legible part reads:

[illegible]。[illegible]，[illegible]? ?……

[483] Photo from ECMS 28, 42.

> Copied[484] by the scribe Zjwị ·o Gjṳ rjur śjow. When persons who are inferior in intelligence[485] see it, [they] only dislike…

The scribe's name consists of three parts. Zjwị ·o [Tangut] is no doubt his clan name, which is fairly common among the Tanguts.[486] Gjṳ rjur [Tangut], which literally means "glorious" (< Ch. *jixiang* 吉祥, Skt. *śrī*, Tib. *dpal*) seems to be a part of his religious name. The last part, the śjow [Tangut], literally means "iron," and is also a common component of Tangut names.[487] But we are not a hundred percent sure that it should be counted as part of his religious name, *Dpal lcags, or whether it is his layman's name. What we can tentatively infer from the available information is that the scribe was a Tangut and probably also a monk. The second sentence here is also of interest. It seems to be a cautionary tale, suggesting that many people might indeed be disappointed by this text because of its philosophical sophistication. But it can be interpreted in several ways. It could be that the manuscript was copied at an early stage when Gsang phu scholasticism was just being introduced to the Tangut State.

All four manuscripts are scrolls. But, since all of them are fragments, none of them actually cover the full text of the first volume of the text in two or three volumes. Fortunately, by joining them together, we can in fact acquire the entire text of the first volume. Among these fragments,

---

484 While the Tangut [Tangut] literally means "to write," just like the Tibetan *'bri*, it should mean "to copy" here in this context.

485 The expression [Tangut] here is reminiscent of the Tibetan *blo gros dman pa*.

486 See Han, *Xixiawen cidian*, 4:217. Several other persons bearing that clan name also appear in Khara-Khoto texts, for which see Kychanov, *Katalog Tangytckix byddiyckix pamyatnikov Institut Boctokovedeniya Pocciyckoy Akademii Hayk*, 673–674.

487 We see that, in Tangut registers, there are names such as Zjwị ·o Gjṳ rjur nẹw [Tangut] and Zjwị ·o Thu ɣie śjow [Tangut] (Han, *Xixiawen cidian*, 4:217). The first, excluding the clan name, would mean "glorious excellence," which would well be religious name reflecting the Sanskrit name Śrībhadra or the Tibetan name Dpal bzang po. The second, excluding the clan name, would mean "drawing-force-iron," which does not seem to be a religious name.

M2 is the longest, covering roughly 85% percent of the text from the end. M1 is the second longest, covering about 65% of the text from the beginning. M3 covers about 45% of the text from the end. And M4 covers about 40% of the text from the end. The distribution of their spans in the text of the first volume of the *Clarification* is shown in the following chart:

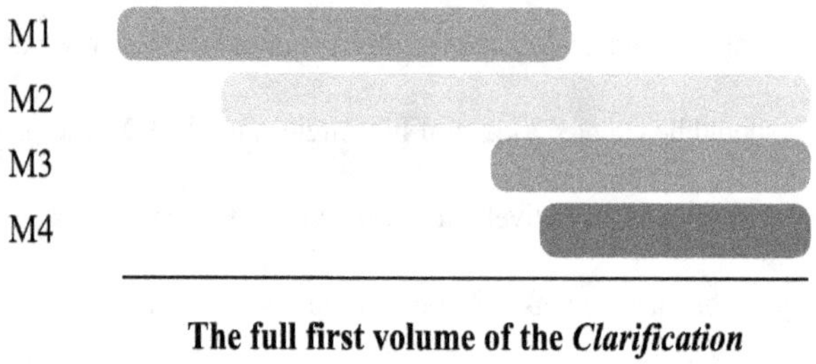
M1
M2
M3
M4
The full first volume of the Clarification

Figure 2. The distribution of the spans of M1–M4 in the first volume of the *Clarification* (only proximate).

This study makes use of the facsimiles of the manuscript fragments that are published in vol. 28 of the *Heishuicheng Manuscripts Collected in Russia* (see ECMS). However, there is a fatal and disastrous problem with the publication, namely, the facsimiles of M1, M3 and M4 are all incomplete. While the first four frames of M1 are consecutive, there is a break between the fourth and the fifth frame, which is the end of the manuscript. Therefore, about ten frames are missing from the facsimile of M1. M3 has only two frames of its beginning and end, and the same applies to M4. This means that about eight or nine frames for each one of them are missing from the publication.[488] While one can hope that the actual manuscripts in Russia will become accessible

[488] Kychanov (*Katalog Tangytckix byddiyckix pamyatnikov Institut Boctokovedeniya Pocciyckoy Akademii Hayk*) has the following lengths for these manuscripts: M1, 980 cm; M2, 997 cm; M3, 982 cm; M4, 790 cm. Obviously, the facsimiles for M1, M3, M4 are all too short if M2 has 22 frames.

again in the future, we now can only make use of the facsimiles for the present translation since the frames of M1 and M2 are sufficient for restoring the full text of the first volume of the *Clarification*. A *hyparchetype*[489] of the text will be produced based on the comparison of M2 and the available parts of M1, M3 and M4. Given the complicated nature of the versions of texts in Khara-Khoto, I dare not to speak of a critical edition or an Ur-text of any sort.[490] However, I believe collating the manuscripts to form a *hyparchetype* is justified as it will form a tangible textual ground for the translation.

The corpus of manuscripts of our text has but a few annotations. The situation is then similar to the relatively clean manuscripts of the Tangut translation of the *Nyāyabindu*. But the situation is in the reverse where the manuscripts of the Tangut translations of Phya pa's *Epistemology* (work no. 16) and Rma bya's *Introduction to Speculative Thinking* (work no. 15) are concerned because these have ample annotations. This issue will be further dealt with in Section 8.

3. Author

The authorship statement at the beginning of M1 says:

[illegible]

Composed by Central Tibetan Great Master, Monk "Wisdom-Conqueror"

---

[489] For *hyparchetype*, see Silk, "Editing without an Ur-text," esp. 154–155. Without probing into the historical relations between the texts, a *hyparchetype* is a product of the editor's editorial choices on the preferable readings.

[490] Tangut texts were generally edited over time, thus resulting in different versions. For example, a sutra translated during the reign of one Tangut emperor would often be proofread/edited/revised (but not completely retranslated) during the reign of another emperor; see Shi, *Xixia Fojiao shi lue*, 79–84.

Most of the information here is straightforward: the author is a Tibetan, he is from Central Tibet, and he is a monk. To say that he is a "great master" means he had made a name for himself, at least in his own time. But who is "Wisdom-Conqueror" (Źjɨr ɣwie 𗧓𗂧)? First, it is obviously the monk's name in religion. Second, since both characters have religious meanings and their phonetic reconstructions do not make a reasonable sound in Tibetan, we should take it as a translation of the monk's name rather than a transcription. The Tangut character *źjɨr* 𗧓 would literally mean "wisdom," which is usually used to translate the Chinese character *hui* 慧. In most cases, it translates Tibetan *shes rab*. But sometimes it also translates Tibetan *blo gros*. The second character *ɣwie* 𗂧, which literally means "to conquer," normally translates Tibetan *rgyal ba*. We can, of course, do a search for the name Shes rab rgyal ba and Blo gros rgyal ba[491] in all the available e-texts of Tibetan literature. However, we should also bear in mind that the author must have been someone who flourished before the demise of the Tangut State in 1227 and who was closely connected to the Gsang phu tradition. This will greatly reduce the scope of our search.

While we do not find any Gsang phu master bearing exactly the name Shes rab rgyal ba or Blo gros rgyal ba, in chapter twenty of the *Red Annals* where Tshal pa narrates the abbatial succession of Gsang phu Monastery, there is the following passage:

> Zhang e ba[492], the student of Dkar chung ring mo and Khu [Shes rab brtson 'grus], spoke the Buddhist Teaching to the student monks of the four communities of Mdo smad [who lived] in places such as Mon 'dra, Rgya grong, 'Or skyo reg, Me reg, and 'On lcang rdo.[493] He brought an uncountable number of people to spiritual

[491] Or simply Shes rab rgyal or Blo gros rgyal.

[492] Alternatively, as Zhang e pa and Zhang g.ye ba, etc.

[493] Most of these place names cannot be identified at the moment. Rgya grong probably refers to 'Phan yul rgyal grong, a place north to Lhasa; 'On lcang rdo, alternatively as U shang rdo, 'U shang rdo, etc., is located in the southwest to

> maturity, such as the scholar Bsod [nams] rin [chen], Gnyal pa zhig po[494], Rgyal ba so ston. He placed [in his lecture hall?] rows of cushions made of silk used/enjoyed boiling about 50 large blocks of tea leaves at a single religious assembly. However, he was only famous at that time. After him, the abbot Bsod [nam] rin [chen] took the see. He was the eldest son of the *siddha* La stod Dmar po. He also composed many treatises such as *The Mirror of Karma*.[495] [With him,] the tradition of subjectively explaining the Buddhist Teaching[496] appeared. Thereafter, 'Gral Sher rgyal took the see. In the latter half of his life, he established a college in Shab 'Bre sgang. His students were Ra Grags she, etc.[497]

Toward the end of the passage, a name "'Gral Sher rgyal" appears. 'Gral is of course his clan name and Sher rgyal is his name in religion. Sher rgyal is further a contraction of either Shes rab rgyal ba, Shes rab rgyal po, or Shes rab rgyal mtshan. And the first option immediately rings our bell. Could this 'Gral Sher rgyal, then, be our author?

Lhasa. These two are then places in Central Tibet. But Mdo smad would refer to a part in today's Amdo and/or Kham areas. Did Zhang e ba taught his Mdo smad students in Central Tibet? This remains unclear.

[494] The text has *zhig pa* here. But *zhig po* is how his name is normally presented.

[495] Bsod nam rin chen's auto-commentary on this treatise is extant. See Bsod nam rin chen, *Las kyi me long gi gtam rgyud rnam par bshad pa*.

[496] Tib. *chos blo bshad byed pa'i srol*. According to Dung dkar Blo bzang 'phrin las, this means to explain the teachings without relying upon books (Tshal pa, *Deb ther dmar po*, 381, n. 358).

[497] Tshal pa, *Deb ther dmar po*, 69:

> *dkar chung ring mo dang / khu'i slob ma zhang e bas mon 'dra dang / rgya grong / 'or skyo reg / me reg / 'on lcang rdo la sogs su mdo smad tsho bzhi'i grwa pa la chos gsungs shing / mkhas pa bsod rin dang / gnyal pa zhig pa / rgyal ba so ston la sogs dpag tu med pa smin par mdzad cing / gral stan za 'og la byed pa dang / dus chos re la ja sig chen lnga bcu re tsam skol ba la sogs longs spyod kyang de dus kho na che bar grags / de'i rjes su mkhan po bsod rin gyis gdan sa byas / de grub thob la stod dmar po'i sras che shos yin / las kyi me long la sogs bstan bcos kyang du ma mdzad / chos blo bshad byed pa'i srol byung / rjes su 'gral sher rgyal gyis gdan sa mdzad / sku tshe'i smad la shab 'bre sgang du gra sa btsugs / de'i slob ma ra grags she la sogs pa yin no /.*

Parallel texts are found in Yar lung jo bo, *Yar lung jo bo chos 'byung*, 130; Dpa' bo, *Chos 'byung mkhas pa'i dga' ston*, 1:734–735. Variants are insignificant.

Let us now closely examine the passage quoted above. The abbatial succession of Gsang phu Monastery has been well researched.[498] However, this passage presents a subsidiary lineage, which has not received much attention. We can, provisionally, identify it as the *prajñāpāramitā* lineage, as many of the figures was specialized in that subject.[499] The line started with 'Bre Shes rab 'bar, a direct disciple of Rngog Lo. His disciple Khu Shes rab brtson 'grus (1075–1143) was active in Thang po che[500] and taught "approximately more than ten thousand student monks" (*grwa pa khri lhag tsam*).[501] Zhang E ba, the student of Khu, was extraordinarily popular at this time, as indicated by the passage. He was evidently succeeded by Bsod nams rin chen. But here, we have a small problem: the text mentions that Bsod nams rin chen "took the see" (*gdan sa byas*); but the "see" (*gdan sa*) appears here abruptly since it was never explicitly stated before. It cannot be Gsang phu Monastery because Bsod nams rin chen is not included in that line of succession. We can only assume that this refers to the residence of Zhang E ba, although it might have been established even earlier by Zhang E ba's masters. Nevertheless, we know for certain that the abbotship taken by Bsod nams rin chen was further passed down to 'Gral Sher rgyal, and the master-disciple lineage from 'Bre Shes rab 'bar to 'Gral Sher rgyal is clear.

There is yet another subsidiary lineage within the *prajñāpāramitā* lineage, that began with Gnyal pa Zhig po 'Jam pa'i rdo rje, one of Zhang E ba's students. Kun dga' rdo rje further writes in his *Red Annals*:

---

498 See van der Kuijp, "The Monastery of Gsang-phu ne'u thog and Its Abbatial Succession from ca. 1073 to 1250"; Onoda, "The Chronology of the Abbatial Successions of the Gsang phu sne'u thog Monastery." A key source here is the *Red Annals*. See Tshal pa, *Deb ther dmar po*, 67–68.

499 This is briefly touched by Sparham, "A Note on Gnyal zhig 'Jam pa'i rdo rje, the Author of a Handwritten Sher phyin Commentary from about 1200," 23, although Sparham does not use a specific term to indicate the lineage.

500 In present day 'Phyongs rgyas Prefecture, south of Rtse thang.

501 Tshal pa, *Deb ther dmar po*, 69.

> Furthermore, Gnyal pa zhig po, the student of Zhang E ba and Dan 'bag taught in places such as 'On lcang rdo. On account of it, there appeared those who were known as the "nine spiritual sons", namely, [1] Bzad [pa] rings [mo] , [2] Phu thang Dar [ma] dkon [mchog], [3] Gtsang drug, who were known as the three early graduates; [4] 'U yug pa Bsod nams seng ge, [5] Bo dong rin po che, [6] the master Jo [sras?] nam [mkha'], who were known as the three middle graduates; and [7] Rgya 'Chims ru ba, [8] the religious lord 'Jam gsar, [9] and Skyel nag Grags [pa] seng [ge], who were known as the three later graduates.[502]

Then, after describing the careers of several of the graduates, Kun dga' rdo rje focuses on the life of Jo nam:

> Gtsang pa Jo nam, having become a student of 'Gral, took the see of 'Gral. While he was holding the see, in [Gsang phu] ne'u thog, Bzad pa Don grub handed over the see [to him]. Having taken two sees, he incorporated the monastic estates and held the see for fifteen years.[503]

[502] Tshal pa, *Deb ther dmar po*, 69:

> *yang zhang e pa dang / dan 'bag gi slob ma gnyal pa zhig pos 'on lcang rdo la sogs su bshad pa las bu dgur grags pa byung ste / bzad rings / phu thang dar dkon / gtsang drug gsum la snga tshar gsum zer/ 'u yug pa bsod nams seng ge / bo dong rin po che / slob dpon jo nam gsum la bar tshar gsum zer/ rgya 'chims ru ba / chos rje 'jam gsar / skyel nag grags seng gsum la phyi tshar gsum zer bar grags pa.*

[503] Tshal pa, *Deb ther dmar po*, 70:

> *gtsang pa jo nam gyis 'gral gyi slob ma byas nas / 'gral gyi gdan sa mdzad kyi yod pa la / ne'u thog tu bzad pa don grub kyis gdan sa gtad de / gnyis ga'i gdan sa mdzad nas chos gzhi rnams dril te lo bco lnga'i bar du gdan sa mdzad.*

Although Zhang E ba was formally succeeded by Bsod nams rin chen, it seems that it was Gnyal pa Zhig po who really expanded the glory of his lineage. He was once the abbot of the upper college of the Gsang phu Monastery and had several prominent students. And Jo nam was one of them. By attending to both Gnyal pa Zhig po and 'Gral Sher rgyal, he merged together the main and the subsidiary *prajñāpāramitā* lineages. Not only that, but he also received the abbotship of Gsang phu Monastery (lower college) from Bzad pa Don grub, who, as we know, served as the abbot until around 1218. This means that after more than a century since Rngog Lo's death in 1109, his legacy of the Gsang phu institutions, once split by Zhang Tshe spong Chos kyi bla ma and 'Bre Shes rab 'bar, were once again unified by Gtsang pa Jo nam, despite the continuing division between the upper and lower colleges. We can, then, produce the following chart that illustrates the transmissions of the above-mentioned three lineages:

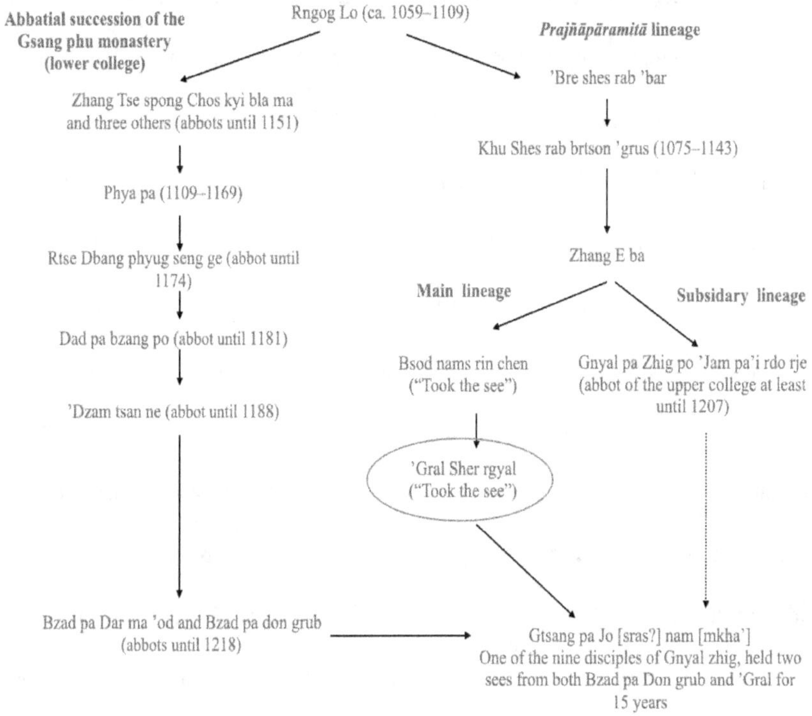
Abbatial succession of the Gsang phu monastery (lower college)
Rngog Lo (ca. 1059–1109)
Prajñāpāramitā lineage
Zhang Tse spong Chos kyi bla ma and three others (abbots until 1151)
'Bre shes rab 'bar
Khu Shes rab brtson 'grus (1075–1143)
Phya pa (1109–1169)
Rtse Dbang phyug seng ge (abbot until 1174)
Zhang E ba
Main lineage
Subsidary lineage
Dad pa bzang po (abbot until 1181)
Bsod nams rin chen ("Took the see")
Gnyal pa Zhig po 'Jam pa'i rdo rje (abbot of the upper college at least until 1207)
'Dzam tsan ne (abbot until 1188)
'Gral Sher rgyal ("Took the see")
Bzad pa Dar ma 'od and Bzad pa don grub (abbots until 1218)
Gtsang pa Jo [sras?] nam [mkha']
One of the nine disciples of Gnyal zhig, held two sees from both Bzad pa Don grub and 'Gral for 15 years

Figure 3. The abbatial succession of the Gsang phu Monastery and the *prajñāpāramitā* lineage.

We can then further assess 'Gral Sher rgyal's relevance. We know nothing about this figure except for the mention of him here in the lineage. We have, to date, no copy of his writings or references to him in other authors' works. However, based on the previous discussion, we know that he was a Tibetan monk of the Gsang phu tradition who was active in Central Tibet. Since he succeeded Bsod nams rin chen in the main lineage of the *prajñāpāramitā* lineage and served as an abbot, he certainly enjoyed substantial prestige, at least socially. We also notice that Kun dga' rdo rje uses the honorific form *mdzad*[504] for 'Gral while he uses the informal verb *byas* for Bsod nams

[504] It would in general mean "to do," "to make," etc. Here, it should mean specifically "to take" [the see].

rin chen. We do not know the dates of most of the figures discussed above. Jo nam had already succeeded 'Gral before taking the abbotship from Bzad pa Don grub in around 1218. Roughly that year, appears to be our *terminus ante quem* for 'Gral. So, if he were the Wisdom-Conqueror, he could have easily completed the *Clarification* well before the destruction of the Tangut State in 1227. Therefore, up until this point, there is nothing that really contradicts the identification of Wisdom-Conqueror with 'Gral. The fact that Zhang E ba had many students from Mdo smad is also telling. We have already seen in Chapter Four that Rngog Lo once sent an open letter to the monastic community in Tsong kha. It seems that Zhang E ba strengthened the ties between the Gsang phu tradition in Central Tibet and the monastic communities along the northern borderlands. It is possible that Zhang E ba's enterprise was continued by Bsod nams rin chen and 'Gral, which could mean that the Tanguts could very well have been acquainted with 'Gral or with his writing.

There are two more issues to be dealt with before we proceed to the next section. The first is related to 'Gral's expertise. If he was a member of the lineage of *prajñāpāramitā*, why would he be skilled in epistemology? This can be answered quite easily. It does not necessarily mean that every member must be an expert in that subject exclusively. The second issue is about the reconstruction of the Tibetan name of Wisdom-Conqueror. Wisdom-Conqueror, as indicated before, can surely be reconstructed as Shes rab rgyal ba. However, it cannot be reconstructed in any way as Shes rab rgyal mtshan, which would be Źjɨr dźjow [illegible], Wisdom-Banner, or Shes rab rgyal po, which would be Źjɨr njij [illegible], in Tangut. But I argue 'Gral could still be Wisdom-Conqueror even if his name were indeed Shes rab rgyal mtshan or Shes rab rgyal ba. If his name was normally presented in its contracted form as Sher rgyal – not his full name Shes rab rgyal mtshan or Shes rab rgyal ba – then the Tanguts would still translate his name as Źjɨr ɣwie [illegible] due to the "morpheme-to-morpheme" principle. The syllable *rgyal* would be translated fixedly as *ywie* 𗼃 regardless of the actual word it stood for.

4. Date

Since neither the colophon of the text nor the scribe's colophon in M2 contain any information about dates, we will have to find out the date of the composition of the *Clarification* in other ways. If we push the identification that Wisdom-Conqueror is 'Gral, then we can use the possible dates of 'Gral for the dating of the *Clarification*. But let us avoid that approach for the moment and instead base ourselves on the internal evidence of the text. As I will show in detail in Section 7, the *Clarification* cites a number of Gsang phu masters, including Rngog Lo, Khyung Rin chen grags, and Rgya dmar ba. Since the latest figure we see is Rgya dmar ba, it effectively helps us to set up a *terminus post quem* for the work – that is, it must not predate Rgya dmar ba, who flourished in the first several decades of the twelfth century.

The *terminus ante quem* for the work is more difficult to determine. While we know it was composed before 1227, we want to further narrow the range of the period. To say Rgya dmar ba is the latest person quoted in the text means that Phya pa, one of the towering figures in the Gsang phu tradition, is not at all present in the first volume of the *Clarification*. This, in general, is not the case for all the post-Phya pa Gsang phu scholars whose works we have access to since Phya pa had greatly reshaped the intellectual landscape of the tradition. Not citing Phya pa's ideas in a work like the *Clarification*, which contains many citations of names, would be highly unlikely in the post-Phya pa period, especially given the fact that Rgya dmar ba, the teacher of Phya pa, is already cited. Therefore, we can come up with the following several possibilities regarding the date of the composition of the *Clarification*:

1. The *Clarification* was composed before the ascendency of Phya pa's intellectual influence in the mid-twelfth century.

2. The *Clarification* was composed after the ascendency of Phya pa's intellectual influence in the mid-twelfth century. But the author decided not to cite Phya pa due to his disbelief of Phya pa's philosophical position.

3. The *Clarification* was composed after the ascendency of Phya pa's intellectual influence in the mid-twelfth century. But the author did not cite Phya pa simply because he was not aware of Phya pa's thoughts that had recently flourished.

The first is the most plausible scenario. For one thing, it is simple and straightforward. When we apply Occam's Razor to our analysis, the first possibility is where we would want to go. Furthermore, as indicated in Section 7, our author follows Rgya dmar ba closely on almost every point in the discussion, which suggests that he may have been a disciple of Rgya dmar ba. This will, then, place him as a contemporary of Phya pa. There are also other less direct pieces of evidence. For example, two topics, namely the compartmentalization of awareness (*blo dbye*) and the workings of definition (*mtshan nyid*), are typical in Phya pa and post-Phya pa epistemological works. But neither is evident in the *Clarification*. Also, in terms of textual parallels, our author's sentences are in general closer to those of Rngog Lo than to Phya pa (see Section 7, table 2). Finally, when discussing the idea of factive assessment (*yid dpyod*), our author's position shows a strong transitional characteristic between the positions of Rgya dmar ba and Phya pa. These all speak in favor of the first possibility.

The second option is not impossible. In fact, when we consider, as mentioned above, that our author is probably a contemporary of Phya pa, it might indeed be the case that he intentionally moved away from him on account of their competitive relationship. What contradicts this assumption, however, is that the register of our author is, in most places, not polemical at all. If he disbelieved Phya pa's interpretations, he could have first presented his ideas and then refuted them. But such a case is never seen. There is only one place where Phya pa is a possible candidate for the "some" (𭇹, *kha cig*).[505] But, for almost all other cases, our author is obviously more interested in how Rgya dmar ba's position is superior to the positions of Rngog Lo and Khyung.

The third possibility can be in one way or the other regarded as a cognate of the first one because both possibilities are predicated on our author's ignorance of Phya pa's intellectual framework. But it is less straightforward than the first one. And even if the third option is the case, the composition cannot be too late to be reasonable. It seems, then, the work should be composed not later than the *floruit* of Rma bya (d. ca. 1185) and Gtsang nag pa (d. after 1195), who were direct disciples of Phya pa. Otherwise, it would not make much sense to state that our author was still ignorant of Phya pa's thoughts. I suggest, when having only the first and third possibilities at hand, we should of course prefer the first possibility.

Now, let us see how the dates of 'Gral may be mapped onto these possibilities. Of the *prajñāpāramitā* lineage, the dates of one person, namely Khu Shes rab brtson 'grus, are clear. He was born in 1075. If we suppose that every transmission occurred between two generations and each generation is 20 years later, then Zhang E ba was born around 1095, Bsod nams rin chen in 1115, and 'Gral in 1135. We also know that 'Gral could have passed away before 1218 as his see

[505] There, our author sticks to the fourfold typology of the possible mistakes as opposed to a fivefold typology.

was passed down to Jo nam that year. Then we have ca. 1135–before 1218 for 'Gral. However, we now have a problem: 'Gral is now at least one generation after Phya pa, which does not accord well with our P1, the ideal choice. Alternatively, we can push 'Gral one generation back and put him as a contemporary of Bsod nams rin chen. This is possible, as Bsod nams rin chen might have died early. But in that case, the life span of 'Gral might then be a bit unreasonably long. We know the dates of 'U yug pa Bsod nams seng ge, a supposed classmate of Gtsang Jo nam under Gnyal pa zhig po, to have been ca. 1195–after 1267.[506] Even if Jo nam might have been born a bit earlier, it seems that 'Gral had to spend his last years at least in the first decade of the thirteenth century in order for Jo nam to become his student and take his see. In all probability, then, it is justifiable to assert that 'Gral's dates are ca. 1135–ca. 1215. Based on this, we can try the third possibility instead, which would work well with the dates. But the flaw with the third possibility here is if 'Gral was born in 1135 or even later, it is then unlikely that he could become a direct disciple of Rgya dmar ba, whose thoughts are dominant in the *Clarification*.

While we can further dive into more nuanced possibilities, at this point, I feel it is necessary to waive a white flag and confess that the problem of the inconsistency between the efforts of identifying the author and the date of the composition is something that I cannot solve at this moment. It is perhaps more reasonable to stick to the dating in the first possibility than to opt for the identification of the author because the former is based on the internal, direct evidence and the latter is more or less a hypothesis drawn from external and indirect clues. In regard to the foregoing, I will consistently call the author of the *Clarification* "our author".

---

[506] For 'U yug pa, see van der Kuijp, "Studies in Btsun pa Ston gzhon's *Pramāṇavārttika* Commentary of 1297 Part Two(a)."

5. Content and Structure

The title of the work, *The Clarification of the Words and Meaning of the "Nyāyabindu,"* directly reveals its nature – it is a commentary on Dharmakīrti's *Nyāyabindu*, the shortest treatise of his three discourses on Buddhist epistemology and logic. Dharmakīrti's text contains three chapters: I. Direct Perception (*pratyakṣa*, *mngon sum*), II. Inference for Oneself (*svārthānumāna*, *rang don rjes dpag*), and III. Inference for Others (*parārthānumāna*, *gzhan don rjes dpag*). The first volume of the *Clarification* covers the whole first chapter. This means that the *Clarification* in Tangut translation may have three volumes – as in Chinese *shang* ("upper"), *zhong* ("middle"), and *xia* (lower) – each covering one chapter in Dharmakīrti's treatise. It is not impossible that it only has two volumes because of the very dense philosophical content in the first chapter despite its conciseness. Chapters II and III, could be potentially included in the length of one volume. But I think this is hardly likely.

As a commentary, the *Clarification* quotes the basic text of Dharmakīrti. The twenty-one passages in the first chapter of the basic text that are isolated by Dharmottara (ca. 800) in his commentary on the *Nyāyabindu*, are quoted sometimes in part and sometimes in full. Only I.3 and I.11 are not explicitly quoted. But this is because they are quoted together with the passage that immediately precedes them. This supposition is supported by the particle "etc." (*nji* 𗍫, **la sogs pa*) at every end of their preceding quotes. The following table summarizes the relevant information about these quotes:

Passage No.	Text	Way of Quoting	The Translation of the Basic Text

1	"[illegible]" / "[illegible]" / "[illegible]" / "[illegible]" / "[illegible]" / "[illegible]" / "[illegible]" / "[illegible]"	In full but in pieces[507]	Inapplicable[508]
2	"[illegible], [illegible]" [illegible]	In full	
3	None.	Implicitly quoted with the previous	
4	"[illegible], [illegible], [illegible]"	In full	
5	"[illegible], [illegible]"	In full	
6	"[illegible]" / "[illegible]" [illegible]	In parts	
7	"[illegible], [illegible]"	In full	
8	"[illegible]"	In full	
9	"[illegible]" [illegible]/ "[illegible]"	In parts	
10	"[illegible]" [illegible]	In a part	Missing [illegible], variant insignificant
11	None.	Implicitly quoted with the previous	Inapplicable
12	"[illegible]" [illegible]	In a part	Exact
13	"[illegible]" [illegible]	In a part	Missing [illegible], text in the *Clarification* better
14	"[illegible]" [illegible]	In a part	Exact
15	"[illegible]" [illegible]	In a part	Exact
16	"[illegible]" [illegible]	In a part	Exact
17	"[illegible], [illegible]"	In full	[illegible] for [illegible]; [illegible] for [illegible] ,variants insignificant.
18	"[illegible]" [illegible]	In a part	Exact
19	"[illegible]" [509]	In a part	Exact
20	"[illegible]" [illegible]	In a part	Exact
21	"[illegible], [illegible]" [illegible]	In a part	Exact

Table 1. Basic text of the *Nyāyabindu* quoted in the *Clarification*.

[507] The first passage is divided into eight sections. For this approach in the Gsang phu tradition, see Section 6. We can reconstruct the Tangut translation of the first passage based on the eight segments of the sentences: [illegible][[illegible]], [illegible][[illegible]][illegible][[illegible]][illegible], [illegible] [= 1. *yang dag pa'i shes pa ni*, 2. *skyes bu'i don*, 3. *thams cad*, 4. *'grub pa'i* 5. *sngon du 'gro ba can* 6. *yin pas na* 7. *de* 8. *bstan to /*]. The three Tangut particles added in the brackets make the language follow the Tibetan even more closely, but they are not necessary for the meaning.

[508] The beginning of the manuscript fragment of the Tangut translation of the *Nyāyabindu* is missing.

[509] There is a reason for the lack of the particle [illegible] here. I. 18 and 19 are quoted in the same sentence with the construction "from…to…" (…[illegible]…[illegible], *…*las*…*bar du*). Since [illegible] (*phyir ro*) is the ending point, there should not be a [illegible] there.

Elsewhere, I studied the Tangut translation of just the *Nyāyabindu*.[510] This version can now be compared to the quotation of the *Nyāyabindu* in the *Clarification* on the basis of the rightmost column of the table. The comparison shows that, in most places, both texts are completely identical. The several remaining variants do not bespeak a substantial discrepancy. Only in passage no. 13 does the quoted text better reflect the Tibetan original. The relatively close relationship of both texts shows that the translator of the *Clarification* might have referred to an existing version of the Tangut translation of the *Nyāyabindu*, which is slightly different from the version that we currently have.[511]

The phrase "word-meaning" (𗼃𗧓, **tshig don*) can be usually interpreted in three ways. It can mean either the "meaning of the words" (*tshig gi don*) or "words and meaning" (*tshig dang don*) "category." The ultimate source of this term is Sanskrit *padārtha*. The content of the *Clarification* evidently shows that it should fall into the second category, which means it does not merely provide glosses of the words in the basic text but also prefaces these with general considerations of their meaning in the larger context of Buddhist epistemology. Hence, the *Clarification* is not merely an explanatory work like Vinītadeva's commentary on the *Nyāyabindu* but is more of an argumentative work like Dharmottara's commentary. We will have more discussion of this feature of the *Clarification* below.

In the *Clarification*, our author provides a topical outline (*sa bcad*) for his commentary on the first chapter of the *Nyāyabindu*. It consists of five uppermost level topics:

---

[510] Ma, "The *Nyāyabindu* in Tangut Translation." The Tangut translation is based on Rngog Lo's revised Tibetan translation of the Sanskrit. See text no. 8 in Chapter Four, Section 3.

[511] The Tangut translation of the first chapter only has one manuscript fragment (Or.12380/2145) as its witness. So, it is likely that there were other slightly different versions of the first chapter circulating in the Tangut State.

1. The connected purpose.
2. The compartmentalization of the types of knowledge.
3. The definition of direct perception.
4. The clarification of the cognitive object.
5. The posit of the cause and result of perceptual knowledge.

As we will see in Section 6, the division of the five topics is similar to Rngog Lo's topical outline.

6. Parallel Textual Sources

One of the most salient features in the Gsang phu scholastic literature is the so-called "text re-use," especially in epistemological texts.[512] In modern terms, it would partly mean to appropriate previous textual material in one's own work without citing so.[513] This was, however, not considered as plagiarism in the premodern practice of these Tibetan masters. Instead, it was a virtue, as it helped spread the truth preached by the Buddha as much as possible. For modern scholars, on the other hand, the phenomenon of text re-use produces an excellent opportunity for us to see how the works of different scholars are interrelated. Does one work belong to the Gsang phu tradition? What thoughts remained relatively stable within the tradition and what thoughts did not? What position is favored by an author and what is not? These are questions to which the text re-use phenomenon can potentially provide answers. Therefore, when analyzing the *Clarification*, we want also to bring in other Tibetan epistemological works that have textual parallels to it. To this end, then, all the Gsang phu epistemological works are potential candidates. However, to

[512] For text re-use, see Hugon, "Text Re-use in Early Tibetan Epistemological Treatises.".

[513] Hugon includes the acknowledged text re-use under the term as well. Here, I focus only on the unacknowledged text re-use.

effectively limit the scope of our study, we will only choose four sources from them. And we will further add one pertinent Indic work in Tibetan translation. These five are:

- Dharmottara's *Nyāyabinduṭīkā*, i.e., *The Commentary on the "Nyāyabindu"* in Tibetan translation (henceforth the *Commentary*).[514]
- Rngog Lo's *Concise Guide to the "Nyāyabinduṭīkā"* (henceforth the *Concise Guide*).[515]
- Rngog Lo's *Explanation of the Difficult Points of the "Pramāṇaviniścaya"* (henceforth the *Difficult Points*).[516]
- Phya pa's *Epistemology*.[517]
- 'Jad pa Gzhon nu byang chub's *Compilation of the Essential Nature of Epistemology* (henceforth the *Essential Nature*).[518]

---

[514] See NBṬ for the Sanskrit text. See Stcherbatsky, *Buddhist Logic*, for a study of the work and an English translation of it. See Nakamura, "Indo ronrigaku no rikai no tameni I: Darumakīruti *Ronrigaku shōron*," for a Japanese translation and Wang, *Facheng "Zhenglidi lun" yu Fashang "Zhenglidi lun zhu" yizhu yu yanjiu,* for a Chinese translation.

[515] For a study of the work, see Hugon, "Tracing the Early Developments of Tibetan Epistemological Categories in Rngog Blo ldan shes rab's (1059–1109) Concise Guide to the *Nyāyabinduṭīkā*." The manuscript of the text originally had the title "A Work of Buddhist Philosophy" (*mtshan nyid kyi chos*). But this is more of a general reference to the content of the work than its actual title. It was identified by Hugon as a "concise guide" to the *Nyāyabindutīkā*. I suppose it is appropriate to use "concise guide" as the name for the work here.

[516] For a brief examination of the content of the work, see Hugon, "Tracing the Early Developments of Tibetan Epistemological Categories in Rngog Blo ldan shes rab's (1059–1109) Concise Guide to the *Nyāyabinduṭīkā*," 196.

[517] Work no. 16 in Chapter Four, Section 3 is the Tangut translation of the work. For a study of the *Epistemology* and translation of its first chapter, see Hugon and Stoltz. *The Roar of a Tibetan Lion.*

[518] The work was first attributed to Klong chen rab 'byams pa (1308–1364) at its publication. However, having examined the content of the work, van der Kuijp ("A Treatise on Buddhist Epistemology and Logic Attributed to Klong chen rab 'byams pa (1308–1364) and Its Place in Indo-Tibetan Intellectual History") pointed out that Klong chen rab byams pa could not be the author and the author had to be from the Gsang phu tradition. Recently, Stoltz ("On the Authorship of the *Tshad ma'i de kho na nyid bsdus pa*") identified the author with 'Jad pa Byang chub gzhon nu (ca. 1150–1210), whose teacher was a direct disciple of Phya pa.

While all the five contain words and expressions similar to those in the *Clarification*, the ways these works are related to it vary. The first two works are structurally related to the *Clarification*. While Dharmottara's text does not have a topical outline, but its structure is made clear by Rngog Lo in his *Concise Guide*. Although Rngog Lo does not have an uppermost-level outline of how Dharmottara's text should be compartmentalized, he manifestly indicates through his section titles that the first chapter of Dharmottara's *Commentary* should consist of the following five parts:

1. *Dgos 'brel.*
2. *Tshad ma'i dbye ba.*
3. *Mngon sum gyi mtshan nyid.*
4. *Mngon sum gyi spyod yul.*
5. *Tshad ma dang 'bras bu.*[519]

These titles are presented on purpose in Tibetan rather than in an English translation as those who read Classical Tibetan will immediately realize if we translate them, the result would be nothing but a slightly different version of topics 1–5 presented in Section 5. This means our author reused Rngog Lo's topical outline – here I do not mean *the* outline of the *Concise Guide* but *an* outline of it that reveals the internal structure of Dharmottara's *Commentary*. When we go deeper into the subtitles under these five, we find many more connections between the outline of the *Concise Guide* and the *Clarification*. Let us examine one example here. When analyzing Dharmottara's commentary on the first passage of the *Nyāyabindu*, Rngog Lo says:

[519] *Concise Guide*, 3, 15, 17, 27, 29.

tshig gi don la rnam pa brgyad de / yang dag pa'i shes pa dang / sngon du 'gro ba dang / skyes bu'i don dang / 'grub pa dang / thams cad dang / yin pas na dang / de bstan to zhes bya ba'i tshig gi don to /[520]

The meaning of the words and phrases are eightfold, namely, the meaning of the words and phrases of [1] "correct cognition," [2] "preliminary," [3] "the goal of the person," [4] "accomplishment," [5] "all," [6] "because," [7] "that," [8] "explained."

Dharmottara explains these words and phrases one by one in this order. But he never explicitly states that there are eight and that the first passage should be divided so.[521] Rngog Lo, again, having based himself on the internal structure of Dharmottara's *Commentary*, provides this outline. Then, we soon realize that the *Clarification*, when explaining the words and phrases of the first passage, contains exactly those eight subtopcis. Therefore, our author's framework of his *Clarification* is heavily predicated on the internal structure of Dharmottara, which is further made clear by Rngog Lo.

Rngog Lo's *Difficult Points* is, in many ways, a supplement to his *Concise Guide* in our analysis of the *Clarification*. To be sure, it comments on another epistemological work of Dharmakīrti. Yet, it is still related to the *Clarification* in several aspects. First, it contains sections that find their equivalents in the *Clarification* but are otherwise unseen in other textual sources. For example, when commenting on Dharmakīrti's statement in the *Pramāṇaviniścaya* that the means of knowledge is twofold, Rngog Lo discusses the "purpose of compartmentalization" (*dbye ba'i dgos pa*), which finds its equivalent in the second topic of the *Clarification*. It is not stated in his *Concise Guide* as Dharmottara does not explicitly discuss it. It is not included in Phya pa's

[520] *Concise Guide*, 8.

[521] See Stcherbatsky, *Buddhist Logic* 2:4–11.

Epistemology and 'Jad pa's *Essential Nature* as those two are summaries and not commentaries of a specific Indic work.

Second, in terms of the closeness between the text of the *Clarification* and other works, the *Difficult Points* at times have the closest expressions to those in the *Clarification*. For example, in the second topic, the *Clarification* explains the difference between the denominational cause ([illegible], *'jug pa'i rgyu mtshan*) and the explanatory cause ([illegible], *bshad pa'i rgyu mtshan*). Although not completely identical, the very beginning of the explanation matches quite well with a passage in the *Difficult Points*. In the following table, I have showcased the four relevant passages from the *Clarification*, *Difficult Points*, *Epistemology*, and *Essential Nature*:

Clarification	*Difficult Points*	*Epistemology*	*Essential Nature*
[illegible]	*bshad pa'i rgyu tshan* [read: *mtshan*] *dang 'jug pa'i rgyu mtshan gyi khyad par ci lta bu zhe na / brda'i yul ni 'jug pa'i rgyu mtshan yin te / dper na mtsho skyes kyi sgra pad ma la brdar byas pas pad ma 'jug pa'i rgyu mtshan yin pa lta bu'o /*[522]	*phyir sgra 'jug pa'i gzhi ni don ste / brda'i yul du bya bas tha snyad kyi sgras rtogs par bya ba ste / ba lang zhes pa lkog shal la sogs pa 'dus pa la 'jug pa lta bu'o /*[523]	*phyir sgra 'jug pa'i rgyu mtshan dang bshad pa'i rgyu mtshan gnyis las dang po ni gang la brda' chad yas pa la de'i ming du grags pa ste / de yang dper na nog dang lkog shal dang ldan pa 'di ba lang ngo zhes brda chad byas pas de'i ming du grags pa lta bu'o /*[524]
Well, then what is the distinction between the explanatory cause and the denominational cause? As for the	How is the distinction between the explanatory cause and the denominational cause like? The cognitive	In general, the basis for denominating a word is the meaning. On the basis of that which is made the cognitive object of a	In general, from among the two – the denominational cause and the explanatory cause – the first is the following: that which

[522] *Difficult Points*, 70.

[523] *Epistemology*, 41a9–b1.

[524] *Essential Nature*, 157.

first:[525] what has become the cognitive object of a convention that is set particularly is the denominational cause, just like, on the basis of stating the word "lake-born"[526] as the convention for the lotus, the lotus being denominated.	object of a conventional designation is the denominational cause, just like, on the basis of making the word "lake-born" a conventional designation for the lotus, the denominational cause for denominating the lotus is involved.	conventional designation, one would understand [the meaning] by means of the word of the convention, just like "cow" denominating a collection of things such as dewlap.	is established as a conventional designation for something is known as the name of that thing, thus, just like, on the basis of establishing a conventional designation: "that which possesses hump and dewlap is cow," ["cow"] is known as the name of it.

Table 2. Relevant passages on the denominational cause in parallel textual sources

The close connection between the *Clarification* and the *Difficult Points* is apparent. Thus, I will not elaborate on it further. Phya pa's text is different in several aspects. It does not have the introductory question; it does not explicitly state the terms "denominational cause" and "explanatory cause"; it changes the example from "lake-born" to "cow." While 'Jad pa does state the two causes, it is obviously still much closer to Phya pa's text than to Rngog Lo's *Difficult Points*. They even both have the phrase "in general" (*spyir*) at the beginning. As briefly mentioned in Section 4, the fact that the *Clarification* is closer to Rngog Lo's text in terms of text re-use indicates it was likely composed prior to the rise of Phya pa, who, to a certain extent, reformed the textual model for his successors.

[525] On the basis of the introductory question, "the first" should be the explanatory cause. However, the actual explanation is in the reverse order.

[526] The Tangut [illegible] would literally mean "sea-born". But there is no doubt that it must be translated from *mtsho skyes* (Skt. *saroruha*), "lake-born." It is possible that the Tanguts understood the Tibetan *mtsho* as *rgya mtsho* here. I have used "lake-born" to translate it for consistency.

Finally, the *Difficult Points* serves as a practical sourcebook for identifying Rngog Lo's ideas mentioned in the *Clarification*. Ideally, the treasury of Rngog Lo's epistemological thoughts would be his larger commentary on the *Pramāṇaviniścaya* and his commentaries on the *Pramāṇavārttika*.[527] However, these works are not currently available. Since the *Difficult Points* is more substantial than the *Concise Guide*, we can locate his representative philosophical positions in it. Indeed, we are able to find most of the references to him in the *Clarification* in the *Difficult Points*.

In regard to the foregoing, Phya pa's *Epistemology* then shows some distance from the *Clarification*. However, Phya pa's work is likely the closest to the *Clarification* in terms of the chronology (see Section 4). This provides us with an excellent opportunity to see how they illuminate each other based on the differences they have. We will then be able to see the pre-Phya pa ethos manifested by the *Clarification* and the innovations of Phya pa.

The relevance of the *Essential Nature* is more nuanced. We cannot say it is, in terms of its phraseology, closer to the *Clarification* than the *Difficult Points*, though at times it does seem to be closer to it than the *Epistemology*. The resemblance here is about their shared typology as a primer to Buddhist epistemology. Granted, the *Essential Nature* is not commentary. But the goal of the composition is to make people familiar with what has been learned rather than giving a whole set of inspiring new thoughts and ideas. This is apparent in 'Jad pa's opening verse:

> I pay homage to him who, by means of having the resolve to become a buddha and the unobstructed intelligence,
> has become the refuge of all beings!
> I will write a memorandum which summarizes the nature of epistemology,

[527] See Kramer, *The Great Tibetan Translator*, 112, work nos. 29, 32, 33.

on the basis of the stainless texts of the authors[528] of the sutra and the commentary.[529]

Hence, 'Jad pa conceives his work to be a memorandum rather than a cutting-edge work. Contrarily, Phya pa's verses of his statement of purpose demonstrate his aim at "extending Dignāga and Dharmakīrti's endeavor in the field of epistemology, and providing tools to progress on the path to omniscience."[530] Therefore, even though the textual modal in the *Essential Essence* is more like Phya pa, the goal of the composition is in fact closer to that of our author, who has the following opening verse[531]:

> I pay homage to the all-knowing one,
> who works for the benefits of self and others!
> In order to avoid the fear of conceptual proliferation,
> I will elaborate briefly on the words and meaning of this.

---

[528] The "sutra" (*mdo'*) here refers to the "sutra of epistemology" (*tshad ma'i mdo*), i.e., Dignāga's *Pramāṇasamuccaya*, whereas the "commentary" (*rnam 'grel*) refers to the *Pramāṇavārttika* of Dharmakīrti.

[529] *Essential Nature*, 1:

> */ **byang chub** sems dang blo gros thogs pa med mnga' bas /*
>
> */ 'gro ba rnams kyi **skyabs** gyur de la phyag 'tshal te /*
>
> */ mdo' dang rnam 'grel mdzad pa'i dri med gzhung rnams las /*
>
> */ tshad ma'i de nyid rab tu bsdus pa'i brjed byang bri /.*

'Jad pa's teacher Byang chub skyabs' name is hidden in the first two lines. For this, see Stoltz, "On the Authorship of the *Tshad ma'i de kho na nyid bsdus pa*," 59–60.

[530] Hugon and Stoltz, *The Roar of a Tibetan Lion*, 349.

[531] See the text and the translation in Part Two.

Of course, our author does not say he would write a memorandum. But the attitude here is equally conservative rather than innovative. Our author obviously wants his work to keep a low profile without infringing on the existing tradition.

Their similar attitudes are also reflected in their respective contents. A noticeable shared tendency is that they both seldom give their own voices. This does not mean they do not take their philosophical positions. But they do so by basing themselves almost completely on the positions taken by their immediate predecessors. For 'Jad pa, this means his teacher Byang chub skyabs and his teacher's teacher, Phya pa. For our author, this would mean Rgya dmar ba, which will be further discussed in the following section. Another feature related to the phenomenon is they both cite frequently the positions taken by other Gsang phu masters.[532] In general, by first arranging these positions hierarchically, they will finally reach the positions they acknowledge.

Having examined the relationships between these parallel textual sources and the *Clarification*, where then should we place the *Clarification* in the Gsang phu tradition of epistemology, and what is the significance of the work in Tibetan intellectual history? These are the questions that will be dealt with in the next section.

7. The Significance of the *Clarification* for Tibetan Intellectual History

The *Clarification* serves as an important work that may further develop our understanding of Tibetan intellectual history. While it is clear that the Tibetan study of Buddhist epistemology

[532] For the phenomenon of the many citations in the *Essential Nature*, see van der Kuijp, "A Treatise on Buddhist Epistemology and Logic Attributed to Klong chen rab 'byams pa (1308–1364) and Its Place in Indo-Tibetan Intellectual History," 415–418; Stoltz, "On the Authorship of the *Tshad ma'i de kho na nyid bsdus pa*," 60, 66–68.

started with the *Nyāyabindu* in the Imperial Period,[533] there is no clear sign that any Tibetan author ever composed a comprehensive commentary on it.[534] At the dawn of Tibetan Buddhist scholasticism from the eleventh to the thirteenth centuries, a large number of Tibetan commentaries were indeed composed on Indic epistemological texts. However, the *Nyāyabindu* seems to have never become a subject of interest for Tibetan commentators. Rngog Lo, as we have seen, did write the *Concise Guide* to Dharmottara's *Commentary*. Nevertheless, Rngog Lo's *Concise Guide* "is indicative of his specific interest in Dharmottara's thought rather than of an interest for the NB [=*Nyāyabindu*]."[535] We would need to wait for three more centuries until Rgyal tshab Dar ma rin chen (1364–1432) composed a Tibetan commentary on the *Nyāyabindu*. Now, with the discovery of the *Clarification*, we take hold of the earliest Tibetan indigenous commentary on the *Nyāyabindu* available to us, albeit partially and in the translation of another language.

The discovery, then, has two implications for the Gsang phu epistemological tradition, which I have briefly discussed elsewhere.[536] The first is that the *Nyāyabindu* might have been used as the fundamental textbook for the Gsang phu scholastic training in epistemology. The *Nyāyabindu* is concise yet comprehensive, which is an ideal compendium. But it is hardly readable

---

[533] See van der Kuijp, *An Introduction to Gtsang nag pa's "Tshad-ma rnam-par nges-pa'i ṭi-ka legs-bshad bsdus pa*, 8–9; Hugon, "Tracing the Early Developments of Tibetan Epistemological Categories in Rngog Blo ldan shes rab's (1059–1109) Concise Guide to the *Nyāyabinduṭīkā*," 203.

[534] Under the section of the "commentaries of sutras and treatises composed by Btsan po Khri srong lde btsan" (*Mdo sde dang bstan bcos kyi ti ka / btsan po khri srong lde btsan gyis mdzad pa*) in the 'Phang thang catalog, an early catalog of Tibet, there are a *Memorandum of the Nyāyabindu* (*Na ya bin dhu'i brjed byang*) and a *Memorandum of a Chapter of the Nyāyabindu* (*Na ya bin dhu'i skabs kyi brjed byang*). See Bod ljongs rten rdzas bshams mdzod khang, *Dkar chag 'phang thang ma / Sgra sbyor bam po gnyis pa*, 56. However, these two works do not appear in the Lhan kar catalog, another important early catalog of Tibet. Since the former is one *bam po* and the latter is one *śloka*, the lengths of both do not seem to make them comprehensive commentaries of the text. The basic text of the *Nyāyabindu* is one *bam po*.

[535] Hugon, "Tracing the Early Developments of Tibetan Epistemological Categories in Rngog Blo ldan shes rab's (1059–1109) Concise Guide to the *Nyāyabinduṭīkā*," 205.

[536] See Ma, "The *Nyāyabindu* in Tangut Translation," 789–791.

without a commentary due to its very nature as an extremely terse treatise. The discovery of the *Clarification* means that the basic text was not studied alone but most likely with this commentary by our author.[537] This enhances the possibility that there was an established curriculum in the Gsang phu tradition for the novices to first get trained in the *Nyāyabindu* before turning to more difficult texts. We will examine this further in the next section. Another implication is that the *Nyāyabindu* was, to some extent, a subject of interest among some Gsang phu masters for a short period before the attention was shifted to the *Pramāṇaviniścaya* and *Pramāṇavārttika*.[538] While previously scholars tended to regard the *Pramāṇaviniścaya* as the predominant object to comment on in the Gsang phu tradition, the reason that there was no trace that they had actively engaged in commenting on the *Nyāyabindu*. Now, the reasoning seems to be the opposite: the earlier commentarial literature might have become obsolete and forgotten because of the rise of the interest in *Pramāṇaviniścaya* in figures such as Phya pa.

These implications are also echoed by some Tibetan sources, though only piecemeal. For example, in the *Red Annals*, Kun dga' rdo rje mentions in the Gsang phu lineage a certain Rigs thigs pa, who was distantly connected to Bzad rings[539] and obviously taught Bu ston (1290–1364).[540] The name "Rigs thigs pa" is apparently a nickname and it implies the person was an

---

[537] The direct evidence for this is the very last line that appears in one manuscript (#4363) of the Tangut translation of the *Nyāyabindu*, which reads [illegible], "of the meaning and words of the *Nyāyabindu*". This is very likely a portion of the title of the *Clarification*, [illegible]. But, for some reasons, the scribe decided not to continue copying the commentary on the same paper.

[538] van der Kuijp, *An Introduction to Gtsang nag pa's "Tshad-ma rnam-par nges-pa'i ṭi-ka legs-bshad bsdus pa*, 9–11, 19–22.

[539] See student no. 1 of Gnyal pa zhig po.

[540] Tshal pa, *Deb ther dmar po*, 72–73.

expert in the *Nyāyabindu*.[541] The fact that he taught Bu ston means he lived a part of his life already in the 14th century. Another source is 'Jad pa's *Essential Nature*. Notwithstanding the many citations of the *Pramāṇaviniścaya*, the name *Nyāyabindu* also occurs therein quite frequently. Most of these citations appear in places where 'Jad pa wants to give quick definitions or conclusions. For example, he quotes from the *Nyāyabindu* to define direct perception.[542] This nature of the citations suggests that the *Nyāyabindu* is 'Jad pa's "muscle memory," with which he set forth the most basic concepts. We even notice that at one point 'Jad pa reportedly tells us that Phya pa gives his argument by directly quoting the II.28 of the *Nyāyabindu*.[543] This indicates that even Phya pa, an innovative philosopher who was interested primarily in the *Pramāṇaviniścaya*, would, as a habit, draw from the *Nyāyabindu*. Although 'Jad pa was earlier than Rigs thigs pa, he was no doubt also a post-Phya pa figure. In short, the tradition of using the *Nyāyabindu* as the entry-level textbook persisted, perhaps even continued to the time of Rgyal tshab. And the interest in the *Nyāyabindu* never fully faded away; there would be scholars who engaged in it once in a while, like Rgyal tshab and Bo dong Paṇ chen Phyogs las rnam rgyal (1376–1451)[544]. What is compelling here is that 'Jad pa's *Essential Nature* itself was a forgotten book for a long time until its publication two decades ago (even so, not until most recently are we certain about its author). The shared ethos of the *Clarification* and the *Essential Nature*, as made clear in Section 6, is likely what made them silenced witnesses for the *Nyāyabindu* tradition.

---

[541] *Rigs [pa'i] thigs [pa]* is the Tibetan for *nyāyabindu*.

[542] *Essential Nature*, 158: *mngon sum ni rtog pa dang bral zhing ma 'khrul ba'o zhes rigs thigs la sogs par bshad pa.*

[543] *Essential Nature*, 112: *mi rmongs pa dran pa'i 'du byed bsgrub pa'i mngon sum 'das pa 'jal ba'i rjes dpag dang zhes rigs thigs nas bshad pa dang 'gal lo zhes phya pa zer ro /.* Although the quoted passage here is not completely identical with what we see in the II.28 in the Tibetan translation of the *Nyāyabindu*, it cannot be identified otherwise, especially given that the text says clearly it is "explained by the *Nyāyabindu*" (*rigs thigs nas bshad pa*).

[544] The full Tibetan text of the Nyāyabindu is quoted in Bo dong Paṇ chen's *Epistemology: Appearance of Reasoning, Tshad ma rigs pa'i snang ba*.

Similar to the situation of the *Essential Nature*, a key value of the *Clarification* is the many citations of the early Gsang phu masters such as Rngog Lo, Khyung, and Rgya dmar ba. In other words, the *Clarification* curates an exquisite exhibition of the pre-Phya pa Gsang phu epistemological thoughts. While we now have Rngog Lo's *Difficult Points*, by means of examining his citations in the *Clarification* we are able to identify those positions that were inherited by his followers and those that were not. There is little doubt that Khyung, a direct disciple of Rngog Lo, once was a leading figure in Gsang phu epistemology. Gser mdog Paṇ chen Shākya mchog ldan (1428–1507), one of the major contributors to the later development of Tibetan epistemology, recalls:

> Those who had become the principal ones of his [spiritual] sons are four: the one who held the throne of [his] body was Zhang Tshe spong ba Chos kyi bla ma; the one who held completely the teaching of [his] speech was Gro lung pa Blo gros 'byung gnas; the one who held the exegetical system of the *Prajñāpāramitā* in 100,000 lines was the Great 'Bre Shes rab 'bar; the one who held the exegetical system of the Middle Way (*dbu* [*ma*]) and epistemology (*tshad* [*ma*]) was Khyung Rin chen grags.[545]

However, likely due to the rise of his predecessors Rgya dmar ba and Phya pa, who disagreed with Khyung on a series of issues, Khyung's ideas were already little seen in the writings of Phya pa's direct disciples such as Gtsang nag pa. By the time of Shākya mchog ldan, Khyung seems to have been, in most cases, only known by name. Recent scholarship has revealed a large number of

[545] Gser mdog Paṇ chen, *Rngog lo tsā ba chen pos bstan pa ji ltar bskyangs tshul mdo tsam du bya ba ngo mtshar gtam gyi rol mo*, 450: *de la sras kyi thu bo byung ba ni bzhi ste / sku'i gdan sa 'dzin pa zhang tshe spong ba chos kyi bla ma / gsung gi bstan pa rdzogs par 'dzin pa gro lung pa blo gros 'byung gnas / yum shes rab kyi pha rol du phyin pa'i bshad srol 'dzin pa / 'bre chen po shes rab 'bar / dbu tshad kyi bshad srol 'dzin pa / khyung rin chen grags rnams so /.*

references to Khyung in the *Essential Nature*,[546] thus providing us with substantial material for the study of his ideas. The *Clarification*, then, is now another treasury for that purpose. It is not surprising that, in many places, Khyung's positions can be cross-referred between the *Clarification* and the *Essential Nature*. For example, when listing the definitions of knowledge given by earlier figures, our author says Khyung approves the idea that "non-deceiving" and "realization of the veridical object" are definitions that can be used interchangeably. And this is evidently attested by 'Jad pa in the *Essential Nature* as well.[547]

The case with Rgya dmar ba is equally fascinating. As I have briefly noted in the previous sections, our author does not only quote Rgya dmar ba but also sticks closely to his philosophical position by always putting him at the top of the hierarchically arranged presentations of the masters' thoughts. This suggests that the *Clarification* is essentially a facsimile of Rgya dmar ba's work. We know from later sources that Rgya dmar ba composed a commentary on the *Pramāṇaviniścaya* as well as a summary of epistemology.[548] But these works are no longer extant. With the help of the *Clarification*, we can now see how Rgya dmar ba's ideas are systematically presented, albeit in the form of a commentary on the *Nyāyabindu*.

Finally, let us summarize some of the major philosophical positions taken by our author. The definition of knowledge should be the realization of the veridical object, namely, eliminating superimpositions with regard to the veridical cognitive object. In terms of the relationship between the color of something and the touch of it, the non-erroneous cognition of the color cannot be the

[546] Khyung appears in the *Essential Nature* under the title Jo btsun ("Noble Lord"). But we now know Jo btsun is no one else but Khyung. See Hugon "Wonders *in margine*—Mapping the Madhyamaka Network of Gyamarwa Jangchupdrak," § 3.2.1; Ma, "Unveiling Gsang phu Madhyamaka Thought in Xixia," § 5.3.

[547] See note **Error! Bookmark not defined.**.

[548] van der Kuijp, *Contributions to the Development of Tibetan Buddhist Epistemology*, 60–61.

knowledge of the touch. If one is in error about a certain exclusion property of a non-conceptual object, then it is necessary that one is erroneous about all of them; if one is non-erroneous about a certain exclusion property, then it is necessary that one is non-erroneous about all of them. There are four types of mistakes with regard to the definition: 1. Impossibility, 2. Inexhaustive, 3. Fallacy, and 4. Being different defining exclusion properties. Knowledge is determined either reflexively or transitively. These are all reportedly held by Rgya as well. The other positions all follow the general Gsang phu stances.

In short, we may regard the *Clarification* as a repository for pre-Phya pa Gsang phu epistemological thoughts. And its value is further supplemented by other relevant texts documented in Chapter Four, Section 3. They, together, reveal some important aspects of the scholastic training in the Tangut State as well as allude to a possible curriculum in the Gsang phu monastery. This will be the theme for the next section.

8. The Relevance of the *Clarification* to the Scholastic Training in the Tangut State

A fascinating aspect of the group of Tangut literary remains related to the Gsang phu tradition examined in this dissertation is that they are not only texts that convey textual information but are also physical manuscripts that reflect, to no less extent, the actual context in which these texts were produced, circulated, and utilized. Of course, just like the so-called "Library Cave" in Dunhuang might never have been a library as such, it is not necessarily the case that the corpus of texts discovered in Khara-Khoto would be a mini collection representative of all the texts the Tanguts had. Nevertheless, the status and structure of these manuscripts cannot be completely random and must be considered capable, in one way or the other, of projecting a larger picture of what texts the Tanguts had and how they used them in the twelfth to the thirteenth centuries.

Keeping this in mind, we are now ready to take a look at certain aspects of the scholastic training in the Tangut State.

The first point to make is that the Tanguts chose to use a Tibetan indigenous commentary on the *Nyāyabindu* rather than opting for an Indic composition. Intriguingly, there seems to be little doubt that Dharmottara's *Commentary* would have been the natural place to go. The *Commentary* was not only translated and read in the Imperial Period but was also evidently read by the monks in the Ta bo monastery (est. 996),[549] which flourished after the demise of the Tibetan empire. However, there is no sign that the *Commentary* was ever translated into Tangut. And, as mentioned in the last section, the basic text is obviously read together with the *Clarification*. This shift is telling. It is of course not the case that the Tanguts would always go to a Tibetan commentary instead of an Indic one. For example, it seems quite clear that Haribhadra's *vṛtti*-commentary served as the companion for the basic text of the *Abhisamayālaṃkāra* (see Chapter Four, Section 3, work no. 2). A factor that could have potentially led the Tanguts to avoid Dharmottara's *Commentary* would be the flawed new Tibetan translation of the Sanskrit.[550] But I suggest the major reason concerns the philosophical disagreements between the Gsang phu tradition and Dharmottara. While Dharmottara remained an influential figure in the Gsang phu tradition and provided the bedrock for many of the intellectual frameworks of the tradition, he was opposed by the Gsang phu masters in some specific philosophical positions. Rngog Lo had already rejected some of Dharmottara's arguments. And some of these rejections were further inherited by our author of the *Clarification*. For instance, Dharmottara's position on the definition of

549 Lasic, "Fragments of *Pramāṇa* Texts Preserved in Tabo Monastery."

550 There are many mistakes and corruptions in the revised translation of Rngog Lo of the text, probably due the carelessness of his scribe. See Lasic, "Placing the Tabo *Tshad ma* Materials in the General Development of *Tshad ma* Studies in Tibet, Part 1: The Study of the *Nyāyabindu*."

knowledge is not accepted; Dharmottara's explanation of the subject dealt with in the *Nyāyabindu* is judged as incorrect; Dharmottara's explanation of the workings of the subsequent expression and the establishment is regarded as inappropriate. Our author, by means of smartly keeping the general structure of Dharmottara's *Commentary*, overwrote some of Dharmottara's philosophical positions without sabotaging the value of the *Commentary* as a useful guide to the *Nyāyabindu*. We should also note that this characteristic is not applicable to the *Abhisamayālaṃkāra*, which is a much less debated philosophical tradition.

The fact that the Tanguts adopted the *Clarification* is then not insignificant. In this case, a Tibetan commentary – and more specifically a Gsang phu commentary – was considered closer to Dharmakīrti's original intention than an Indic counterpart. The reason might be simple: the Tanguts only had Tibetan teachers who thought the Gsang phu thoughts were better. But the implication is far-reaching: Tibetan Buddhism was held as an authoritative form of Buddhism that was credible and reliable, and at times even superior to the commentarial tradition developed by Indic masters. It is then also relevant to our discussion of the Buddhist Complex, a subject we will return to at the conclusion of the dissertation.

Building up on the previous discussion, the second point here is also related to the authoritative nature of Tibetan epistemological literature that flourished in the Tangut State. The Tanguts obviously knew that Dharmakīrti composed seven treatises as they read the introductory survey of the *Clarification*.[551] However, we have not yet so far seen the Tangut translation of either one of the rest six treatises. Now, if we believe that the Tangut texts that we currently have are somewhat representative, then even if some other works of Dharmakīrti were once translated into

[551] Tanguts' knowledge of the seven treatises is also attested in a Tangut indigenous commentary on Mahāmudrā. See Ma, "Facheng de 'Qibu liang lun' zai Xixia."

Tangut, they did not become the central objects for scholastic training among the Tanguts. Instead, the Tanguts heavily relied upon the Tibetan works as a medium for their knowledge of epistemology since the other texts we have are things such as Rma bya's *Introduction to Speculative Thinking* and Phya pa's *Epistemology*. Hence, we might say that the Tanguts were in fact more interested in Buddhist epistemology as a scholastic subject introduced by the Tibetans rather than in Dharmakīrti and his Indic predecessors' thoughts.

We further notice that, other than the *Clarification*, all the Tibetan epistemological works translated into Tangut are summaries rather than commentaries. Even though Phya pa wrote a commentary on the *Pramāṇaviniścaya*, which would have indeed provided the Tanguts with a great opportunity to study Dharmakīrti's work, we do not currently see it in Tangut translation. The phenomenon of summaries then further supports our supposition that the Tanguts were more inclined to use Tibetan sources for their training in Buddhist epistemology. Perhaps the *Nyāyabindu* was translated mainly because it was an easy-to-use textbook. Therefore, there is also a practical aspect here. For modern scholars, studying Buddhist epistemology would mean starting with Dharmakīrti, making sense of the thoughts of his predecessors, and then finally reaching the works of Tibetan thinkers. But this cannot be true for the Tangut monks, who were trained not for modern scholarship but for more practical goals such as building up a way of philosophical thinking, understanding the reality of the world, and the possible final liberation. As a result, these Tibetan summaries, despite "secondary sources" in our modern eyes, are clearly ideal sources to achieve those goals.

Furthermore, when we try to organize the available Tangut texts of the Gsang phu epistemological tradition, they show a systemic nature that may allow us to probe into the actual curriculum of Buddhist epistemology implemented in the Tangut State. The first piece of evidence is based on the correlation between the popularity of a text and the number of manuscripts we have for it. We have 3–4 manuscripts[552] for the basic text of the *Nyāyabindu* and we have 4 manuscripts for the *Clarification*. 2–4 manuscripts of Rma bya's *Introduction to Speculative Thinking* are extant[553] and only 1 manuscript is found for Phya pa's *Epistemology*.[554] Hence the *Nyāyabindu* and the *Clarification* were likely the most studied texts. Then, it is hard to imagine that someone could investigate Phya pa's *Epistemology*, which is the most philosophically sophisticated, without first studying the entry-level *Nyāyabindu* and its commentary. On the other hand, apparently, not everyone could have the ability to get trained in the *Epistemology* after finishing the *Nyāyabindu*. Also, as mentioned in Section 2, all manuscripts of the *Clarification* are relatively clean without annotations. The same applies to the four fragments of the *Nyāyabindu*. However, both the manuscript fragments of the *Introduction to Speculative Thinking* and those of the *Epistemology* have ample annotations, thus indicating the very demanding lectures on these texts and the engaging attitude of the users of them.

In regard to the foregoing, if we believe that the quantitative distribution of the manuscripts that we currently have reflects the actual scholastic training of the Tanguts, then we can reconstruct a part of the tiered curriculum of Buddhist epistemology in the Tangut State, as shown in the following chart:

---

[552] Among the four manuscript fragments, #4363, #832, and #5609 overlap, so they cannot be from the same manuscript.

[553] There are at least two manuscripts since #5114 and #5112 overlap at the beginning. #5073 and #5801 could be considered as the fragments of the same manuscript because of their identical size, format, and handwriting. #7905, which is highly fragmentary, is uncertain.

[554] The three fragments are identical in terms of their size and format. The handwritings of #4851 and #5933 are identical (#5923 has not become accessible). The three are from the 4th, 5th, and 6th volume of the text respectively.

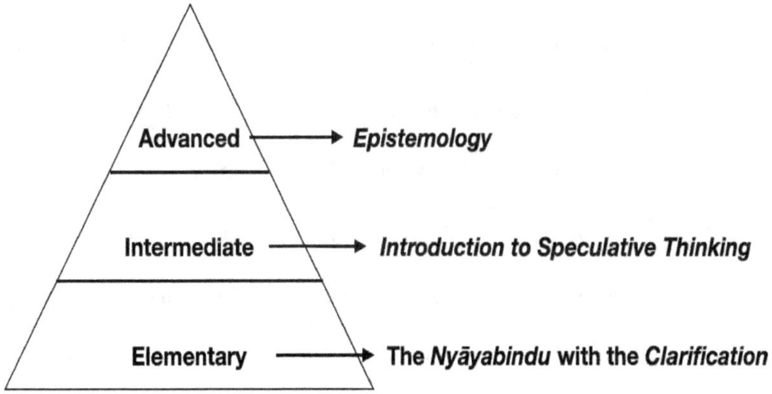
Advanced
Epistemology
Intermediate
Introduction to Speculative Thinking
Elementary
The Nyāyabindu with the Clarification

Figure 4. Reconstructed tiered curriculum on Buddhist epistemology in the Tangut State

This curriculum cannot be said to be the comprehensive one, as there is still a number of Tangut epistemological texts from Chapter Four, Section 3 that I have not yet examined. And we do not know if there were in fact other texts that are not preserved in Khara-Khoto. But the above chart is supposedly the core courses in the curriculum. Students who are trained in the program of Buddhist epistemology would first study the *Nyāyabindu* with the *Clarification*. Then, having entered the intermediate level, students would study Rma bya's *Introduction to Speculative Thinking* and probably also some other texts. Finally, for those who have reached the advanced level, the central focus would be Phya pa's *Epistemology*. This curriculum also makes sense in terms of the chronological development of Gsang phu epistemological thoughts. As the *Clarification* represents the typical pre-Phya pa thoughts, it should be studied before engaging in Phya pa's discourse, which updates the previous views. Although Rma bya postdates Phya pa, the *Introduction to Speculative Thinking*, which is an easier read than the *Epistemology*, follows faithfully Phya pa's model without a significant hint of Rma bya's own intellectual innovations that are regarded as his signature.[555] So, the students would, during the course of an elevating difficulty, also see the chronological development of the Gsang phu epistemological thoughts.

Can we map this curriculum onto the curriculum established in the Gsang phu monastery at the same time as well? To date, we know very still little about any curriculum in premodern Tibetan monasteries. If we could say the curriculum in the Tangut State mirrors what was established in the Gsang phu monastery, then it would greatly deepen our understanding of the Gsang phu scholasticism. However, direct evidence that allows us to do so does not exist, although it is reasonable to think that the ones who introduced the Gsang phu scholasticism to the Tanguts simply transplanted the original curriculum. What we do have is indirect evidence. For example, in Section 7, we have seen some hints on the *Nyāyabindu* being the text that provided 'Jad pa and Phya pa "muscle memories" of fundamental concepts, definitions, and arguments. It is, therefore, not entirely impossible that they started their career learning the *Nyāyabindu* just as the Tanguts did, and probably even with the *Clarification*.

[555] See Ma, "Introduction to Speculative Thinking," 31–32.

PART TWO: TRANSLATION

The translation covers from the very beginning of the text to the end of the author's discussion of the connected purpose of Dharmottara's *Nyāyabindu*.

《[illegible]》[illegible]
[illegible]

The Clarification of the Words and Meaning of the "Nyāyabindu," Upper Volume
Composed by Central Tibetan Great Master, Monk "Wisdom-Conqueror"

[illegible]，[illegible]。
[illegible][556][illegible]，[illegible]。

I pay homage to the all-knowing one,
who works for the benefit of himself and others!
In order to avoid[557] the fear of conceptual proliferation[558],
I will elaborate briefly on the words and meaning of this [*Nyāyabindu*].

[illegible]：[illegible]，[illegible]《[illegible]》[illegible]。[illegible]，[illegible]。[illegible]，[illegible]，[illegible]，[illegible]。[illegible]，《[illegible]》[illegible]，《[illegible]》[illegible]，《[illegible]》[illegible ?][illegible]。

As for the seven treatises[559] of Dharmakīrti: if we follow the way Master Rngog deals with[560] the proposition of Jñānaśrī,[561] then all seven treatises are commentaries on the intention of

---

[556] The character *ljɨ¹* [illegible] ("tired") is likely a phonetic loan of *ljɨ¹* [illegible] ("discourse").

[557] [illegible], Tib. **spang*.

[558] [illegible] is a Chinese style term that comes from *xilun* 戲論 (Skt. *prapañca*, Tib. *spros pa*), thus "conceptual proliferation."

[559] The seven treatises of Dharmakīrti: 1) *Pramāṇavārttika*, 2) *Pramāṇaviniścaya*, 3) *Nyāyabindu*, 4) *Hetubindu*, 5) *Saṃbandhaparikṣā*, 6) *Saṃtānāntarasiddhi*, 7) *Vādanyāya*.

[560] [illegible], literally means to "take up." Normally, it translates the Tibetan *len/blang*. I have chosen to translate it in a more neutral register as it might also mean Rngog Lo developed Jñānaśrībhadra's idea.

[561] The Tangut phrase *nja̱¹ nja² sjɨ² rjir¹* [illegible] is most likely a phonetic transcription of the Sanskrit name Jñānaśrī. The only problem with this identification is that the syllable *sjɨ²* is not retroflex, thus different from the usual Tangut character for transcribing this sound, *śji¹* [illegible]. But it is hard to identify this phrase in other ways. Jñānaśrī here would most likely refer to the Kashmirian master Jñānaśrībhadra (11th century), who wrote a commentary on the

the *Pramāṇasamuccaya*[562]. Among them, three treatises are like the body; and four treatises are like the limbs.[563] And they make seven. Further, the first three are commentaries summarized in the ways of the extraordinarily extensive, slightly summarized, and extraordinary summarized. They are the *Pramāṇavārttika*, the *Pramāṇaviniścaya*, and the *Nyāyabindu*.[564]

[illegible]

Further, as for the four limbs, the limbs for one's own benefit are two. Since the realization that derives from the three characteristics involves one's own benefit, the propositions of one characteristic or six characteristics, etc.[565] are the mistaken understandings of other people in connection to the particular three characteristics themselves. For the purpose of rejecting the inferences that that entail such mistaken understandings, that which explains the definition [of the inference for oneself] to be just the three characteristics is the *Hetubindu*. Since the condition for

---

Pramāṇaviniścaya. The piece of information is somewhat significant here as it may indicate the origin of the body-limb division of the seven treatises of Dharmakīrti. There is no textual evidence showing their intellectual connection. But, considering the fact that Jñānaśrībhadra and Rngog Lo were contemporaneous, it is quite possible that they corresponded on certain issues like this one.

562 [illegible], **kun btus*, i.e., Dignāga's *Pramāṇasamuccaya*. Cf. 'Jad pa's *Essential Nature*, 2: "At that time, the master called Dharmakīrti listened to the teachings from Master Īśvarasena, the one who became a direct disciple of Dignāga. Then, by means of the spontaneously arising insight, he had a knowledge of the meaning of the *Pramāṇasamuccaya* as it is. And he thought, 'It is really not ideal that these [people] belittle Master Dignāga and the treatise composed by him. Hence, I composed the treatise that is like a commentary on it. And those sentient beings should understand [Dignāga's treatise].' Having thought so, he composed the seven treatises of epistemology" (*de'i tshe slob dpon dar ma kir ti zhes bya ba phyogs glang gi slob ma dngos su gyurd pa'i slob dpon dbang phyug sde la chos gsan pa dang lhan cig skyes pa'i shes rab kyis kun las btus pa'i don ji lta ba bzhin du shes pa zhig byung ste / des bsams pa 'di rnams kyis slob dpon phyogs glang dang des brtsams pa'i bstan bcos la skur ba 'debs pa ma legs pas/ de'i 'grel ba lta bu'i bstan bcos brtsams la sems can de dag gis go bar bya'o snyam nas tshad ma sde bdun mdzad do /*).

563 The text here is likely the earliest available account of the three-body-four-limb theory of the seven treatises. A very similar parallel section, including even the quoted verses from Dharmakīrti's works, is found at the beginning of 'Jad pa's *Essential Nature*. I have discussed this in some detail in Ma, "Facheng de 'Qibu liang lun' zai Xixia." Therefore, I will not repeat it here. Note that Gtsang nag pa also engages in the theory in his commentary on the *Pramāṇaviniścaya*: "[Dharmakīrti] wrote seven treatises. The first three treatises, the extensive one, the medium one, the condensed one, are like the body. The four limb-treatises reject the mistakes about parts of the body. They are the two that reject the mistakes about the relations of the defining characteristics of the reason and branches of the inference for oneself, and the two that establish the refutation and examine the language of the refutation at the point of setting up the inference for others" (*bstan bcos sde bdun mdzad de/ rgyas 'bring bsdus pa gtso bo lus lta bu'i bstan bcos gsum dang / rang don rjes dpag gi rgyu rtags kyi mtshan nyid 'brel pa la 'khrul pa spong pa gnyis dang / gzhan don rjes dpag dgod pa'i yul phyir rgol bsgrub pa dang rgol ba phyir rgol gyi ngag brtag pa gnyis sde lus kyi cha shas la 'khrul pa spong pa yan lag gi bstan bcos bzhi'o/* [Gtsang nag pa, *Tshad ma rnam par nges pa'i ṭi ka legs bshad bsdus pa*, 2a1–2]).

564 For the Tangut translations of the names of the seven treatises, see Ma, "Facheng de 'Qibu liang lun' zai Xixia."

565 For the position of the six characteristics, which is held by Īśvarasena, see Steinkellner, *A Splash of the Logical Reason*, 43.

one to be not mistaken about the logical reason and is to be established as the relation, the propositions of some cases of relation, such as the relation of possession and the relation of collection[566], which are different from that which [truly] possesses the relation, are mistaken understandings of other people in connection to it. For the purpose of rejecting such propositions, that which explains the relation to be of just two types – the relation of identity[567] and the relation of causality[568] – is the *Saṃbandhaparikṣā*.

[illegible]

The limbs for others' benefit are also two. Among them, as for the first one: the posit of the statements of proof and disproof is not for the benefit of the cognitive object; instead, they are posited for the benefit of other persons. In this connection, through analyzing the establishment of others' minds, the *Saṃtānāntarasiddhi* is stated as a response to the question "how are other minds established," just like the explanation such as "having seen the preliminary deed of the intellect of one's own body, in others, that..."[569] (prove other's mind)

[illegible]

As for the second one: when debating the opponent, how does one develop the statements of proof and disproof? That which explains the mistaken and the unmistaken is the *Vādanyāya*. It states things such as "Not stating the branches of the (parts of proof) condition of the proof and stating something that is not mistaken are the two that involve the occasion of defeat. Since it is not appropriate [for the defeat] to be of other kinds, they are not claimed."[570] An argument with an

---

[566] The relation of possession ([illegible], **ldan pa'i 'brel ba*) and the relation of collection ([illegible], **'du ba'i 'brel ba*) are two of the five relations proposed by the Sāṁkhya; see *Sāṃkhyakārika*, v. 10. An example of the former would be the fire that possesses the smoke; an example of the latter would be the horn and that which has the horn. These are all rejected by the Dharmakīrtian tradition.

[567] [illegible], **de'i bdag nyid* (Skt. *tādātmya*).

[568] [illegible] **de las byung ba* (Skt. *tadutpatti*).

[569] The first two lines of the introductory verse in the *Saṃtānāntarasiddhi*: */ rang lus blo sngon 'gro ba yi / / bya ba mthong nas gzhan la de /* (*Bstan 'gyur* 98, 941). Also, cf. 'Jad pa's *Essential Nature*, where he quotes exactly these two lines to introduce the *Saṃtānāntarasiddhi*. These two lines are quoted as: */ rang lus blo yi sngon 'gro ba'i / / bya ba mthong nas gzhan la de /...* (*Essential Nature*, 3).

[570] The introductory verse of the *Vādanyāya*: */ sgrub pa'i yan lag mi brjod cing / / skyon mi brjod pa gnyis po dag / / tshar gcad pa yi gnas yin gyi / / gzhan ni mi rigs phyir mi 'dod /* (*Bstan 'gyur* 98: 863). Also, cf. 'Jad pa's *Essential Nature*, where he quotes exactly these four lines to introduce the *Vādanyāya*. These two lines are quoted as: */ sgrub byed yan lag mi brjod cing / / skyon min brjod pa gnyis po dag / / tshar gcad pa yi gnas yin te / / gzhan du mi rigs*

incomplete proof such as the lack of the presence of the reason in the subject (*pakṣadharma*) or with unestablished proof, accordingly, involves the occasion of defeat. It is not appropriate for the complete proof that is not pseudo to involve the occasion of defeat. Also, as for disproof, unable to state the mistake derived from the logical reason of others and stating the unmistaken as mistaken are occasions of defeat. Stating the mistake of what inheres in the ontological status is not proposed as the occasion of defeat.

[illegible], [illegible], [illegible], [illegible]: [illegible], [illegible], [illegible][+[illegible]] [illegible], [illegible], [illegible], [illegible]。

In that connection, here, among the three principal body-like treatises, this extraordinary summarized one [=the *Nyāyabindu*] has three chapters. The first chapter, direct perception, has five topics:

1. The connected purpose.[571]
2. The compartmentalization of the types of knowledge.
3. The definition of direct perception.
4. The clarification of the cognitive object.
5. The posit of the cause and result of perceptual knowledge.

[illegible]、[illegible]、[illegible]:

1. The connected purpose

It further contains three topics:[572]

1.1. The meaning of the purpose.
1.2. The summary.
1.3. The meaning of expressions.

[illegible]: [illegible], "[illegible], [illegible], [illegible]" [illegible]。[illegible]。"[illegible]" [illegible], [illegible], [illegible], [illegible]。

1.1. The topic of the purpose.

If we were to follow the explanation of non-Buddhists, then we would claim: "By means of relying upon the statement of purpose, the idea definitely arises that the treatise has a purpose, etc. Because of this, one engages with the treatise." That is not the case. Just like the statement

---

phyir mi 'dod / (*Essential Nature*, 2–3). The Tangut text is closer to the text quoted in the *Essential Nature* as [illegible] reflects *skyon min* instead of *skyon mi*.

571 [illegible], **dgos 'brel*.

572 These three items are common in Buddhist hermeneutics, as prescribed by Vasubandhu in his *Vyākhyayukti*. See Nance, *Speaking for Buddhas*, chap. 4.

"On the side there is a cart filled with sugarcane,"[573] that statement would not have been established as connected to the meaning of the statement. Hence, it is unreasonable that [the purpose] definitely arises from the statement [of the purpose].

[illegible]

Great Master Dharmottara explains the purpose with three topics:

1.1.1. The essence of the purpose of positing the statement that does not have a proof.
1.1.2. Eliminating the idea that it has no purpose.
1.1.3. Eliminating the idea that it is incapable [of letting people engage in the treatise].[574]

[illegible]

1.1.1. The substance of the purpose of positing the statement that does not have a proof

Question: If, by means of the statement, there is no certainty with regard to the meaning of the statement, then wouldn't it be useless to posit the statement of the connected purpose at the beginning of the treatise?"

Answer: "Even though there is no certainty, the doubt about the argument that there is a purpose in the statement and the meaning of the statement would arise. To engage in the treatise because of that is the result of the statement."

[illegible]

1.1.2. Eliminating the thought that it has no purpose

Question: Since both the statement and the doubt are not established in a positive and negative logical concomitance[575], isn't it the case that, with the onset of doubt, the statement has no purpose?

---

[573] This is a statement that I do not currently understand.

[574] These three topics seem to correspond to the following three segments in Dharmottara's *Commentary*, 104: Topic 111 to the part from *rab tu byed pa nyan pa'i sngon rol du* to *the tshom las kyang rab tu 'jug par 'gyur ro*; Topic 112 to the part from *rtog pa dang ldan pa rnam don la the tshom yod pa ni* to *brjod par rigs so*; Topic 113 to the part from *'chad pa po rnams kyi tshig ni* to *the tshom bya bar rigs so*.

[575] [illegible], Tib. **rjes su 'gro ba dang ldog pa* (Skt. *anvayavyatireka*). The meaning here is, even if there is doubt, it is not necessarily because of the statement. Cf. Rngog Lo's *Concise Guide*, 8: "By 'if it was not shown,' etc., the negative logical concomitance is stated; by means of 'if the subject, etc. was spoken, that,' the positive logical concomitance

> Answer: Even though the statement would have no purpose with regard to giving rise to mere doubt, it has the purpose with which the non-doubting about the argument that there is a purpose arises. If the substance of purpose is not stated in words, then the argument that there is a purpose would be doubted, resulting in the non-doubting about the argument that there is no purpose.

Likewise, if the subject was not stated, then there would be a doubt that it could not be established. If the purpose of the purpose was not stated, then there would be the doubt that, then even though there is a purpose, there would be the doubt that it is not something to be devoted to. If the connection was not stated, then one would doubt that it is not connected to this treatise.

[illegible]

So, just like the absence of the doubt about the argument that there is a purpose on account of the absence of the statement, the establishment of the positive concomitance on account of the establishment of the negative concomitance itself also rejects the idea that the statement, with which doubts the argument that there is a purpose, has no purpose.

1.1.3. Eliminating the idea that it is incapable [of letting people engage in the treatise]

[illegible]

> Question: Does this statement, by means of the established existence of the purpose, etc., eliminates the non-existence or not? If the first, then, since there would be certainty already, it would be a fault that there would be no doubt; if the second, it could not just give rise to the doubt about the argument that there is a purpose.[576]
>
> Answer: Without probing into the two—establishment and elimination, it is the mere posit of the statement. Because of the two assertions—"not seeing the reason for a mistaken statement" and "have not seen [anyone who] engage in a mistaken

---

is stated. The meaning of this is the following: in general, the statement of the connected purpose and the doubt are established as negative and positive logical concomitance. Hence, without the words, doubt would not arise" (*ma bstan na ni zhes pa la sogs pas ldog pa brjod pa dang / brjod par bya ba la sogs pa smras na ni / de zhes bya bas rjes su 'gro ba brjod do / 'di'i don ni spyir dgos 'brel gyi ngag dang / the tshom ldog pa dang / rjes su 'gro ba grub pas tshig med par the tshom mi skye'o /*).

576 That is, it could also fail to do that because the statement does not necessarily entail the doubt.

statement,"[577] it has the capacity to give rise to the doubt about the argument that there is a purpose. Hence, positing the statement as a way to reject the doubt is what is explained by other masters [but not the position we accept]. Master Rgya says, "The statement [makes] one engage in [the treatise] on the basis of the definite rise of the doubt; it eliminates the mistaken understanding and beautifies the text. Without contradicting any philosophical system, it does not undermine them due to adhering to individual philosophical systems."

[illegible]

1.2. The summary

It contains two topics:

1.2.1. The explanation of the treatise that has the connection with the purpose.
1.2.2. The purpose connected to it.

[illegible]

1.2.1. The explanation of the treatise that has the connection with the purpose

The ultimate meaning explained for the occasion[578], the essence that summarizes the many words and expressions, appears to the discriminative cognition[579] as the linguistic universal[580]. What attends[581] to it [=linguistic universal] is the treatise, which involves things such as the linguistic particular[582] or the marks of form[583]—the cognitive objects of eyes and ears.[584]

[577] Cf. Dharmottara's *Commentary*, 104: "While it is possible that the words of narrators may be something else in order to be playful, as for the writing of treatise by writers, the purpose of mistakenly showing the subject, etc., is not seen. There is no engagement [in it] either" (*'chad pa po rnams kyi tshig ni brtse ba la sogs pa'i don du gzhan du srid kyi / bstan bcos mdzad pa rnams rab tu byed pa rtsom pa la ni brjod par bya pa la sogs pa* [*pa* Pe cing; *pa'i* Sde dge] *log par ston pa'i dgos pa ma mthong la 'jug pa yang med de /*).

[578] [illegible], Tib. **skabs su bab pa*.

[579] [illegible], Tib. *rnam par rtog pa'i shes pa*.

[580] [illegible], Tib. **sgra'i spyi*.

[581] [illegible], Tib. **zhen pa*.

[582] [illegible], Tib. **sgra rang* [*gi*] *mtshan nyid*.

[583] [illegible], Tib. **gzugs* [*kyi*] *mtshan nyid*. It seems we should supply [illegible] (*rang*) here and make it [illegible] (*gzugs rang* [*kyi*] *mtshan nyid*) as well. But we are not sure of this.

[584] The section aims at showing the relationship between the treatise and the meaning it urges the audience to obtain. Rngog Lo's *Concise Guide* contains a lengthy discussion of this. It first rejects the idea that the treatise involves the "sole language [=linguistic particular]" (*'bab' zhig gi sgra*) because it is "connected to the agency of conveying [the

[illegible]

1.2.2. The connected purpose in it

It contains four topics:

1.2.2.1. The compartmentalization of the connected purpose.
1.2.2.2. Identifying them in the words.
1.2.2.3. The determination of the number.
1.2.2.4. Clarifying the essence.

[illegible]

1.2.2.1. The compartmentalization of the connected purpose

It involves the subject, the purpose, the purpose of the purpose, and the connection. Among them, the subject is the meaning one should understand on the basis of engaging in this text. It further involves the actual topic of discourse and the attended subject. The first one is the conventional concept. The second is direct perception and inference, which are the attended subject.

[illegible]

However, even that is the case, "Any meaning that is understood on the basis of the explanation of it by means of language should be demonstrated as the meaning of the language, and not as having a separate mark of meaning." The purpose that explains so is the insight[585] that determines the meaning by means of the language.

[illegible]

---

meaning]" (*rjod byed dang 'brel ba*). It does not involve "language [=linguistic universal]" (*sgra*) either, because the particular that we engage as the audience is not the linguistic universal. It is not the "meaning [particular]" (*don*), which is the result of the treatise. Neither is it the "meaning universal" (*don spyi*) because, as the universal, it is "casually ineffective" (*don byed mi nus pa*). The right way to frame it is the treatise is "connected to the meaning, to which the phenomenon of language attends" (*sgra'i chos zhen pa'i don dang 'brel ba*). See *Concise Guide*, 4. The implied 4-step model here is that we must first start from the linguistic particular, which leads to the linguistic universal, and then move to the meaning universal, which is signified by the linguistic universal, and finally reach the meaning particular. For a detailed discussion on these concepts and the model, see Gold, *Sa-skya Paṇḍita's Buddhist Argument for Linguistic Study*, esp. 166, who alternatively translates *sgra spyi* as "term universal", *don spyi* as "object universal", and *zhen pa* as "to conceive."

585 [illegible], Tib. **shes rab.*

The connection is the fact that the insight through which one understands it relies upon the treatise.

[illegible]

The purpose of the purpose is the achievement of a person's goal[586] on the basis of relying upon the purpose.

[illegible][587][illegible]

1.2.2.2. Identifying them in the words.

Until "accomplishment," it explains the purpose of the purpose. By means of "it," it explains the subject. By means of "taught," it explains the purpose.[588] The connection is implied[589].

[illegible][590][illegible]

> Question: Among the many qualities of the treatise, what is the reason for only stating the fourfold connected purpose?
>
> Answer: By means of eliminating the mistaken understanding that obstructs one's engagement in the treatise, the four state the causes that [make] one engage in the treatise without remains. If fewer than the four, it [=the connected purpose] is incapable; if more than the four, it is purposeless. Hence, it is only fourfold.

---

[586] I.e. Dharmakīrti's definition of knowledge in the *Nyāyabindu*: *puruṣārthasiddhi* (Tib. *skyes bu'i don 'grub pa*).

[587] [illegible]] M2; M1 om.

[588] The words quoted here are from the *Nyāyabindu* I.1: "Since the accomplishment of all person's goals is preceded by correct cognition, it is taught" (Skt. *samyagjñānapūrvikā sarvapuruṣārthasiddhiriti tadvyutpādayate* /; Tib. *yang dag pa'i shes pa ni skyes bu'i don thams cad 'grub pa'i sngon du 'gro ba can yin pas na de bstan to* /). "accomplishment"=*siddhi* (*'grub pa*); "it"=*tad* (*de*); "taught"=*vyutpādayate* (*bstan to*).

[589] [illegible], Tib. **shugs kyis*.

[590] [illegible]] M1; M2 om.

"[illegible]? [illegible]?" [illegible]; [illegible]: [illegible], [illegible][591], [illegible]。[illegible], [illegible]、[illegible]、[illegible]、[illegible]。

Well, then what is the mistaken understanding? How is it eliminated?

Answer: Engaging in the treatise does not mean to desire wealth, etc. But even that is the case, the pursuit of the many purposes of the purpose is in fact the pursuit of the purpose of the treatise. Hence, it [=the mistaken understanding] is doubting that there is no purpose of the treatise, that it cannot be established, that it is not something to be devoted to, and that the purpose is not connected to the treatise.

[illegible], [illegible], "[illegible]" [illegible], [illegible]; "[illegible]" [illegible], [illegible]; [illegible], [illegible], [illegible], [illegible] "[illegible]" [illegible], [illegible], [illegible]。"[illegible], [illegible]" [illegible], [illegible], [illegible], [illegible], [illegible], [illegible], [illegible], [illegible], [illegible]。

As for the way to eliminate it: the statement of the connected purpose, by means of stating "the purpose of the treatise involves the understanding of the correct cognition," eliminates the doubt that there is no purpose; by stating "the subject of this is the correct cognition," it rejects the doubt that it cannot be established; if it was not connected to other later purposes, then, it is not ultimate that it is something desire by a person.[592] Hence, when other people have not yet engaged in the treatise, this statement that precedes the present moment, in stating, "I composed this treatise, which explains the correct cognition that has become the cause for the accomplishment of a person's goal," explains the connection between other later purposes and the accomplishment of a person's goal. By means of that, it cuts off the doubt that the purpose is not something to be desired. In stating, "For the purpose of making the correct cognition understood, I composed this treatise," it explains both the treatise and the purpose as the skillful means and the connected meaning that arises from the skillful means. By means of that, it rejects the doubt that the purpose is not connected to the treatise. Therefore, the branches that eliminate the mistaken understanding that obstruct one's engagement are stated as the four, such as the existence of the purpose. If more than those, than it is purposeless; if fewer than those, it is incapable. Hence, it is determined that they are four.[593]

---

591 [illegible], [illegible]] M2; [illegible] M1.

592 That is, the purpose of the purpose has to be unconditioned rather than conditioned.

593 Cf. Rngog Lo's *Concise Guide*, 8: "Likewise, if any one of the four were not to be stated, then the doubt about whether it would be meaningful would not arise. And it is not necessary to have more than four either. Hence, the determination of the number is also established" (*de bzhin du bzhi la sogs pa gang rung zhig ma smras na don du mi 'gyur ba'i the tshom mi skye la / bzhi las mang ba yang mi dgos te / des na grangs nges pa yang grub bo zhes bya ba'o /*). Note the doubt in Rngog Lo's work here means the inquisitiveness that makes a person engage in the treatise.

[illegible][594] [illegible]

1.2.2.4. Clarifying the essence

In a certain person's mind[595] to which the discourse appears, a certain mind that understands the subject arises. With regard to that mind, on the part[596] of being what is held[597], it is the subject; on the part of being the agent of holding[598], it is the purpose. The fact that the part of being the agent of holding relies upon the first mind where the agent of explanation appears is the connection. So, the three [members of] the connected purpose are identical in terms of being the nature of a single mind. The purpose of the purpose, having relied upon the purpose, is the achievement of later persons' goals. Furthermore, because the purpose of the purpose is explained as the meaning of the statement, it is stated as it is. Because the other three are explained as the meaning of the words, they are implicitly stated.

594 [illegible]] M1; [illegible] M2.

595 [illegible], Tib. **blo*.

596 [illegible], Tib. **phyogs* [*su*].

597 [illegible], Tib. *'*dzin pa*.

598 [illegible], Tib. **bzung ba*.

Conclusion

A Roadmap to the Answers

At the beginning of the Introduction, I put forward three questions. It might be useful to recapitulate them here:

1. Why do the ethnic, political, and religious landscapes of China and Inner Asia after roughly the year 1000 look so different from what they were before?
2. What roles did Buddhism play in making these changes?
3. How did the Tangut State structure Buddhism within its realm in a particular fashion so that it could play the roles?

As previously stated, answering these questions is not a simple task, and my aim in this dissertation was to propose a roadmap.

For the first question, I suggest examining the period from approximately 1130 to 1230, immediately before the establishment of the Mongol Yuan Empire. This timeframe is significant because it saw the intensified interactions between three regions: the Tibetan Plateau, the Northern Areas, and the Eastern Lowlands. Using Fletcher's theory of "integrative history," we can explore how these interactions gave rise to the Yuan Empire, which was a political realization of integrative Inner Asian imperial history. The continuity of this history can be seen in the subsequent Ming and Qing empires, which were also predicated on integrative history and dramatically different from the histories of China and Inner Asia prior to 1000. By delving deeper into these interactions, we may gain a better understanding of the factors that led to the emergence of the Yuan Empire and the continuity of this integrative history in later empires.

For the second question, I proposed to examine how Tibetan Buddhism influenced the integrative history. I introduced the concept of a Buddhist Complex and suggest that a Sino-Tibetan Buddhist Complex replaced the previous Indo-Chinese Buddhist Complex. Tibetan Buddhism became the primary religious force that connected the three regions of this integrative history. The institutions and doctrines of Tibetan Buddhism played a vital role in maintaining the Yuan and Qing empires. And they were also integral parts of the Ming Empire, albeit being less important. By exploring the impact of Tibetan Buddhism on the integrative history, we can gain a better understanding of the complex religious and cultural interactions that helped shape the history of Inner Asia.

The third question is closely related to the first two questions, as it seeks to understand the role of Tibetan Buddhism in the Tangut State, which was, geographically, located in the overlapping area of the three regions of the integrative history and, temporally, fell into the formative period of that history. In this dissertation, the Tangut State is seen as a prototype of the later Inner Asian empires, containing many of the factors that were essential in the formation of those empires, including Tibetan Buddhism. Therefore, the dissertation chooses to focus on how Tibetan Buddhism became a central theme in the religious life of the Tangut State, and how it contributed to the state's political and cultural integration.

Tibetan Buddhism in the Tangut State

When exploring the rise of Tibetan Buddhism in the Tangut State, it is important to take note of several aspects of its history. Firstly, Tibetan Buddhism was introduced into the Tangut

State as it was well-suited for the framework of Tangut State Buddhism. This is evident in the first set of scriptures translated from Tibetan into Tangut in roughly the 1140s. These scriptures, primarily consisting of *dhāraṇī*s and *mantra*s, offered the Tangut State with new resources to safeguard the state and enhance the collective welfare of its people.

The Kashmirian scholar Jayānanda played a crucial role in promoting Tibetan Buddhism in the Tangut State during the mid-twelfth century. Interestingly, Jayānanda, despite being a state preceptor of the Tangut court, did not directly communicate with the Tangut audience. Instead, he was a revered Buddhist master among the Tibetans in the Tangut State. It is important to note the power dynamics here: Indic Buddhist masters were respected by Tibetan Buddhists, who, in turn, were revered by the Tanguts. However, the Tanguts did not necessarily view the Indic masters as superior to the Tibetans. The Tangut State intentionally made Jayānanda a center of attraction to draw Tibetan Buddhists close to him, and the latter could then spread Buddhist teachings to the Tanguts.

The emergence of local Tangut traditions in Buddhism can be compared to the development of Geyi Buddhism in early Chinese Buddhism. This is evident in Tśhja źjɨr's application of some Huayan concepts to Mahāmudrā practices. However, the Tangut integration of Chinese and Tibetan Buddhist traditions is more than a provisional method of making a path for the influx of Tibetan Buddhism. The local traditions can be seen as the results of the Tanguts' effort to build a comprehensive understanding of Buddhism, in which all Buddhist traditions could work together seamlessly. In this regard, preexisting Chinese Buddhist traditions never posed a barrier to the Tangut reception of new Tibetan teachings.

The success of Tibetan tantric Buddhism in the Tangut State was not accidental. Tibetan tantric Buddhism effectively integrated the trends of State Buddhism and Individual Buddhism, creating a single stream. Tantric practices served as a powerful tool on the state level to protect the state and elevate the ruler's legitimacy, as evidenced in the accounts of Ti shri Ras pa. Additionally, they were essential for individuals to achieve soteriological aims. The popularity of Tibetan tantric practices in the Tangut State is well attested by the large number of tantric texts translated into Tangut. The role of Tibetan masters in combining the two forms of Buddhism in the Tangut State was also significant, with their charisma leading them to be venerated as the preeminent spiritual leaders of the Tangut State in its final years. As a result, Buddhist institutions such as the imperial preceptor also matured.

However, Tibetan tantric Buddhism did not exist in isolation in the Tangut State. As discussed, the Gsang phu scholastic tradition played a significant role in the rise of Tibetan Buddhism in the Tangut State. Many works from this tradition were translated into Tangut and studied by Tangut monks. Rather than hindering the ascendency of Tibetan tantric Buddhism, the Tangut assimilation of the Gsang phu tradition actually aided it. This is because tantric practices could only be fruitful when combined with scholastic training. The establishment of the scholastic tradition in the Tangut State also allowed the state to effectively regulate the monastic population within monastic institutions, without losing control and allowing them to become free-roaming practitioners.

When examining the rise of Tibetan Buddhism in the Tangut State, it is crucial to consider how that process developed in parallel with the evolution of Tibetan Buddhism in Tibet. Rtsa mi Lo tsā ba, a cultural Tibetan, born a Tangut, and spiritual an Indian, played an important role in the Bka' brgyud tradition and inspired Bka' brgyud masters like 'Jig rten mgon po to establish a connection with the Tangut State. The Bka' brgyud school's rise to power in the Tangut State was not accidental, as some Bka' brgyud subsects struggled to find political and financial support in

Tibet during the late twelfth century, prompting them to look beyond its borders for patronage, with the Tangut State being an ideal destination.

The establishment of the Gsang phu scholastic tradition in Tibet paved the way for its assimilation by the Tangut State. The tradition had a significant impact on Tibetan intellectual history by introducing Tibetan indigenous systems of thinking through the philosophical topics posed by Indian philosophers. During this process, the Tanguts were exposed to Tibetan interpretations of Buddhist thought rather than the Indian versions. As seen in the case of the *Clarification*, The Tanguts were mainly introduced to Buddhist epistemology mainly based on the philosophical position of Rgya dmar ba, rather than those of Dharmottara and others. This solidified Tibet's position as an authoritative source of Buddhist transmission. This study of the Tangut assimilation of the Gsang phu tradition sheds light on the dynamic interactions between Tibet and Inner Asia and contributes to our understanding of the transmission of Buddhism in the region.

From a Prototypical Inner Asian Empire to Inner Asian Empires

This dissertation highlights how the historical phenomena resulting from the rise of Tibetan Buddhism in the Tangut State persisted into later periods. As demonstrated, certain Tibetan Buddhist practices that were prevalent in the Tangut State were also adopted by the Mongol Köden Khan. Additionally, the institution of the imperial preceptor, which originated in the Tangut State, was subsequently practiced by the Yuan and further by the Qing.

What this dissertation has not yet specifically addressed is how the practices of Tibetan Buddhism in the later Inner Asian empires differed from those in the prototypical Inner Asian empire, namely, the Tangut State. This is a very intriguing question that worth exploring as well.

One major difference between the practices of Tibetan Buddhism in the Tangut State and the later Inner Asian empires is the absence of a unified monastic system in the latter. The Tangut State had a prescribed monastic system, in which Tangut monks played a crucial role, as seen in the *Tiansheng Legal Code.* In contrast, the Yuan Empire did not establish a Mongol monastic community intentionally, and the same was true for the Qing Empire. The audience of Tibetan masters was limited to the royal family and a few noble persons, resulting in fewer Tibetan Buddhist texts being translated into Mongol and Manchu languages compared to Tangut translations. Additionally, Chinese Buddhists, who were regulated by the monastic institutions of the Tangut State, were introduced to Tibetan Buddhism. Many Tibetan masters had Chinese followers, as evidenced by Chinese translations of Tibetan tantric texts. However, Chinese monastics were not incorporated into a unified system for actively receiving teachings from the Tibetan side. Buddhist exchanges between Tibet and China continued but on a much smaller scale. Therefore, Tibetan Buddhism remained Tibetan in nature and was not translated into languages accessible to other ethnic groups in later empires. Consequently, Tibetan Buddhism had very limited influence on Chinese Buddhists until the fall of the Qing Empire. Further studies are necessary to pursue the implications of this transformation.

Re-Making Sense of the Middle Period China and Inner Asia

This dissertation, on the most general level, aims to demonstrate the value of a transregional history of Middle Period China and Inner Asia. "Middle Period Chinese history" has been, for a long time, concerning models such as the "Tang-Song transition" or "Song-Yuan transition." Much of the dynamics in the Inner Asian world, like the development of Tibetan Buddhism in the Later Diffusion, seems to be completely external and irrelevant to the models.

However, the limitations of the nation-state narrative have become apparent. While a transregional approach has been difficult to achieve, except in the case of the Tang dynasty, this study shows that a broader perspective can reveal new dynamics of the period. For instance, as shown in the dissertation, the Yuan political, ethnic, and religious landscapes were shaped by the interactions among the three regions, and not just a continuation of the Song dynasty.

This dissertation also aims to contribute new insights to the ongoing debates surrounding late imperial Chinese history. Since the emergence of narrative New Qing history, scholars have debated whether this narrative accurately reflects the reality of late imperial China and to what extent the concept of an "Inner Asian empire" is valid. In order to address these conflicts and offer new perspectives, it is necessary to move beyond the limits of a single dynasty and examine the dynamics of diachronic development. As mentioned in the earlier chapters of the dissertation, some scholars have argued that the Ming Empire inherited many legacies of the Yuan Empire and thus also possessed Inner Asian characteristics. This represents an important effort in this direction. Building on this perspective, this dissertation expands the temporal scope to the Tangut period and argues that the Tangut State was a prototypical Inner Asian empire imbued with the impetus that later gave rise to subsequent Inner Asian empires.

The examination of the rise of Tibetan Buddhism in the Tangut State represents a small step towards re-evaluating our understanding of the Middle Period China and Inner Asia. It is my hope that this project will inspire further scholarship, including a further pursuit of this dissertation topic.

www.ingramcontent.com/pod-product-compliance
Lightning Source LLC
Chambersburg PA
CBHW051422290426
44109CB00016B/1399
* 9 7 8 0 6 2 4 7 0 7 7 5 2 *